# JANEITES

# JANEITES

## AUSTEN'S DISCIPLES AND DEVOTEES

*Edited by Deidre Lynch*

PRINCETON UNIVERSITY PRESS PRINCETON AND OXFORD

Published by Princeton University Press, 41 William Street,
Princeton, New Jersey 08540
In the United Kingdom: Princeton University Press,
3 Market Place, Woodstock, Oxfordshire OX20 1SY


***Library of Congress Cataloging-in-Publication Data***

Janeites: Austen's disciples and devotees/edited by Deidre Lynch
p. cm.
Includes bibliographical references and index.
ISBN 0-691-05005-8 (cl : alk. paper)—
ISBN 0-691-05006-6 (pbk. : alk. paper)
1. Austen, Jane, 1775–1817—Criticism and interpretation—History.
2. Women and literature—England—History—19th century.
3. Austen, Jane, 1775–1817—Appreciation. 4. Austen, Jane,
1775–1817—Influence. 5. English fiction—Appreciation.
6. Reading interests. I. Lynch, Deidre.
PR4037.J39 2000
823′.7—dc21 00-021205

This book has been composed in Galliard

The paper used in this publication meets the minimum
requirements of ANSI/NISO Z39.48-1992 (R1997)
(*Permanence of Paper*)

www.pup.princeton.edu

Printed in the United States of America

(Pbk.)
1 2 3 4 5 6 7 8 9 10

1 2 3 4 5 6 7 8 9 10

# *Contents*

*Acknowledgments* vii

*A Note to the Reader* ix

**Introduction:** Sharing with Our Neighbors 3
*Deidre Lynch*

**1.** The Divine Miss Jane: Jane Austen, Janeites, and the Discipline of Novel Studies 25
*Claudia L. Johnson*

**2.** Jane Austen's Friendship 45
*Mary Ann O'Farrell*

**3.** Sensibility by the Numbers: Austen's Work as Regency Popular Fiction 63
*Barbara M. Benedict*

**4.** Austen's Earliest Readers and the Rise of the Janeites 87
*William Galperin*

**5.** Decadent Austen Entails: Forster, James, Firbank, and the "Queer Taste" of *Sanditon* (comp. 1817, publ. 1925) 115
*Clara Tuite*

**6.** The Virago Jane Austen 140
*Katie Trumpener*

**7.** Free and Happy: Jane Austen in America 166
*Mary A. Favret*

**8.** In Face of All the Servants: Spectators and Spies in Austen 188
*Roger Sales*

**9.** Jane Austen and Edward Said: Gender, Culture, and Imperialism 206
*Susan Fraiman*

*Notes on Contributors* 225

*Index* 227

## *Acknowledgments*

I WOULD LIKE to thank the University at Buffalo, State University of New York, for the sabbatical that enabled me to write the introduction, and Kerry Grant, Dean of the College of Arts and Sciences, for his generous financial support.

Jane Austen and her most caustic critic would each have enjoyed this irony: my courses on Austen's novels and their adaptations have for the last six years taken place in Samuel Clemens Hall. For permitting me to reuse in this irreverent manner space meant to be dedicated to Mark Twain's memory, I am grateful to Stefan Fleischer.

I owe much to colleagues and friends, at Buffalo and elsewhere, for conversation, for ensuring that my mailbox would overflow with a steady supply of Austeniana, and for readings of the introduction. To Barbara Bono, Robert Devens, Mary Favret, Nancy Glazener, Susan Howe, Claudia Johnson, Tom Keirstead, Devoney Looser, Richard Maxwell, Azar Nafisi, Suzanne Pucci, Julia Saville, Clifford Siskin, Katie Trumpener, Bill Warner, and the readers for Princeton University Press: thank you. Lauren Lepow edited the manuscript with grace and precision. Mary Murrell's encouragement made all the difference.

My primary debt is to the contributors to *Janeites*, whose intelligence, humor, and patience have made our collaboration so much fun.

## *A Note to the Reader*

ALL QUOTATIONS from Jane Austen's works are based on the edition of R. W. Chapman, *The Novels of Jane Austen: The Text Based on Collation of the Early Editions*, 3d ed., 5 vols. (Oxford: Oxford University Press, 1933), along with a sixth volume covering *Sanditon*, the juvenilia, the "Plan of a Novel," and "Opinions of *Mansfield Park* and *Emma*," edited by Chapman and published in 1954 as *The Works of Jane Austen*, vol. 6 (Oxford: Oxford University Press). In Chapman's edition, vol. 1 contains *Sense and Sensibility*; vol. 2, *Pride and Prejudice*; vol. 3, *Mansfield Park*; vol. 4, *Emma*; vol. 5, *Persuasion* and *Northanger Abbey*; and vol. 6, the *Minor Works*.

A number of contributors quote extensively from the materials compiled by B. C. Southam in his *Jane Austen: The Critical Heritage* (London: Routledge and Kegan Paul, 1968), followed by and reissued as vol. 1 with vol. 2, *Jane Austen: The Critical Heritage, 1870–1940* (London: Routledge and Kegan Paul, 1987). These editions are referred to hereafter as Southam 1968 and Southam 1987.

# JANEITES

# Introduction: Sharing with Our Neighbors

DEIDRE LYNCH

> [H]er faithful followers . . . do not want to share their pleasure with their neighbours. It is too intimate and too individual.
>
> *(Agnes Repplier, 1931)*

> It is possible to say of Jane Austen, as perhaps we can say of no other writer, that the opinions which are held of her work are almost as interesting, and almost as important to think about, as the work itself.
>
> *(Lionel Trilling, 1957)*

## Whose Austen?

Were Lionel Trilling alive today, he might be forgiven for deciding that there were too many opinions of Austen's work to "think about." At the end of the millennium the evidence for Austen's appeal is plentiful. Through the 1990s opinions of Austen's novels and of Austen herself have been tendered in a staggeringly various array of venues. And denizens of the English literature classroom are far from monopolizing the conversation.

The newspaper article reporting the formation of the Connecticut Chapter of the Jane Austen Society of North America tells interested parties to arrive at the first meeting prepared to vote for their favorite Austen character and then suggests that persons who see themselves as "expert lecturers" had better stay away: "This attracts readers, not academics." The World Wide Web is another place one is likely to encounter a definition of "reading" that, like that of the Connecticut Chapter, challenges the prerogatives customarily claimed by those of us who *assign* it. Multiple discussion groups convene on the Internet in order to trade observations about Austen's characterization and themes as well to keep tabs on the ever-more-numerous adaptations and sequels that replay or prolong her stories. To visit, for example, the particular corner of cyberspace occupied by "the Republic of Pemberley" is quickly to realize that the work of interpreting Great Books and of adjudicating between their acceptable and unacceptable appropriations goes on in forums besides those administered by professional scholars and journalists. And, indeed, as its witty toponym suggests, this republic—a host site that welcomes the "huddled masses" and adheres unapologetically to a "matriarchal" form of "governance"—may come closer than either the university or the press can to implementing the democratic potential of the eighteenth century's republic of letters.[1]

Visitors to that Pemberley do not suffer from any shortage of topics for conversation. (In this they differ from Elizabeth Bennet and her relations, visitors to the original Pemberley who are somewhat daunted both by its master's presence and by anxiety over the seeming impropriety of their visit.) Right now, Austen's admirers have an Austen Boom to discuss—still. Consider—to linger with the electronic media—the numerous interpretations of her work proposed by the recent movie and television adaptations (Patricia Rozema's film adaptation of *Mansfield Park*, released by Miramax in late 1999, Andrew Davies's serial *Pride and Prejudice* [A&E/BBC, 1995], Roger Michell's telefilm version of *Persuasion* [BBC/WGBH, 1995], Ang Lee and Emma Thompson's film of *Sense and Sensibility* [1995], and three *Emma*s, if one adds Amy Heckerling's film *Clueless* [1995] to Doug McGrath's film *Emma* [1996] and the ITV/A&E adaptation of the novel [1996]). And should we opt, following Trilling's lead, to move on from the works and trace the opinions held about Austen herself, we must now do more than engage the latest biographies (by Claire Tomalin, David Nokes, and Valerie Grosvenor Myer). We must also take into account Stephanie Barron's putative discovery of a certain "Jane Austen, Detective," a cross-dressed Regency Sherlock Holmes who has to date exercised her crime-busting skills in three mystery novels: Austen's reappearance in the guise of a detective, a character type who may be revived repeatedly to investigate case after case in a series that postpones closure indefinitely, in itself testifies to Austenians' desire to keep talking. Assessment of that talk might appropriately consider the debates spurred in 1997 and 1998 by Helen Fielding's *The Diary of Bridget Jones*, a modernized *Pride and Prejudice* that made headlines for (as several feminists noted ruefully) the ostensibly postfeminist terms in which it also managed to revive "the marriage plot." Perhaps an assessment of Austen's contemporary reception should also acknowledge—although this evidence file is already overflowing—the popular acclaim granted of late to the ostentatiously Austen-inflected Aubrey-Maturin novels. Setting the twenty adventure yarns in his series aboard the ships of the navy in which Austen's brothers served, Patrick O'Brian transports Austen's novels of manners into the war zone.

It has been hard to get out of earshot of all of this talk of Jane Austen. Who hasn't tired lately of all the rip-offs of her good lines? The *Economist* recently gave the headline "Pride and Petroleum" to an article about a possible "match" between Mitsubishi and Volvo; the latter, *if* Austen had written about European car companies, "would surely have been her favorite character."[2]

And yet at the same time that this talk engrosses growing numbers of readers, and even those who, preferring the cineplex, refrain from reading altogether, there continue (as several contributors to this volume observe) to be a worrying number of propositions about the woman and her works that get to count as gospel truth. The Austenmania manifested nowadays by Hollywood studios, television networks, and the publishers of sequels is motivated, we are often told, by their faith in her broad commercial appeal—their sense, that is, that, ever the well-mannered lady, Jane Austen is "safe." Where Austen is concerned, not only do these institutions feel sure of getting a return on their monetary investment. There is a matching certainty that she and her works present few interpretive or political challenges, that the culture has already got her number.

However, to scrutinize a little more closely what people do and have done with Austen's books quickly leads us away from the hackneyed truths ("universally acknowledged") that make up much of the current Austenian punditry. Committed to such scrutiny, the essays on reception history that are collected here work together, although not always in perfect harmony, in order to interrogate just how much there really is that can "safely" be said about the nature of these works or their influence—or, by extension, about the status of the novel, about the category of women's writing, about the politics of realism, or even about the relationship between "great books" and greatly liked books.

*Janeites: Austen's Disciples and Devotees* is generated out of three premises. The contributors to this anthology concur with Lionel Trilling in perceiving something "interesting and important" in the record of adaptations, reviews, rewritings, and appreciations of Austen that have accumulated in the almost 190 years since her publication of *Sense and Sensibility.* The second assumption we make is that there are more productive things to do with this record than to adjudicate between faithful and unfaithful readings. To concentrate on whether the meanings of the novels have been "misrepresented," by either Austen's admirers or her detractors, is to defer more interesting if more difficult questions: about the diverse frameworks within which audiences have claimed interpretive authority over those meanings; about the varying motives audiences have had for valuing the novels and for identifying with or repudiating Austen's example; about the divergent uses to which such alternative Austens have been put in the literary system and the culture at large. For professional literary historians, approaching the reception history with these questions in mind, acknowledging that the cultural Jane Austen has been a crossover phenomenon, and acknowledging that Austenmania straddles the divides between high and low culture, and between the canon and the cineplex, can be humbling experiences. We are reminded that we are far from having exclusive title to the real Jane Austen. Popular appropriations have on occasion preempted academic criticism in recovering aspects of Austen's works that our professional protocols—for instance, our narratives about the novel's "rise" or our habit of slicing up literary history into eighteenth-century, Romantic, and Victorian slices—may occlude from view.[3]

The third premise informing this collection concerns the prior readings that intervene between contemporary approaches to Austen's texts and the Regency context in which she produced them. This collection argues quite strenuously for the significance of past appropriations of Austen, often discovering, in the past, evidence for a less gentle Jane than the one we have encountered of late. For other decades knew an Austen whose status as a safe subject was less than self-evident. There is a considerable contrast, for example, between the idealization of the country village (Meryton and Highbury) that features prominently in the modes of Austen loving which occupied the late Victorians and the idealization of the great house (Pemberley and Donwell Abbey) that draws audiences into the cinema and then onto National Trust properties a hundred years on.[4] It is that kind of tension between alternative Austens—between the historical conditions in which these alternatives are produced and between the dominant fictions of Englishness and of home by which each is inflected—that makes inquiry into readerships and their readings productive and politically pertinent. Through acquaintance with earlier reading practices, we learn the limitations of our own. The orientation toward the past that marks this collection should not therefore be condemned as testimony to our nostalgia (a term too readily used to malign Austen's admirers); rather, it evidences our desire to reactivate the past in ways that empower us to revise the future.

As it implements the alliance of cultural studies and cultural history I invoke above, this book unfolds in a roughly chronological way, moving forward from accounts of Austen's earliest readers, to the late nineteenth century, the era of high modernism, and the American 1960s, and then to the two contemporary ways of talking about Jane Austen that are placed in juxtaposition by our concluding chapters: on the one hand, those of television and the cineplex and, on the other, those that also involve our talk, within university literature departments, about empire and postcoloniality. One point *Janeites* makes is that the path which takes us from our early-nineteenth-century starting point to the present conjuncture—a moment when cultural continuity seems challenged both by new modes of global cultural relationships and by new communications technologies that marginalize traditional uses of print—is perhaps less smooth than we have acknowledged. Following that path, we encounter challenges, in the form of issues, particularly those surrounding sexuality and race, that we didn't expect to confront, and in the form of company (the belated Decadent Ronald Firbank; servants who use blackmail to take a class revenge on their employers; Scarlett O'Hara) that we didn't think we would keep. Contemporary scholarship has demonstrated just how hard conservatives have had to work at their mythologizing in order to depict Austen's classic novels as products of an era of classicism, "a world that seems to have been the same from everlasting to everlasting, . . . a kind of ideal centre of calm which was conceived, and for a time . . . actually realised by the eighteenth century."[5] We certainly see ourselves as following the lead of recent feminist and cultural materialist work on Revolutionary-era and Regency history. But there can also be something misguided, and equally wishful, about the historicist privileging of the originary moment of a text's production. Or there can be if that privileging involves the notion that "the values and insights of literary texts are fully actualized at the moment of their creation," if it means proceeding as if two centuries' worth of reproductions of Austen do not themselves count as history.[6] The very diversity of the representations reported on by this anthology signals our determination to do otherwise. It is now time to put not only Austen herself but also our readings of her back into the fray.

## Austen and the Literary Canon; or, The Bard in Petticoats

And fray there is. Calling attention to the "interesting and important" dimensions of her reception history, Lionel Trilling omits (but only initially) reference to its disputatiousness. Yet if we wish to find other things to "say of Jane Austen" that could be said of "no other writer," we might do well to consider the vehemence of the partisanship that her life and works inspire (we are dealing with true love, not mere admiration), and, as the counterpart to such devotion, the equally passionate expressions of acrimony they can provoke (the very writers whom we might reasonably decide to classify as Austen's disciples are capable of switching abruptly from emulation to resentment). We should turn to the contentiousness that surrounds Austen's popularity—and, correspondingly, to the apologetic murmurs that are the background noise to many discussions of her canonicity. Are there any other writers who have seemed so vulnerable to being loved by so many in so wrongheaded a way? Repeatedly over the last 190 years, certain admirers of her novels have seen fit to depreciate the motives and modes of every one else's admiration. Indeed, a customary method of establishing one's credentials as a reader of Austen has been to regret that others simply will insist on liking her in inappropriate ways. With some regularity, other people's admiration is disrespectful, based on a misreading, or embarrassingly hyperbolic (given the humble pretensions of its object). The opening that D. W. Harding supplied for "Regulated Hatred: An Aspect of the Work of Jane Austen," the 1940 essay that helped inaugurate the scholarly study of Austen's novels, exemplifies this attitude toward the Other Reader. Austen's fate, Harding remarked, had been "to be read and enjoyed by precisely the sort of people whom she disliked." As a professional, his task was to uncover this irony, which had escaped a popular audience. His prerogative was to show that, in contradistinction to that audience, he knew better.[7]

Of late such claims to sophistication are encountered more frequently in the popular media than in scholarly journals. In the journalism occasioned by the recent Austen movies, it is a standard move for the film critic or media pundit to forge an alliance, comparable to the one Harding forges, between Austen and his self. (Often, it does indeed seem to be "his" self.) In column after column, commentators have lambasted what theory-obsessed academics do with the novels or lambasted the white middle-class women (the so-called frilly bonnet brigade) who go to the movies for the costumes and for romance. By such means, Jane has been rescued from undeserving claimants to her hand. According to Louis Menand, writing in the *New York Review of Books*, "Austen is surely the novelist most thoroughly embarrassed by her admirers." Boyd Tonkin concluded his review of the movie *Emma* with a call to arms: "It's time to rescue Jane from the Janeites."[8]

Choosing his terms more carefully than Tonkin, Lionel Trilling wrote, in the 1957 essay that is cited in my second epigraph, of how Austen had often been the object of "illicit love," and how response to her novels had often been "carried outside the proper confines of literature." The stakes are higher in this comment than in Tonkin's. It suggests one reason it is worth analyzing carefully the impassioned exercises in mutual reproach that have occupied large sectors of Austen's audiences. It is not only that Trilling disengages Austen from licit love—from that marriage plot to which so many commentaries have wedded her. Here, anxiety over what other readers do with Austen also seems to shade over into anxiety over Literature—over the viability of that category, that way of cordoning off some texts from others, which was invented in Austen's lifetime (as Barbara M. Benedict suggests in "Sensibility by the Numbers"), and which is said to be losing currency in our own. If it is possible to read Austen in ways that transgress the boundaries of properly literary reading, it must follow that the location of those limits is far from being apparent or fixed. In this way, the worry that Austen has been afflicted by the wrong sort of popularity seems a backhanded acknowledgment of the tenuousness of the boundaries between elite and popular culture, and between the canonical and the noncanonical.[9] Indirectly, the guardians of Austen's reputation who worry about whether a canonical figure can or should have a cult audience are admitting that the distinctions which her classic example is supposed to shore up—those between a degraded romance and a normative realism, for instance—may be untenable. "Romance" and "realism" may have little to do with stable categories of writing. They may do no more than index the varying uses to which readers may put a single text.

But it may be Austen herself who has an improper relation to the literary, not just reprehensible readers who love her too much, nor just, conversely, those reprehensible literature professors whose theorizing might pollute the shrine. In their discussions here of the varying ways in which Austen's legacy was identified by Henry James and E. M. Forster, on the one hand, and by Virginia Woolf and other women modernists, on the other, Clara Tuite and Katie Trumpener each hint at how Austen's gender can destabilize literary history's orthodox narratives about tradition and the individual talent. At recurring intervals, Austen has caused trouble for literary history—this despite her reputation as the quintessential good girl. Her problematic femaleness is compounded by her spinsterhood and childlessness. For readers in our post-Freudian century especially, the distance that Austen put between herself and marriage represents a topic of ongoing, almost obsessive fascination. Witness the vile yet venerable hypothesis that the novels represent "a plain and obscure spinster's written revenge on an uncaring world."[10] Witness the nervous jokiness with which one critic after another has made a match for Jane or offered to wed her himself (possibly to make his love a licit rather than, as Trilling would have it, an illicit one).[11] It is not clear that those who devise these arrangements or make these offers have Austen's interests at heart. But arguably the matchmakers and suitors *are* safeguarding the interests of Literature. For, as an institution, Literature is also invested in narratives about the legitimate transmission of a patrimony. It is fundamentally troubled by the unattached woman's lack of a legitimate relation to the official mechanisms of cultural transmission and cultural memory.

It is not only, that is, that multiple attempts have been made to pinpoint Austen's place in the genealogy of English Literature—casting Austen, as, variously, the "daughter" of Samuel Johnson or "mother" of Henry James. (Such efforts are undermined by the novels' persistent interest in daughters who lack a patrimony.) The very frequency of those attempts suggests a certain defensiveness. Commentators seem unsure about exactly how a woman *could* claim a space within the cultural heritage. Certainly, it was Austen's prestige that originally legitimated the respectable, academic study of prose fiction. R. W. Chapman's 1923 edition of the novels for Clarendon Press was the first to bestow on a novelist the sort of editorial care previously reserved for the English canon's dramatists and poets. But Austen's example can also make orthodox ways of accounting for cultural reproduction—our concepts of influence, tradition, literary legitimacy, and canon; our schemes for segregating the literary from the popular—seem strange and skewed.[12]

So, scrutinizing the designation of Austen as a "prose Shakespeare," a commonplace since Archbishop Whately and Thomas Babington Macaulay offered accolades to Austen in the early nineteenth century, we might do well to remark the distinction between the kinds of canonicity that a Bard and an Austen can claim—even though the account of the cultural Jane Austen that this anthology proffers has as its inspiration recent cultural studies of Shakespeare's multiple functions as folk hero, English export industry, cult object and tutelary deity. On the testimony of those studies, there are few signs in Shakespeare's reception history of any counterpart to the disputatiousness that distinguishes Austen's. As I have indicated, the popularity or, worse still, the marketability of the novels has represented a problem for some custodians of Austen's reputation.[13] As the disputes about how best to like Austen and the ideas about rescuing her suggest, popularity and marketability appear in some way to threaten Austen's canonicity. Their being greatly liked compromises the novels' status as Great Books.

In fact, it may be that the complaints against those who read Austen outside the disciplinary and disciplined parameters of the literary tradition are spurred by something more than the perception that the others' love goes beyond those "proper confines." The complaints may also draw on the complainants' private conviction that what the ravening and unwitting fan gets in Austen's works is in fact Great Books Lite, the output of a lady amateur, not of a "conscious literary artificer." In their concern over the impropriety and extravagance of the pleasures other readers find in the works, the most zealous defenders of the novels sometimes seem to signal that they might not be so classic after all.[14]

Shakespeare fans, we should note, can act like fans, parade through Stratford-upon-Avon every April 23rd sporting sprigs of rosemary, and not put at risk the plays' claims to be taken seriously. No one, it seems, feels compelled to take this cult audience to task for their excesses and their failure to blush over them. But numerous readers of Austen have enlisted her in projects of cultural intimidation and regulation, making her into the knuckle-rapping schoolmistress of English letters. The novels are not simply *safe* reading, then, but in this guise a kind of boot camp. The roles Austen has been assigned often involve her teaching the reader and/or would-be writer a lesson, about morality, about linguistic propriety, or even about the renunciation of literary ambition. *She* chooses her words carefully. *She* knows her place. (These portraits of Austen as pedagogue are scrutinized by many contributors to this collection—Mary Ann O'Farrell, for instance, when she revisits the George Henry Lewes–Charlotte Brontë debate about Austen's merits and demerits; Katie Trumpener, when she shows us a proprietary Edmund Wilson administering Austen's female fans a lesson in how the "art" that she practiced transcended common feminine concerns with "emotion" and "gossip"; William Galperin, when he traces how the reality effects of Austen's fiction, initially perceived as anarchic and even surreal, were reinvented by the Victorians as a normative, regulatory realism.) When a commentator like D. W. Harding asserts that Austen would be embarrassed by how she is being read, he is intimating just how mortifying it would be for us in our turn should we be exposed as bad pupils to her lessons.[15]

Those who claim custody of the real Austen have had one other approach to opt for when coping with the popularity of the novels—with the idea that people with motives and values unlike "our" own read her too, people who might be, variously, lay readers or working-class readers or Americans. In the past many commentators have chosen to deny the existence of a general audience for the works (a move more difficult to pull off now). That denial has spirited away much conflict. It allays the anxiety provoked when the mass production of the tokens of elite culture threatens to undo their elite cachet. Over the last century and a half much has been invested in the premise that the appreciation of Austen's excellence is a minority taste. Within this scheme, the novels—by someone who was herself, it is stressed, a member of select society—are said to appear tame and commonplace to "the multitude" (this, according to J. E. Austen-Leigh in the *Memoir* of his aunt he published in 1870); the novels' virtues are "of an unobtrusive kind, shunning the glare of popularity" (or so George Henry Lewes concluded in 1859, tacitly reassuring the reader that such modesty was among the authoress's virtues too); unlike Dickens (or so Sheila Kaye-Smith asserted in 1943), Austen "exerts no mass appeal."[16]

Introducing the second volume of his invaluable *Jane Austen: The Critical Heritage* (1987), B. C. Southam demonstrates how this refrain has been picked up by one Austen commentator after another. He reveals just how shameless these efforts to turn Austen's works into caviar for the deserving few can be. In the hothouse atmosphere of these commentaries, Austen's popularity is a function of her *not* being popular. Hence Agnes Repplier's half reassuring, half sarcastic assertion that "Jane is not for all markets."[17] One should not, of course, disregard the attractions of hothouse atmospheres. Surveying Austen's reception, we can discern the outlines of a sort of history of homemaking, in which, time after time, a spirit of clubbability is ascribed to the novels and then celebrated for how it knits tight-knit family circles tighter, or for how it sponsors fellowship in tight places—among them, as Claudia L. Johnson suggests here, the tight place of the closet. (Even the nation-state can be scaled down to the dimensions of a snug home, if one imagines, as, for instance, Anne Thackeray

Ritchie did in 1883, all of the English reading Austen together and proving their insidership by getting allusions the French would miss.[18] It is hard to miss, too, the undertone of nationalist self-satisfaction imbedded in the later, apparently depreciatory suggestion that "Miss Austen" may be "one of those writers whom it is impossible to export.")[19]

Southam does not explicitly acknowledge the appeal of this home-loving way of loving Austen, but he does not, on the other hand, entirely resist the allure of its compound of togetherness and exclusivity. His introduction proposes that until Austen-Leigh published the *Memoir*, *real* interest in Austen was confined to a discriminating minority.[20] But Southam, as he proposes this, seems not to notice how he echoes the self-styled coteries whose claims to exclusivity he analyzes. As Barbara M. Benedict points out in her essay, given the difficulty of ascertaining anything from early-nineteenth-century sales figures, which date from a time when much novel reading was done under the auspices of the circulating library, there is a certain wishfulness to Southam's conviction that Austen's works were at first perceived as highbrow literature, and that they were only later commercialized and assimilated to the category of "popular novels."

## Austen's Popularity; or, Janeite vs. Janeite

Even Southam projects into the past a golden age of a unified readership, an audience at once unswayed by hype about best-sellers and above the snobbish pursuit of cultural capital, who would have read as "we" think Austen's readers ought to. We might say that Southam is envisioning a time before the "Janeites." For this is the term that Austen's audiences have learned to press into service whenever they need to designate the Other Reader in his or her multiple guises, or rather, and more precisely, whenever they need to personify and distance themselves from particular ways of reading, ones they might well indulge in themselves. "Janeite" can conjure up the reader as hobbyist—someone at once overzealous and undersophisticated, who cannot be trusted to discriminate between the true excellence of *Emma* and the ersatz pleasures of *Bridget Jones* or Barbara Pym or a Regency romance, and who is too *nice* in the modern sense of the word, not nice enough in Henry Tilney's. This figure is soul mate to the avid consumer whose purchases of Austeniana—coffee mugs and Regency writing paper—help sustain, along with additional purchases of potpourri and porcelain from National Trust shops, what is a conspicuously female-centered and female-staffed gift culture (and what is, in addition, a mode of engaging past times that proves endlessly vexatious to the professional historian).[21] Conversely, "Janeites" designates and accuses in their turn a cohort of cultural purists who, likewise transgressing against common sense but in their own way, haughtily find fault with all the nice methods of enacting a devotion to Austen. According to this particular, populist fable about the motives that impel *other* people to read Austen, those Janeites-cum-elitists manage to find in the novels' portrait of patrician society an endorsement of their own anachronistic reverence for cultural hierarchies, and of their equally anachronistic, obsequious Anglophilia. (More than other figures in the English literary canon, in fact, Austen seems a lightning rod for the anxieties provoked by that odd, ironic vestige of Britain's imperial past, the fact that English literature is a curricular staple in schoolrooms overseas. In certain contexts, to some observers, Austen loving looks symptomatic of a bad case of cultural cringe: the activity of a not-yet-decolonized mind. Yet Austen's "Englishness" need not be taken as an article of faith. We cannot always count on either her rootedness in English literature's Great Tradition or her usefulness to the heritage cinema that promotes past times and old money—or so the essays here by Mary A. Favret, Susan Fraiman, and Roger Sales argue in diverse ways.)[22]

The problem with Southam's assertion that Austen was thought of as a popular novelist only after 1870 is that it obscures the intimate relation between the history of the novel, Austen's chosen genre, and the histories of mass literacy and the commodity form. It distracts us from the instability of the opposition between canonical and popular writing: from how uses of the classic text and passions for tradition shift shape when, as the difference between Bardolatry and Janeiteism suggests, we move from one sort of classic text and one sort of tradition to another. To map, as I did above, the myriad locations in which people have discovered the Janeiteism they deplore is to remark that instability. A canon-loving insider who, nonetheless, insists on behaving like an outsider, and who through doing so delineates the inconsistencies that are internal to the institution Literature, the Janeite holds the secrets of the literary. And in this capacity the Janeite is a figure who, pace Southam's chronology, has needed to be there all along.[23] The Janeite—s/he who has responded too eagerly to the invitations to alliance that the Austen novels extend—is the necessary negative exemplar in a cultural order that since Austen's lifetime has called on us to love literature but not let our feelings get out of hand. This odd, abjected centrality is one reason Janeites receive star billing in the title to this collection.

And much can be learned from the peculiarities and peculiar history of their moniker. These go beyond the odd grammatical convention according to which "Janeite" can be used only in the second person or third. The term, now used almost exclusively about and against *other* people, was used differently a century ago: when literary scholar George Saintsbury coined it, he meant to equip himself with a badge of honor he could jubilantly pin onto his own lapel.[24] It is worth noting the contrast with contemporary codes of scholarly conduct, which would warn the career-conscious critic against letting the wrong people know of her desire to, for instance, wear Regency costume and dance at a Jane Austen Literary Ball. Austen is a safe subject, but in the academy Saintsbury's high-camp style of Janeiteism is high-risk behavior.

The term "Janeite" is also one of a kind. Has the given name of any other writer been made into an epithet like this one? "Shakespearean" or "Dickensian" operate differently. Those labels belong to a chillier idiom. Neither intimates, as "Janeite" does, a reading situation in which writer and fan will be on a first-name basis.

Then, too, "Janeite" works, as corresponding terms do not, to highlight the author's gender and to imply that the reader's is the same. The intimacy of the reading situation the epithet evokes is enhanced by the suggestion that Jane and the Janeite share their gender and more: lately, indeed, some of the annoyance critics express when confronting the spectacle of Janeiteism seems motivated by their suspicion that the novels provide cultural spaces where we girls can all be girls together. But it is worth lingering over the fact that it is George Saintsbury who represents the first self-confessed Janeite, and that it is the artillery officers in Rudyard Kipling's 1926 short story who model the most celebrated examples of Janeite zealotry and esprit de corps. These examples pose a challenge to what contemporary common sense would make of "Janeite." They undermine current dogma about the gendering of Austen's appeal. And, in the same way, when Kipling's Janeites take Austen out of the Home Counties and into the trenches, and when, more recently, Patrick O'Brian makes the conversational skills and ways of killing time that her characters hone in drawing rooms into survival skills for Royal Navy officers, they violate what our culture thinks it knows about Austen's relation to public history.

Careless of Austen's safety, Kipling and O'Brian transport her into the theater of war and so exemplify Trilling's assertion that love for Austen is often carried (and carries her and her novels) beyond the proper confines: in this case, outside the private sphere, and beyond the limits of women's writing and domestic fiction. The examination of Austen's readerships and readings that *Janeites: Austen's Disciples and Devotees* aims to initiate, an examination that ranges widely and does not respect unduly the borders of periodization or the boundaries between academic writing and other ways of talking about Jane Austen, will result in these sorts of displacements. Our common desire in this project is, to reiterate, to make it harder to assign (or consign) Austen to her proper place.

We emphasize accordingly moments when readers' responses to Austen have been shaped by and have shaped their responses to issues of public concern: war, for instance; or the rise of mass literacy in the nineteenth century and the appearance onto the cultural stage of new classes of readers and new ways of settling the boundaries between education, government, and popular culture. If that turn to history reveals Austen's audiences, like Austen herself, as a more worldly set, more tough-minded and even pugnacious, than is sometimes rumored, and if it has revealed to us, in addition, the ways in which our own readings of and trysts with Austen are likewise implicated in processes of social contestation, this does not discount the tributes numerous readers have paid to the Austen novel's power to send them *home* from the world. The Austen novel can make itself into our space of privacy, a power that accounts for recurrent references to its "perfect . . . village geography," to its modeling of knowable communities ("chat rooms" that preexist the Internet) and of ordinary, comfortable familiarity. Repeatedly in the history of Austen's audiences, the act of commodity exchange that is the act of reading is converted into something more tender. Arthur Ransome's 1909 verdict on the Austen novel—"it would almost seem to be written in a letter to the reader"[25]—still rings true. The tricky dimension of writing about the history of Austen's reception is, then, how it tugs the writer in two directions, not only toward the public domain but also toward the spaces of intimacy, where Austen, as the confidante who knows and forgives our hidden desires and dislikes, has allowed our love. What this collection of essays finally proposes, though, is this: even when we turn from Austen's presence in the collective mind to the myriad ways in which involvement with her has given individuals a template for emotional life, we can expect to encounter fracas.

## "More Talk of Jane Austen"

It makes sense, accordingly, that the essays which open *Janeites: Austen's Disciples and Devotees* direct our attention at the outset to what I just described as the risky business of Janeitism. In "The Divine Miss Jane: Jane Austen, Janeites, and the Discipline of Novel Studies," Claudia L. Johnson highlights the confirmed bachelorhood and clubbability Kipling ascribed to his Janeites, alongside the high camp of the real-life Oxbridge gentlemen who in the early decades of this century declared themselves Austen's admirers, in order to recover a nonnormative tradition of reading that recent Austen scholars have forgotten. One outcome of the professionalization of novel studies that occurred in the 1940s and 1950s is that now there appears to be little doubt about the kind of congress Austenian reading promotes. But the fact that accounts of her conservative commitment to "the marriage plot" and to so-called adult sexuality remain orthodoxy in academic discussion has much to do, Johnson argues, with the evaluative strategies a middle-class professorate used to discipline and displace an older and (as these professors claimed) effete and belletristic model of novel criticism.

Johnson's account of the two cultures of Austenian reading communities, which moves from Wilde and Forster to the quiz-taking, ballroom-dancing Jane Austen societies of today, is paired here with Mary Ann O'Farrell's equally wide-ranging examination of the moments since the nineteenth century when readers have imagined Jane Austen as their friend. O'Farrell's aim in "Jane Austen's Friendship," which reads critics' alliances with Austen (as well as Brontë's flamboyant refusal of such an alliance) against the friendships portrayed in Austen's novels, is to reveal friendship—and constructions of authorship and readership as friendly activities—in less idealized and edgier terms than the culture generally allows. The fact that within friendship's uneasy blend of "complementarity and difference," friends deny their friends' imperfections, or deny their friends the capacity to be different from themselves, can explain why readers fall so hard for Austen or feel so let down by her lapses. As well as allowing us to see the novels in new ways (so that, for instance, their author is not so much a celebrant of the marriage plot as a "poet of irrational dislike"), O'Farrell gives us a language for apprehending the narcissistic elements that subsist within all attachments to Austen, including those studied by the other contributors. Tacitly, she reminds us that, alongside the "influence" and "intertextuality" which scholars describe when chronicling Austen's afterlife, they also need to take account of something more emotion-saturated and riskier, better described as identification.

Johnson's and O'Farrell's accounts of the modalities of fellowship in novel reading and promoted by novel reading are succeeded by a pair of essays focused on how Austen's contemporaries responded to her. The first, Barbara M. Benedict's "Sensibility by the Numbers: Austen's Work as Regency Popular Fiction," engages the circulating libraries where Regency-period audiences encountered Austen's work and the now-forgotten novels—anonymously authored, rapid reads such as *Love at first sight, or the gay in a flutter*—those readers would have found right beside that work. Benedict's interest lies with how Austen seems comfortable in packaging her texts as the products of the formulae of popular fiction and not of a unique sensibility, the Romantics' redefinitions of authorship notwithstanding. Indeed, in various ways, Benedict insists, Austen's practice ran athwart Romantic schemes for distinguishing kinds of writings and audiences, and confidence that her work could fit easily into the category of high literature came late. It depended on new claims about popular audiences and their natural proclivity for the sensational, claims that eventually allowed nineteenth-century tastemakers to claim Austen's representations of everyday life as the fulfillment of their own agenda.

In "Austen's Earliest Readers and the Rise of the Janeites," William Galperin is also interested in how critics have used Austen's representations of familiar things to legitimate their own projects—in this case, definitions of the novel's didactic task. If the link, which figures such as Walter Scott and George Henry Lewes helped establish, between a realist aesthetic and projects of social hegemony is now a given, and if literary histories have ascribed to Austen a pivotal role in securing that link, these truths were less self-evident to Regency-period readers such as Annabella Milbanke and Jane Davy. These readers in fact insisted on the novels' *divergence* from the model of probabilistic fiction (fiction that could be trusted to instruct impressionable young women about real life) that had been set in place by the eighteenth-century debate about the novel's superiority to the romance. They commented on the plotlessness of Austen's novels, in which the vivid details seemed to them strangely ungoverned by didactic aims. In this guise, Galperin suggests, these lay readers from the early nineteenth century may be paired with the Janeites as Johnson describes them, as an audience whose ability to wrest an oppositional yield from the fiction (and overlook its marriage plots) counters current orthodoxies not just about Austen but also about the regulatory, policing functions that are said to be enacted by the novel genre itself.

Benedict's and Galperin's studies of Austen's earliest audiences are followed by a trio of essays that take this collection into the twentieth century. These essays address in explicit terms the significance of Austen's legacy and influence, first, for her "queer nephews" (who modeled country-house novels such as *The Portrait of a Lady* and *Howards End* on the works of their foremother even while experiencing such inheritance through the female line as a source of much anxiety); second, for British women novelists in the era of high modernism; and, third, for Americans.

Clara Tuite's essay, "Decadent Austen Entails: Forster, James, Firbank, and the 'Queer Taste' of *Sanditon*," opens by tracing how, in *Pride and Prejudice* and *Mansfield Park*, Austen, preoccupied like her Mrs. Bennet with "how estates will go," endowed canonical literary culture with the genre which provided that culture with its own ways of plotting the (normally patrilineal) transmission of literary influence and legitimacy between the generations. Tuite also highlights Austen's radical departure from the genre of the country-house novel and its plot of heterosexual reproduction in her last, unfinished work, *Sanditon*. She engages the reception greeting that work when it was published belatedly in 1925, a moment of high Janiteism when Austen was herself being made over as a national trust property and image of England's cultural continuity. Forster's iconoclastic response to *Sanditon* indexes the anxiety of influence afflicting Austen's male descendants in the novelistic tradition, nervous about their female-identified genre. His depreciation of Austen also displaces, Tuite suggests, the ambivalence that Forster felt toward his *masculine* predecessors: the Decadents whom, within his review, *Sanditon* seems to predict, both despite and because of its belatedness and "queer taste."

The questions examined by "Decadent Austen Entails" about a woman's place within tradition—and about what it means (as Woolf put it) to think back through our mothers—also preoccupied the British women modernists whom Katie Trumpener studies in "The Virago Jane Austen." Austen's example troubles that idea of a women's literary tradition as much as she anchors the tradition in, for instance, her position as tutelary deity of Virago Press's reprint series of women's fiction. As Trumpener suggests, many early-twentieth-century women worried over the way that Austen-Leigh's story of how his long-suffering aunt wrote in the "common sitting room" was made to stand in, with all its overtones of domestic martyrdom, for the story of women's writing in general. In the wake of the suffrage movement especially, they puzzled over whether their identification with Austen's example and with heroines such as the "creepmouse" Fanny Price represented a luxury that as modern feminists they could no longer afford. Yet E. M. Delafield and F. M. Mayor nonetheless paid homage to Austen's powers as social critic by rewriting *Mansfield Park* and *Persuasion* in the novels from the 1920s that Trumpener analyzes at the close of her essay.

"She never travelled; she never drove through London in an omnibus or had luncheon in a shop by herself." Virginia Woolf assesses her Austenian legacy and measures the difference between her time and her foremother's by gauging varying degrees of domestic entrapment. With change of place, a transatlantic crossing, the emphasis in this way of construing Austen's situation changes too. As Mary A. Favret reveals in "Free and Happy: Jane Austen in America," since the days of James Fenimore Cooper, citizens of the United States, many of them men, have imagined her lighting out for the territory with them and so cocreating what Richard Poirier memorably called "a world elsewhere." Responding to the emotional detachment that positions Austen as somebody who, like an American, is outside English society but also authorized to have fun with it, they have claimed the English novelist as an ally. Favret meditates on the pliability of the concept of tradition and the geographical portability of an aesthetic package that back at home seemed rather to exemplify home: for W. D. Howells in 1900, by contrast, Austen's realism was a democratic project and accordingly her heirs were to be found in New England, not Old. Favret also emphasizes how often, in these American commentaries, the new world Austen made was one marked by Jim Crow: how often the ordinariness of the "ordinary" people that Austen's realism placed in that world was a function of their membership in the white race.

But there are other understandings of who is "ordinarily" admitted into the world of Austen's novels. This volume concludes with two essays that engage Austen's reception at the present moment. As these essays resituate the novels, first in that strange media interzone where high culture gets televised, then among populations coming to terms with the legacies of the British Empire, the homogeneous social world that Austen's American commentators found and celebrated in her work ends up appearing rather more troubled than it did before.

In "In Face of All the Servants: Spectators and Spies in Austen," Roger Sales considers the high profile that retinues of servants have in the recent televisual and filmic adaptations of the novels (the 1995 *Persuasion* primarily). He does so in order to argue for some unexpected effects of the novels' embrace by the institutions of quality television and the heritage industry. The presence of these gardeners and footmen waiting at table does more than exemplify this century's investment in making Austen's high-class settings even classier, and in, more generally, reinventing the past so as to present the stately home as the real home of us all. Sales's point is that in this case the historical details work against the grain of the idyllic qualities of the adaptations, emphasizing the anxieties of a ruling class whose members were forced to act out their lives before an audience of servants. At the moments when they come to seem not just picturesque extras but interlopers, the servant figures reconnect Austen to a set of Regency-period representations of the dangerous servant.

Sales's remarks about the class tensions made visible by the TV *Persuasion* resonate with Favret's suggestion about the strange echoes of *Gone with the Wind* in MGM's 1940 *Pride and Prejudice*: that these echoes register how Americans could not help but inflect their reading of Austen with an acknowledgment of the Americas' traumatic history of racial slavery. By wondering about why *Mansfield Park* has so prominent a place both in *Culture and Imperialism* and in the reviews responding to Edward Said's 1993 book on the inextricable relation between the European aesthetic tradition and European colonialism, Susan Fraiman broaches the question of what Austen's own relation to such an acknowledgment would be. In "Jane Austen and Edward Said: Gender, Culture, and Imperialism," Fraiman, arguing for the confluence of abolitionist and feminist discourses in *Mansfield Park*, portrays Austen as a citizen of a larger world than the country neighborhood with which she is usually associated. Said's attention to how slave labor in distant Antigua sustains the Bertrams in their position of social eminence in their neighborhood also redraws the boundaries of the novel's world. But Said's historicism grants little in the way of a historical consciousness to Austen herself; in his view, her participation in public issues was unwitting, her complicity in imperialism automatic. Said's refusal to wonder about whether Austen was at home in the stately home—and his readers' readiness to embrace his assertion that she was—suggests something about the gendered logic that informs the project of postcolonial theory as *Culture and Imperialism*, a primer for the field, defines it. To make Austen an emblem of empire is to feminize the imperial powers and resecure the masculinity of the oppressed.

---

And why do this with Austen? There are intersections between Fraiman's essay and the essay that provides *Janeites* with its starting point: Johnson's discussion of Austen's usefulness for that middle-class professorate who affirmed their expertise by reappropriating Austen from Bloomsbury and from an effete aristocracy—who didn't just professionalize but simultaneously remasculinized novel reading. Apparently one reason that critics, then and now, center their narratives on Austen is that they rely on her to set gender and sexuality straight. (Whether this is because Austen's attitude to such matters is so evident or so opaque—whether this is a case of sparing the critic the work of interpretation or setting the critic an interpretive challenge—is itself open to question.) On the testimony of this anthology, there are, of course, numerous other reasons why Austen particularly must be the heroine (or villainess) of the stories that readers tell about their relations to the literary tradition or to house and home and nation and history, and why they so often adopt the example of her novels in order to do that telling. She is inside the pantheon of Western culture, a major fact, as F. R. Leavis wrote, in the background of other writers, and yet off-center—as the essays that follow emphasize—with respect to the culture's dominant narratives about literary influence and literary periods, about what realism is and does to us, about the relations of classic literature and popular culture. Such anomalousness may also be an aspect of what keeps us reading.

A reader of Austen, Lionel Trilling wrote, "is required to make no mere literary judgment but a decision about his own character and personality, and about his relation to society and all of life."[26] Trilling is right, but—as if he were hyperconscious of the novels' classic status—his tone is portentous. His Austen is the intimidating schoolteacher, a hard taskmistress. In the place of his exhortation to duty, let us substitute Miss Bates's description of a reader's love: "such a pleasure to her—a letter from Jane—that she can never hear it enough!" (157).

## Notes

1. Susan M. Braden, "Local Jane-ites: Taking a Turn around the Parlor with Austen," *Shore Line Times*, 21 April 1999, "Second Section: Out & About," 1. The Republic of Pemberley may be visited at *www.pemberley.com.*

2. "Pride and Petroleum," *Economist*, 30 March 1996, 58.

3. Roger Sales proposes, similarly, that academic critics have something to learn from popular representations of Austen and of the Regency (which counts as a "period" in popular memory, as Regency romances, fashions for "empire-waist" dresses, and interior decoration all suggest, but has no comparable standing for the academic discipline of English studies). See his introduction to *Jane Austen and Representations of Regency England* (London: Routledge, 1994; rev. ed., 1996).

Practitioners of Shakespeare studies have a better track record than Austen scholars do when it comes to coping with the mobility of the figure whom they study. The readiness of many of these scholars to admit that Shakespeare (like Austen) is wont to move off the pedestal or out of the ivory tower in which the institutions of high culture and higher learning place him has made their work a source of inspiration for this volume. Particularly useful accounts of the cultural Shakespeare may be found in Graham Holderness, ed., *The Shakespeare Myth* (Manchester: Manchester University Press, 1988); Michael D. Bristol, *Shakespeare's America, America's Shakespeare* (New York: Routledge, 1990) and his *Big-Time Shakespeare* (New York: Routledge, 1996); Michael Dobson, *The Making of the National Poet: Shakespeare, Adaptation, and Authorship, 1660–1769* (Oxford: Clarendon, 1992).

4. For an example of how the Regency country house represents the sort of picture of perfection for which we postmoderns should now read Austen, see Susan Watkins's preface to *Jane Austen in Style*, corrected ed. (New York: Thames and Hudson, 1996): "Here we will see *how* the country gentry lived—in an ambience of cultivated politeness. . . . We will also see *where* they lived, the aesthetic perfection of the English country house crowning an almost equally perfect landscape" (7; emphasis in the original). Here, by contrast, is Margaret Oliphant praising the "perfect piece of village geography" that she finds in *Emma*, in her 1870 *Blackwood's Edinburgh Magazine* essay "Miss Austen and Miss Mitford": "Highbury, with Ford's shop in the High Street, and Miss Bates's rooms opposite . . . with windows from which you can see all that is going on. . . . And the vicarage lane at one end of the town, . . . where the young vicar from his study can see the good ladies passing. . . . Nothing could be more easy than to make a map of it, with indications where the London road strikes off, and by which turning Frank Churchill, on his tired horse, will come from Richmond. We know it as well as if we had lived there all our lives, and visited Miss Bates every day" (304). See also Constance Hill, *Jane Austen: Her Homes and Her Friends* (London and New York: John Lane, 1902), which quotes this passage of Oliphant's at length.

5. Paul Elmer More, review of *Jane Austen: Her Life and Letters: A Family Record* (1913), quoted in Southam 1987, 2:86.

6. I quote from Michael D. Bristol's helpful riposte to these purist arguments: see *Big-Time Shakespeare*, 17.

7. Lionel Trilling, "*Emma* and the Legend of Jane Austen," reprinted in *Beyond Culture: Essays on Literature and Learning* (New York: Viking, 1965), 31; D. W. Harding, "Regulated Hatred: An Aspect of the Work of Jane Austen," reprinted in *Jane Austen: A Critical Companion*, ed. Ian Watt (Englewood Cliffs, N.J.: Prentice-Hall, 1963), 167.

8. Louis Menand, "What Jane Austen Doesn't Tell Us," *New York Review of Books* 43, no. 2 (1 February 1996): 15; Boyd Tonkin, "*Emma*," *New Statesman*, 13 September 1996, 39. I encountered the not-so-quaintly sexist phrase "frilly bonnet brigade" in *Facets Features*, February/March 1997, n.p., which attributes this label for fans of heritage cinema to British theater managers.

9. Compare Judy Simons's observation that "Austenmania both restores and distorts the reputation of the literary classic as a signifier of cultural value": "Classics and Trash: Reading Austen in the 1990s," *Women's Writing* 5, no. 1 (1998): 27–28.

10. I quote John Simon's recent version of the portrait of Austen as an envious spinster: see "*Emma* without Emma," *National Review*, 14 October 1996, 87. Simon, who takes pains to show that his remarks are authorized by the scholarly tradition, quotes Harding's "Regulated Hatred." His account of Austen might also be compared to the one on offer in Marvin Mudrick's *Jane Austen: Irony as Defense and Discovery* (Princeton: Princeton University Press, 1952).

11. For critics offering to marry Austen, see, most recently, Richard A. Blake, "Plain Jane," *America*, 9 March 1996, 21: "Ours will be a tryst for the ages!" John Halperin betrays much anxiety about setting the record straight when, responding to a comment on the paucity of Austen's attachments that is made in Austen-Leigh's *Memoir*, construing "attachment" as a term applicable to heterosexual relations exclusively, he ends the title essay of *Jane Austen's Lovers* with a roll call of the names of the eligible men (a dozen, all told) to whom Austen may have felt "attached" (*Jane Austen's Lovers and Other Studies in Fiction and History from Austen to le Carr* [London: Macmillan, 1988], 24–25). Talk of Jane Austen has provided male commentators with a cultural space for exercising the prerogative defining them *as* men: the prerogative of doing the asking. The marriage proposal is an abiding feature of the critical tradition, though W. D. Howells admits of Fanny Price that he is "quite willing Edmund Bertram should have her in the end" (*Heroines of Fiction*, 2 vols. [New York: Harper & Brothers, 1901], 1:77).

12. Compare what Brenda R. Silver says about how popular representations of Virginia Woolf disrupt the boundary between high and low culture: "The boundary . . . mapped by Andreas Huyssen in his study of 'Mass Culture as Modernism's Other' that divides modernism, high culture, and maleness . . . on the one side, from women . . . and mass culture on the other, is a boundary that shivers and dissolves when you introduce an actual woman, Virginia Woolf, and not generic 'Woman' or 'the feminine' into the picture" ("Mis-fits: The Monstrous Union of Virginia Woolf and Marilyn Monroe," *Discourse* 16, no. 1 [fall 1993]: 95). Silver draws on Andreas Huyssen's "Mass Culture as Woman: Modernism's Other," first published in *Studies in Entertainment: Critical Approaches to Mass Culture*, ed. Tania Modleski (Bloomington: Indiana University Press, 1986), 188–207.

13. Another, comparable problem, as Judy Simons notes ("Classics and Trash," 30–31), is Austen's obvious reluctance to polarize "classics" and "trash" as rigorously as modern scholars would like her to: Austen shamelessly enjoyed novels like Mrs. S. Sykes's *Margiana or Widdrington Tower* (1808) and Rachel Hunter's *Lady Maclairn, the Victim of Villainy* (1806) (see *Jane Austen's Letters*, ed. Deirdre Le Faye [Oxford: Oxford University Press, 1995], 10–11 January 1809, 164; 29–31 October 1812, 195). Many women writers, conscious of the gendering of these categories, have been more interested in *collapsing* the boundaries that separate the literary and the popular than in policing them.

14. E. V. Lucas distinguished Austen from "conscious literary artificers" in 1900 as he introduced a new edition of *Pride and Prejudice*: quoted in Southam 1987, 2:28. As Claudia L. Johnson observes in the preface to *Jane Austen: Women, Politics, and the Novel* (Chicago: University of Chicago Press, 1988), Austen "has been admitted into the canon on terms which cast doubt on her qualifications for entry and which ensure that her continued presence there be regarded as an act of gallantry" (xiv). Some of the hostility to the current Austenmania seems to bear out the continuing relevance of Woolf's insights into the gender politics of canonization: "This is an important book, the critic assumes, because it deals with war. This is an insignificant book because it deals with the feelings of women in a drawing-room" (*A Room of One's Own and Three Guineas*, ed. Morag Shiach [Oxford: Oxford University Press, 1992], 96).

15. In thinking about the centrality that the emotion of embarrassment has in the literary system, I have been aided by Joseph Litvak's *Strange Gourmets: Sophistication, Theory, and the Novel* (Durham, N.C.: Duke University Press, 1997), and Mary Ann O'Farrell's discussion of Austen in *Telling Complexions: The Nineteenth-Century English Novel and the Blush* (Durham, N.C.: Duke University Press, 1997).

16. J. E. Austen-Leigh, *A Memoir of Jane Austen*, appendix to Jane Austen, *Persuasion* (Harmondsworth: Penguin, 1965), 361; George Henry Lewes, "The Novels of Jane Austen," *Blackwood's Edinburgh Magazine* 86 (July 1859), anthologized Southam 1968, 150; Sheila Kaye-Smith in Sheila Kaye-Smith and G. B. Stern, *Talking of Jane Austen* (London: Cassell, 1943; published in the U. S. as *Speaking of Jane Austen*), 5.

17. Agnes Repplier, review of *Jane Austen* by R. Brimley Johnson, *Commonweal*, 13 May 1931, in Southam 1987, 2:214. The continuation of this passage supplies me with my first epigraph.

18. Here is Anne Thackeray Ritchie's opening to her discussion of Regency-period women writers, *A Book of Sibyls* (London: Smith, Elder, & Co., 1883): "Not long ago, a party of friends were sitting at luncheon in a suburb of London, when one of them happened to make some reference to Maple Grove and Selina, and to ask in what county of England Maple Grove was situated. Everybody had a theory" (v). If you, embarrassed reader, don't know to consult your copy of *Emma*, there to be reminded that Maple Grove is the name of the former stomping grounds of Augusta Elton, and that Selina is the name of Mrs. E.'s well-to-do sister, then you are like the touring Frenchman who has found his hapless way into this cozy company of initiates.

For Janeite fellowship and friendship, see Mary Ann O'Farrell's and Claudia L. Johnson's essays in this volume. Laura Fairchild Brodie has also discussed the ways in which readers since the nineteenth century have associated Austen with a reading situation that is distinctive for its qualities of intimacy and exclusivity: see "Jane Austen and the Common Reader: 'Opinions of *Mansfield Park*,' 'Opinions of *Emma*,' and the Janeite Phenomenon," *Texas Studies in Language and Literature* 37, no. 1 (1995): 54–69.

19. Raymond Mortimer, introduction to Colette, *Chéri* and *The Last of Chéri*, trans. Roger Senhouse (London: Secker & Warburg, 1951), vii.

20. Introduction to Southam 1987, 2:15; cf. 2:58.

21. Raphael Samuel commented insightfully on the misogynist strain in many of the complaints made about the commodification or Disneyfication of the past (complaints that also function to mark off the practice of history as the prerogative or even invention of professional historians): see *Theatres of Memory: Past and Present in Contemporary Culture*, vol. 1 (London: Verso, 1994), esp. 261–67.

22. See, in addition to those three essays, Ruth Vanita's discussion of how "the English text may either become a means for avoiding our own position as Indian women, or help us come to terms with and endorse it": "*Mansfield Park* in Miranda House," in *The Lie of the Land: English Literary Studies in India*, ed. Rajeswari Sunder Rajan (Delhi: Oxford University Press, 1992), 90–99.

Azar Nafisi, who is completing a book on her experiences writing about and teaching Western novels in the Islamic Republic of Iran, reports that her students at Tehran University find Austen—and not, e.g., Maxim Gorky—the truly "revolutionary" writer on her syllabus. "By the end of the course [*Pride and Prejudice*] becomes the most exciting topic, because they discover [that] a subject like marriage, which in this society is counted as 'trivial,' is really the basis of a lot of values and norms which we call revolutionary" (interview with Jacki Lyden, *Weekend Edition*, 15 April 1995, transcript courtesy of National Public Radio).

23. Clifford Siskin also pairs Austen's afterlife with Literature's. He suggests that study of Austen can provide us with a vantage point that would enable us to stand outside the disciplinary parameters of literary study and see what is culturally contingent about the discipline's classificatory and evaluative principles. Outlining the enigmas that Austen and her canonicity have represented for literary studies (i.e., was Austen a "Romantic"? was Austen a feminist? why, when so many of her female contemporaries were forgotten, has her work been remembered and canonized?), Siskin suggests that these questions should not be adjudicated solely "in terms of her individual beliefs." Instead they represent "problem[s] in the historicity of the category of Literature." See "Jane Austen and the Engendering of Disciplinarity," in *Jane Austen and Discourses of Feminism*, ed. Devoney Looser (New York: St. Martin's, 1995), 63.

24. Saintsbury declared himself a "Janite" in his 1894 introduction to a new edition of *Pride and Prejudice*. On the history of "Janeites," see Lorraine Hanaway, " 'Janeite' at 100," *Persuasions* 16 (December 1994): 28–29.

25. Arthur Ransome, *History of Story-Telling: Studies in the Development of Narrative* (1909), quoted in Southam 1987, 2:78.

26. Trilling, "*Emma* and the Legend of Jane Austen," 32.

# 1

## The Divine Miss Jane: Jane Austen, Janeites, and the Discipline of Novel Studies

CLAUDIA L. JOHNSON

> On the level of common sense it is not hard to wish Mr. Kimball well in his war [against "tenured radicals"]. Even when his examples of academic idiocy are funny, they are also hair-raising. . . . A proponent of feminist studies argues that "gynophobia is structured like a language." Sessions of the annual meeting of the Modern Language Association are devoted to "Jane Austen and the Masturbating Girl" and to "Desublimating the Male Sublime: Autoerotics, Anal Erotics and Corporeal Violence in Melville and William Burroughs."
>
> *(Roger Rosenblatt, "The Universities: A Bitter Attack" [review of Roger Kimball,* Tenured Radicals*],* New York Times Book Review, *22 April 1990)*

> If we now turn to the significance of the macho-style for gay men, it would, I think, be accurate to say that this style gives rise to two reactions, both of which indicate a profound respect for machismo itself. One is the classic put-down: the butch number swaggering into a bar in a leather get-up opens his mouth and sounds like a pansy, takes you home, where the first thing you notice is the complete works of Jane Austen, gets you into bed, and—well, you know the rest. In short, the mockery of gay machismo is almost exclusively an internal affair, and it is based on the dark suspicion that you may not be getting the real article. The other reaction is, quite simply, sexual excitement.
>
> *(Leo Bersani, "Is the Rectum a Grave," in* AIDS: Cultural Analysis, Cultural Activism*)*

JANE AUSTEN always seems to inspire radically contradictory appeals to self-evidence. For Roger Rosenblatt, as for Roger Kimball, "common sense" dictates that Austen is obviously straitlaced and straight, and would have seemed off-limits to the nonsense of sex and gender analysis if tenured radicals had not turned the world, the obviously prim Miss Austen included, upside down. Pressing fantasies about the serenity of Regency England into the service of heterosexual presumption, Kimball and Rosenblatt place Austen *before* the advent of such ills as industrialization, dubiety, feminism, homosexuality, masturbation, the unconscious. In her novels, men are gentlemen, women are ladies, and the desires of gentlemen and ladies for each other are intelligible, complementary, mutually fulfilling, and, above all, *inevitable.* Not that such assumptions are articulated. The whole point is *not* that they do not have to be but that they must never be; as David Halperin has suggested, heterosexuality is the love that dares not speak its name, and argument would denaturalize and *out* it.[1] Recoiling from this possibility as from apocalypse itself, Rosenblatt describes Eve Kosofsky Sedgwick's paper on *Sense and Sensibility* as one of the many "horror stories" that make Kimball seem like a bearded prophet of old: the world may indeed be coming to an end; even Jane Austen is not safe.[2]

For Leo Bersani, the case is different, testifying inadvertently as he does to Austen's status among gay men. His anecdote comes to us as an old and disappointing story. Like Rosenblatt, he relies on "common" knowledge and on an audience that similarly will recognize his anecdote as a *classic*, a story *you*—which is to say, "we gay boys"—all know and that for this reason will require no elaboration. Calling attention to the ambivalences about effeminacy and macho within the gay community itself, Bersani's anecdote shows that homosexuality and the *Oxford Illustrated Jane Austen* are not strange bedfellows. Even as we speak, some leather-clad "butch number" may be "swaggering" up to a not-so-unsuspecting boy in a bar, his mind full of the ball at Netherfield and hot sex. Sure, he is, as Bersani puts it, a "pansy": "you" may pretend "you" had no inkling of this until later, but "you" knew it as soon as he "open[ed] his mouth," and obviously liked it well enough to go home with him in the first place. But his passion for Austen, recognized later, makes him doubly so, guaranteeing that he will be a bottom: "well, you know the rest." Bersani's complex and rather Austenian mockery aside, Austen's novels appear often to have facilitated rather than dampened conversation between men. In 1899, when he was a student at Cambridge, E. M. Forster was whisked to a fellow's room expressly to examine a new deluxe edition of Austen's novels;[3] and Montague Summers remembers "hotly championing the cause of Jane Austen" to the "charming" poet Robert Nichols, a man "distractingly violent . . . but most attractive in his flaming zeal and pale vehemence."[4] The precise nature of these Austenian encounters we do not know. This much is clear, however: the real joke in Bersani's story is not the "complete works of Jane Austen" but the "leather get-up," and their simultaneously denied and desired conjunction.

A comparable clash of assumptions over what Austen is like and what kind of converse her novels promote reerupted in 1995 in the *London Review of Books*, when Terry Castle discussed Austen's intense attachment to her sister Cassandra and claimed that sister-sister relations are just as important as marriage in the novels, if not more so. The editors of the *LRB* sought controversy: why else entitle the review "Was Jane Austen Gay?" without Castle's say-so? But no one expected the vehemence that followed, as scores of people rushed to rescue Austen from the charge of "sister-love": one reader, assuming that "Terry" was a man, damned the "drip-drip" smuttiness of "his" discussions of women's familiarity; some swore up and down that marriages in Austen's novels were perfectly felicitous without requiring the supplemental pleasures of sororal love; others insisted testily, if inanely, that since sisters commonly shared beds in those days, it is anachronistic to imply that their intimacy meant anything "more." Austen scholar B. C. Southam entered the fray: does Austen describe women's bodies with "homophilic fascination," as Castle suggested? Not to worry: Austen was an amateur seamstress and thus had a perfectly innocent reason for attending to how gowns hugged the persons of her female acquaintance. The outcry, extensively covered in the British media, even reached *Newsweek* and *Time*, where one reader grumbled, "So Jane Austen may have been a lesbian. . . . Who cares?" only to continue by complaining about the "questionable practices" of psychoanalyzing historical subjects unable to speak for themselves and of reading too much into the "love language of women." Vainly did Castle plead that she had never asserted the existence of an incestuously lesbian relationship between Austen and her sister: the words *homophilic* and *homoerotic* provoked readers to announce that the limits of tolerance had been reached. Castle had "polluted the shrine," and this would not be suffered.[5]

The heteronormativity of Austen seems as obvious to Rosenblatt, Kimball, and outraged readers of the *LRB* as her queerness does to Castle, Bersani, and the men in his anecdote. How can we account for this anomaly, and why should we bother? In attempting to answer this, I make no claims to neutrality. I cast my lot with the queer Austen and believe that the question of Austen's reception and readerships merits substantial consideration. Such is the enormity of Austen's status as a cultural institution, however, and such is her centrality to the canon of British literature in general, that the issues surrounding these controversies are really much larger. What if Austen *were* "gay" (as the *LRB* put it)? I hope to show that modern Austen criticism labored to occlude this possibility when a middle-class professorate wrested Austen from upper-class Janeites, and when the disciplined study of the novel was being founded. Central to this undertaking, then, is a consideration of different traditions, motives, and modes of valuation regarding Austen.[6] While I will begin by tracing the sexual politics of Austenian valuations and how these get appropriated by constituencies of different class and sexual positions, I will go on to uncover the terms on which Austen's place in the founding of the disciplined study of the novel was established. Although my principal aim will be to illuminate the history of Austenian reception as it sheds light on the institution of novel studies,[7] at the same time, by considering the phenomenon of "Janeiteism," I also hope to genealogize the perceived queerness of many of her readers, as this queerness has been played out euphemistically in (sometimes overlapping) oppositions between macho and "effeminate" standards of masculinity, and between academic and belletristic models of novel criticism.

---

To listen to the readers who attacked Sedgwick and Castle, we might imagine that no one had *ever* doubted Austen's normativity before. This is so far from the case that the wonder is rather that Austen's normality itself now appears beyond question to so many. "Is she queer?—Is she prudish?" (230). So asks the rakish Henry Crawford of *Mansfield Park* as he wonders about Austen's nerdiest heroine, Fanny Price. For some reason, the erotic charm that makes married and unmarried women in that novel yield to Henry's desire fails to make a dent on this mousy, inhibited, and intense girl. Stymied by Fanny's resistance to his allure, Henry tries to determine Fanny's "character" (230). Is something *wrong* with her (is she odd, out of sorts, cold, and thus peculiarly resistant to normal heterosexual seduction)? Or is something "wrong" with him (do his multiple and serial flirtations deserve the censure this unusually, but not abnormally, moral young lady levels against them?)? Fanny decides in favor of the severity of rectitude, but the novel refuses to settle between propriety and pathology, and insists on their confusion.

Henry's reading of Fanny as either queer or prudish describes two traditions of Austenian reception.[8] Ever since Archbishop Whately claimed in 1821 that Austen was "evidently a Christian writer,"[9] many readers have been either pleased or infuriated to find that her novels are given over to orthodox morality, conservative politics, and strenuous propriety. This view is hardly the handiwork of the academic right wing, much less of heterosexist readers. Such are the asymmetries of the sex-gender system brilliantly elucidated by Judith Butler, among others, that it is not hard to find critics working within the camps of feminism, deconstruction, and queer studies who view Austen as Rosenblatt and Kimball might wish.

D. A. Miller, for example, who has done so much for the study of "gay fabulation," reads Austen much as Allan Bloom does: what Bloom admires as wholesomely instructive and disciplinary in Austen's style and narrative structures, Miller can describe as violently hygienic and correctional. Different valuation: same Austen.[10]

Even though Kimball and Rosenblatt cast themselves as righteous amateurs opposing the lunacy rampant in the academy, the Jane Austen prevailing in the British and American academies today actually belongs to this normative tradition. It is only recently, however, that this Austen became the only widely visible one. Starting in the mid–nineteenth century, an antinormative tradition developed. Ever since Mrs. Oliphant praised the "feminine cynicism" and "quiet jeering" of her fiction,[11] another set of readers has been either pleased or infuriated to find that Austen is not committed to the values of her neighborhood or to any values qua values at all, that she is disengaged from dominant moral and political norms, particularly as these are underwritten by the institutions of heterosexuality and marriage.

Because Austen's heterosexuality was not guaranteed by marriage, doubts about her sexuality have been played out in different historical moments as asexuality, as frigidity, and as lesbianism. This "queerness," as we might now term it, has been used to account for her fiction from the get-go. Charlotte Brontë linked the formal perfection of Austen's novels—her attention to "the surface of the lives of genteel English people"—to her indifference to "what throbs fast and full, though hidden, what the blood rushes through."[12] Lionel Trilling attributed many readers' "feral" hostility to Austen to "man's panic fear at a fictional world in which the masculine principle, although represented as admirable and necessary, is prescribed and controlled by a female mind."[13] His explanation, however, misrepresents such animosity as a conflict between the sexes, when it is a conflict about sexuality. It is not because she is a woman that D. H. Lawrence and Brontë deplore her, but because she is a woman whose fiction does not reverence the love of virile men. Thus Lawrence decried "this old maid" for typifying "the sharp knowing in apartness" rather than the "blood connection" between the sexes; and George Sampson complained, "In her world there is neither marrying nor giving in marriage, but just the make-believe mating of dolls. . . . Jane Austen is abnormal . . . because [her characters] have no sex at all."[14]

The history of Austen criticism has often been darkened by the scorn Austen-haters express for novels in which men and women are more absorbed in village tittle-tattle than in each other. For this reason, male admirers of Austen have had much to endure at the hands of a world that frowns upon their love. H. W. Garrod's famous "Jane Austen: A Depreciation," an address delivered to the Royal Society of Literature in 1928, attacks the whole notion of Austen's greatness on sexual grounds. Austen is an "irredeemably humdrum" writer precisely because she holds herself aloof from sexual passion for men, and so "was as incapable of having a story as of writing one—by a story I mean a sequence of happenings, either romantic or uncommon." Garrod's misogynist "Depreciation" is aimed just as much at male Janeites in the audience as at Austen herself: "There is a time to be born and a time to die, and a time to be middle-aged and read Miss Austen." A man content to read novels by "a mere slip of a girl," as Garrod describes her, must be a mere slip of a girl himself. Having unmanned themselves not simply by admiring a woman writer—which is bad enough—but, even worse, by idolizing a sharp-tongued woman unimpressed with men (Garrod takes offense at Austen's quip, "Admiral Stanhope is a gentlemanlike man, but then his legs are too short and his tail too long"), men who *like* Austen are like the "pansy" in Bersani's story, doubly feminized.[15]

The Janeites Garrod ridicules are not the philistine consumers of "their 'dear,' our dear, everybody's dear, Jane" whom Henry James castigated decades earlier, readers who valued Austen as an instance of high culture in its least challenging form, and whose Janeiteism was a badge of gentility.[16] On the contrary, in its most influential forms, the Janeiteism of the early twentieth century was, with the prominent exception of Shakespeare scholar Caroline Spurgeon, principally a male enthusiasm shared among an elite corps of publishers, professors, and literati, such as Montague Summers, A. C. Bradley, Lord David Cecil, Sir Walter Raleigh, R. W. Chapman, and E. M. Forster. At the Royal Society of Literature, in particular, Austen's genius was celebrated with a militantly dotty enthusiasm. Far from regarding their interest in Austen as "work," Janeites flaunt it as the ecstasy of the elect: she was not merely their *dear* Jane, but their *divine* Jane, their *matchless* Jane, and they were her *cult*, her *sect*, her *little company* (*fit though few*), her *tribe* of adorers who celebrate the *miracle* of her work in flamboyantly hyperbolic terms. Although their zeal is genuine, the self-parody implicit in these encomia tells us that we are in an insider's society of scholar-gentlemen at play.[17]

In much the same way the trekkies, fans, and mass culture media enthusiasts of today are, as Henry Jenkins has shown, marginalized by dominant cultural institutions,[18] Janeites constitute a reading community whose practices violate a range of protocols later instituted by professional academics when novel studies emerged—dogmas holding, for example, that you cannot talk about characters as if they were real people; that reading novels requires specialist skills and knowledges developed at universities; that hermeneutic mastery, as exemplified in a comprehensive "reading," is the objective of legitimate novel criticism; that the courtship plot celebrating marriage and maturity is the determinative event in Austen's fiction; and that the business of reading novels is solitary rather than sociable. To exemplify what Janeite reading looked like before novel criticism and readings per se existed, I will turn to Rudyard Kipling's "The Janeites."

---

A story within a frame-story and further enframed by poems, "The Janeites" is set at a London Masonic Lodge in 1920, where shell-shocked veteran Humberstall talks about a secret society into which he was inducted years earlier while serving under the supervision of Sergeant Macklin as an officers' mess waiter with his World War I artillery battery in France.[19] One day, as the officers discuss whether "Jane" (*DC*, 124) died without leaving "direct an' lawful prog'ny" (*DC*, 124), Macklin (who is very drunk) loudly interrupts the officers' conversation with the claim, "She *did* leave lawful issue in the shape o' one son; an' 'is name was 'Enery James" (*DC*, 124). Puzzled that the superior officers, far from punishing this insubordinate intrusion, have the sergeant taken off to bed and cared for, Humberstall finds out more about the secret club whose membership brings such privileges. After selling him the password ("*Tilniz an' trapdoors*," from *Northanger Abbey*), Macklin imparts to him the mysteries of Jane, which make the war front companionable: "It *was* a 'appy little Group" (*DC*, 132), he later murmurs nostalgically. When half the battery is blown up in a German artillery attack, Humberstall is the only Janeite to survive. As he struggles to board a hospital train, only to be pushed back by a woman insisting that the train is too crowded, Humberstall implores a nurse to "make Miss Bates, there, stop talkin' or I'll die" (*DC*, 136), and she—evidently an initiate herself—recognizes a fellow's allusion and obliges, even filching a spare blanket for his comfort.

Unlike most academic readings of Austen's fiction, this story backgrounds the courtship plot. The love story is less than inevitable for Janeites. In their civilian lives, they are chilly toward women (Jane "was the only woman I ever 'eard 'em say a good word for" [*DC*, 123], Humberstall remembers), and chary of domesticity (the senior Janeites are a divorce court lawyer and a private detective specializing in adultery cases). The Janeites recognize that novels are "all about young girls o' seventeen . . . not certain 'oom they'd like to marry" (*DC*, 126). But for them (unlike non-Janeites in the story), this detail is leveled with other details that are also part of what the novels are "all about"—including "their dances an' card parties an' picnics, and their young blokes goin' off to London on 'orseback for 'aircuts an' shaves" (*DC*, 126), a fact that, like the wearing of wigs, intrigues Humberstall, who is a hairdresser in civilian life. As for Austenian plots, "there was nothin' *to* 'em nor *in* 'em. Nothin' at all" (*DC*, 128).

Defended by school lads, equipped with superannuated cannons, and mobilized by a dilapidated train rather than modern transport Caterpillars, the Janeites' battery is pitifully doomed. Indeed, they cathect onto Austen's novels precisely because "there was nothin' to 'em." Unlike current scholars of narrative, for whom plot bears the lion's share of narrative significance, Janeite readers ignore plot with its forward-moving momentums, its inevitabilities, its "maturity," and its closure, and dwell instead on atemporal aspects of narration, descriptive details, catchy phrases, and, especially, characterization (as the appreciations of real-life Janeites such as A. C. Bradley and Spurgeon attest). In this story, identifying people and things in their own experience, and renaming them according to Austen's characters, the soon-to-be-slaughtered Janeites piece together a shattering world.

Because "real-life" Janeites would soon be decried as escapists retreating to the placidity of Austen's world, it is worth stressing that Kipling's Janeites do not do this. Their Jane Austen—as distinct from the Austen celebrated in the prefatory poem as "England's Jane" (*DC*, 120)—is never described by them as a repository of ethical wisdom; nor is she linked with a feminine elegiac ideal of England whose very vulnerability is what knightly menfolk must fight to protect. After the war, Humberstall reads Austen's novels not because they help him recover the prior world unshaken by war but precisely because they remind him of the trenches: "It brings it all back—down to the smell of the glue-paint on the screens. You take it from me, Brethren, there's no one to touch Jane when you're in a tight place" (*DC*, 137).

As for that tight place. We have already seen that many in the academy and outside it assume that Austenian admirers are properly and aggressively heteronormative. For this reason, it is also worth emphasizing that Janeite confederacies had little truck with domesticity. Kipling's story mentions two secret homosocial societies—the Masons and the Janeites—but several details suggest that Austen's fiction promoted a secret brotherhood of specifically homoerotic fellowship, too. When Humberstall chalks the names of Austenian characters onto the guns, he infuriates the battery sergeant major (BSM), who reads his Cockney spelling "De Bugg"—for De Bourgh—as a reference to sodomy. Determined to punish him for "writin' obese words on His Majesty's property" (*DC*, 131), the BSM takes the case to the officers on the grounds that " 'e couldn't hope to preserve discipline unless examples was made" (*DC*, 121). What the BSM does not know, of course, is that the Janeites exist, and that the officers will not discipline one of their own: the officers dismiss the charges, send the BSM away, and entertain themselves by quizzing Humberstall on Jane. Janeite discourse—which would later be trivialized as "gossip" by presumptively masculine professional critics—has the cultural value of promoting fellowship among a group of people living under the aegis of the closet, and their coded and otherwise specialized speech indicates their membership in a "club" that exists covertly within a hostile world.

The narrator of the story, not a Janeite, closes by observing that Austen was "a match-maker" and her novels "full of match-making" (*DC*, 138), and by hinting at a secondary character's marriage to Humberstall's sister. Kipling also attaches a sequel poem, entitled "Jane's Marriage," in which Austen enters the gates of heaven and is rewarded in matrimony by Captain Wentworth. These multiple efforts to reinstate the marriage plot are risible in themselves (Wentworth is not only fictional but already married) and at odds with the Janeiteism elsewhere in the story: the frame-story is thus a sop thrown to "a pious post-war world" (*DC*, 129), which requires what the narrator calls "revision" of the truth. One of these truths is that Janeites are committed to club rather than domestic society. They are as barren of "direct an' lawful prog'ny" as Austen herself, leaving no issue, the surviving Humberstall being a stranger to women. The reproduction they are interested in pertains to the dissemination of Janeite culture itself. Just as Austen brought forth James, Janeites bring forth other Janeites—by recruitment. Macklin is pleased when Humberstall renames the guns after Austenian characters: "He reached up an' patted me on the shoulder. 'You done nobly,' he says. 'You're bringin' forth abundant fruit, like a good Janeite' " (*DC*, 130).

Early-twentieth-century Janeiteism emerges from specific historical needs. Before World War I, Frederic Harrison described Austen as a "rather heartless little cynic . . . penning satires against her neighbors whilst the Dynasts were tearing the world to pieces and consigning millions to their graves."[20] Harrison deplored Austen's isolation, but once the dynasts of our century went at it, many readers loved her presumed ahistoricity, indulging in elegiac yearnings through Austen that Kipling's story both conjures and undermines. To Janeites outside Kipling's story, her novels evoked a world *before* history blew up, before manners were archaic. As Christopher Kent has shown, Austen's novels were recommended to British veterans suffering post-traumatic stress syndrome after the war.[21] For soldiers whose minds were shattered by dynastic history, the famously limited dimensions of Austen's fictional world could feel rehabilitative; her parlors could feel manageable; her very triviality could feel redemptive. Assumptions about *feminine* propriety embedded within this fantasy—about transparency, restraint, poise—shored up masculine lucidity and self-definition when these, along with English national identity itself, were under duress.

D. A. Miller's compelling, latter-day conviction that when he was ill, Jane Austen's novels "did more than accompany [his] return to health; they accomplished it"[22] owes much to this postwar Janeite construction of Austen as a restorative to sensitive men. But as the more ambiguous core of Kipling's story attests, whatever "normality" Austen's novels might foster is attenuated given the indifference to heterosexual passion, domesticity, and heroic masculinity expressed there. In any case, when W. J. Blyton wrote in 1947, "Men as masculine as Scott and Kipling have been Janeites and have been enthralled by her sly humour and fidelity to reality,"[23] his defense of a manful readership demonstrated what he sought to deny: that Janeites were already suspected of being not masculine enough.

This suspicion motivates the emergence of what we now recognize as modern Austenian criticism, which begins with D. W. Harding's "Regulated Hatred: An Aspect of the Work of Jane Austen" (1940). The principle of this pathbreaking essay is that Austen's "books are . . . read and enjoyed by precisely the sort of people whom she disliked."[24] The "people" Harding refers to are clearly Janeites, described by Harding with withering contempt as the "exponents of urbanity," the "sensitive," and the "cultured," the "Gentlemen of an older generation than mine" who disseminate Austeniana "through histories of literature, university courses, literary journalism, and polite allusions" ("RH," 166).[25] Although the Janeiteism of this period was actually more productive than he acknowledges—giving us, for one thing, Chapman's 1923 edition of Austen's novels, the first scholarly edition of any British novelist—Harding dismisses Janeites as weakling escapists who resort to the idyllic figure of Jane as a "refuge" when "the contemporary world grew too much for them" ("RH," 166).[26]

Absolutely foundational to the practice of Austenian criticism in the academy was the discrediting of Janeites such as existed in Kipling's story and in the Royal Society of Literature. Deploying an invidious distinction between the "attentive" and the "urbane," Harding calls Janeites her worst readers: "She is a literary classic of the society which attitudes like hers, held widely enough, would undermine" ("RH," 167). Harding's qualifications as a good reader, it is implied, derive from his alienation from upper-class mores, an alienation Austen is said to have shared. Claiming that Austen would never "have helped to make society what it was, or ours what it is," Harding trumps the Janeite "posterity of urbane gentlemen" by disaffiliating Austen from them ("RH," 179, 170).

Harding's depiction of Austen as subversive was valuable to the next generation of academics, especially feminists. But his motives were hardly emancipatory. In order to champion middle-class values, Harding and others after him reshuffle the relations between gender norms and sexual practices and/or identities. Defining Janeites as upper-class gentlemen of doubtful virility, Harding hinted that Austen was more of a real man—tough-minded, astringent, unblinking—than they were. F. R. Leavis carries this project of reshuffling forward in *The Great Tradition*, which is, among other things, a running diatribe against Janeite extraordinaire Lord David Cecil. Leavis dignifies Austen and the great tradition of fiction she originated by insisting on her moral seriousness; accordingly, the leisured enjoyment of Janeites—with their fondness for entertainment, character, and comedy—is hateful to him. Lord David's influence—detected in books, lectures, exam questions and answers at Cambridge—is so deep that Leavis treats him not as a scholar-dandy but as a downright pervert. The homophobic gender component of Leavis's class-based critique tars Lord David as a homosexual despite his evident heterosexuality. Leavis makes this insinuation by playing up Lord David's Bloomsbury connections, taunting him for regarding Jane Austen as "an ideal contemporary of Lytton Strachey" rather than as a dour moralist and as a formative influence on George Eliot. Assailing Lord David's perceived preference for Austen's stylized comedy over Eliot's "puritan" morality, Leavis champions bourgeois virtue at the expense of Bloomsbury aestheticism: Eliot (like Austen, it is implied)

> admired truthfulness and chastity and industry and self-restraint, she disapproved of loose living and recklessness and deceit and self-indulgence. . . . I had better confess that I differ (apparently) from Lord David Cecil in sharing these beliefs, admirations and disapprovals. . . . [T]hey seem to me favourable to the production of great literature. I will add . . . that the enlightenment or aestheticism or sophistication that feels an amused superiority to them leads, in my view, to triviality and boredom, and that out of that triviality comes evil.[27]

Janeites might be so debilitated or so depraved or so despairing as to enjoy triviality as a reprieve from the business of productive signification, but the brisk and booming Leavis is here to assure us that triviality and its advocates alike are heinous.

What makes Harding's and Leavis's attacks on Janeites different from Garrod's, of course, is that they *like* Austen. They clear themselves from the charge of effeminacy by making Austen safe for real men engaged in real study, driving a wedge between the good (masculine) queerness of Austen and the bad (feminine) queerness of etiolated Janeites. Post–World War II Austenian reception thus participates in that demand to consolidate and reinvigorate masculinity elsewhere visible in the larger context of British and American culture. While such criticism conduced to the rise of Austen studies, some time elapsed before it generated a countermethod of reading that value-coded the marriage plot as the preeminent significance-bearing structural or thematic element of her novels, and devalued Janeite discussions as gossip that promoted the silly sociability of the brethren rather than the production of moral earnestness.[28] Edmund Wilson, for example, chides G. B. Stern and Sheila Kaye-Smith's Janeite book, *Speaking of Jane Austen* (1944), for treating characters "as actual people . . . and speculating on their lives beyond the story."[29] But when Wilson argues that Emma's offstage lesbianism is "something outside the picture which is never made explicit in the story but which has to be recognized by the reader before it is possible for him to appreciate the book," he carries on the Janeite practice of reading beyond what is printed.[30] And when he trails off into a fantasy about how Emma will bewilder Knightley by continuing to invite lovely new female protégées into the household after they are married, he shows that the marriage plot is no bar against the imagination or enactment of futures different from, or even inimical to, it.[31]

It was not until the sixties that the marriage plot gained the prestige it now enjoys in academic readings of classic British fiction. Marvin Mudrick's profoundly influential *Jane Austen: Irony as Defense and Discovery* moved in this direction, but this, too, was by omission. Expecting Austen's novels to narrativize the maturing processes of heterosexual love, Mudrick is scandalized to find that her heart just isn't in this project. Whereas Harding and Leavis attacked the deviance of Janeites, Mudrick dwells on the deviance of Austen; he sees the bachelor toughness they admired in her as a spinster's sick resentment. For him, irony—Austen's most celebrated stylistic achievement—is diagnosed as a defense mechanism against that "great, unknown, adult commitment," that is, "sexual love."[32] Mudrick's book elaborates earlier suspicions about Austen's sexual peculiarity by alluding to same-sex love directly in his chapter on Emma—that heroine deemed most like Austen in her fear of commitment, her coldness, her irony, her penchant for authorship, and her need to dominate, to "play God" by playing *man*: "The fact is that Emma," he writes, "prefers the company of women. . . . Emma is in love with [Harriet]: a love unphysical and inadmissible, even perhaps undefinable in such a society; and therefore safe" (*DD*, 193, 203).[33] Appearing in 1952, when a discourse of psychosexual pathology was readily at hand, Mudrick's book assumes that Austen's queerness is homosexuality tout court. All future attempts on behalf of Austen's normativity would succeed or fail to the extent that they could answer him.

Austen's massively definitive normalization came with Wayne Booth's widely reprinted "Control of Distance in Jane Austen's *Emma*" (1961), which not only passionately defends Emma Woodhouse's heterosexuality but also links the proper reading of Austenian narrative with a proper respect for the self-evidence of marital felicity in novels and outside them: "Marriage to an intelligent, amiable, good, and attractive man is the best thing that can happen to this heroine, and the readers who do not experience it as such are, I am convinced, far from knowing what Jane Austen is about—whatever they may say about the 'bitter spinster's' attitude towards marriage." According to Booth's formalism, marriage is not a matter of pairing character *x* to character *y*, as it is in Stern and Kaye-Smith's book *Speaking of Jane Austen*. If it were, novel studies would be a species of gossip (of the sort in which Janeites revel), novel critics would be lightweights, and novels themselves would not deserve the respect accorded to poetry and drama. Equating the ending of the novel with its telos, Booth elevates the structural and moral import of marriage as the novel's inevitable, its only possible, meaning: plot brings about "the reform of [Emma's] character," and heterosexual love is what Emma must "learn" for the novel to end. Evidence is unnecessary to sustain this standard of value. Countless readers have claimed that the infamous absence of "love scenes" in Austen's novels must mean *something*. Not so for Booth: norms about gender and sexuality are encoded onto plot so that representation in the form of kisses, palpitations, and embraces is superfluous.[34] If you don't see this, you don't know how to read novels.

Rescuing Austen from Mudrick,[35] Booth succeeded in celebrating Austen's mastery over voice and plot as a positive thing, advancing novel studies as an analytic discipline. In the process, he equated the perversity of women who indulge same-sex "infatuations" with the perversity of readers who refuse to credit a happy ending when they see one. Sedgwick has remarked that Austenian criticism belongs to the bottom-spanking "Girl Being Taught a Lesson" mode of criticism.[36] As a description of criticism since the late fifties, this seems quite right. Critics as diverse as Tony Tanner, Ian Watt, and Mary Poovey all concur in maintaining that character development, formal control, voice, and ideological resistance/compliance are mediated through marriage, as an institution and plot device.

Indeed, so entrenched is this respect and so short our institutional memory that we have forgotten that there are other ways to read courtship plots. E. M. Forster, whose *Aspects of the Novel* was still taught in fiction courses when Booth's *Rhetoric of Fiction* was cresting, accorded the courtship plot less power: "A man and woman . . . want to be united and perhaps succeed." The compulsory nature of the love story as described here is acknowledged, and that compulsion has ideological import that we know weighed very heavily on Forster's own career. Still, it seems important to observe that Forster describes these events *not* under the headings "Plot" or "Story" but under the heading "People," classifying it not as an overarching structure but as one among many "facts of human life"—alongside birth, food, sleep, death, and other people—that interest people and novelists who write about them.[37] Many similar Janeite reading practices discussed earlier with respect to Kipling's story flourish today in the Jane Austen Societies, where fans convene to stage teas, balls, games, readings, and dramatic representations; to take quizzes (bringing together minutiae with no hierarchy or agenda-driven priority); and to imagine together how a character in one novel might behave toward a character from another, all of which practices render Austen's novels one loose, baggy middle.

The discipline of novel studies that evolved in England and America during the fifties and sixties was bent first on devaluing Janeites as effete—excessive, aberrant, frivolous, undomesticated, contemptibly weak yet morally pernicious at one and the same time—and next on eradicating everything in Austen and her fiction that might legitimize their way of reading. I began by asking what would happen if Austen *were* "gay," as the *LRB* put it. Now I will venture to answer with a hunch: If the "case" of Rock Hudson showed that our icon of masculinity was gay, the "case" of Jane Austen presented the unnerving possibility that *manners* are gay, that civility (of which Austen has been deemed the preeminent exemplar) may rest on a basis different from what is commonly imagined, and that (the terror of the prophet Kimball about the end of the world notwithstanding) gay manners are profoundly productive. This, indeed, seems to be Leavis's fear, and unless we recognize this, his attacks on Lord David will seem bizarrely out of place. Furiously resisting Lord David's seemingly innocuous statement that Austen's novels are "entertainment," Leavis attacks Lord David for holding that Austen creates "delightful characters" and "lets us forget our cares and moral tensions in the comedy of pre-eminently civilized life." Lord David's opinion might well seem so tepid as not to deserve attacking, but as Leavis sees it, the "idea of 'civilization' invoked [here] appears to be closely related to that expounded by Mr. Clive Bell," which is to say, conducing to "the cult of the stylized, the conventionalized, the artificial, just for their own sakes." In saying this, Leavis is damning the homosexual's Jane Austen, the decadent's Jane Austen, damning all persons for whom manners bear no relation to nature—which, here, is shorthand for bourgeois morality and heterosexual desire. Leavis's target is all readers who take for granted that manners and morality are different things, who regard manners as publicly recognized fictions that make it possible for people with other things on their mind to behave well.[38] Similarly, when Mudrick complained that Austen "was interested in a person, an object, an event, only as she might observe and recreate them free from consequences, as performance, as tableau" (*DD*, 3), he shows that Austen's novels yield up the amoral readings Leavis deplores as Bloomsburian, though Mudrick, of course, shares Leavis's anxiety about them. For Mudrick, Austen queers the courtship narrative so that the love story is presented "not sentimentally, not morally, indeed not [connected] to any train of consequences, but with detached discrimination among its incongruities" (*DD*, 3).

Fearful of the campy space Austen opens up between manners and desire, critics such as Booth and Trilling, as Susan Winnett has suggested, collapse manners into morals, making it possible to bring Austen (along with James) safely into a middle-class canon.[39] C. S. Lewis's essay "A Note on Jane Austen" continues this process for Austen studies by regenealogizing her: "[Austen] is described by someone in Kipling's worst story as the mother of Henry James," he taunts, referring to "The Janeites," "[but] I feel much more sure that she is the daughter of Dr. Johnson." Assailing proponents of the comic, mannered Jane Austen—those who turn her into a Regency James, or, worse, a Regency Wilde—Lewis manfully insists that Austen's comedy is inspired by "hard core morality" and "religion."[40] The process of straightening Austen out, then, occurs in conjunction with the development of a view of narrative that presumes its province to be desire (hegemonic, heteronormative) rather than manners (which may be practiced self-consciously, skeptically, and strategically).

The success of this enterprise is proven by the present invisibility of what was so glaring in the forties and fifties. Even Sedgwick and Castle—in their initial papers, and in their responses to the furor they caused—appear unaware that their positions have ample and rather recent precedent. Likewise, when Southam accounts for Garrod's claim that Janeites liked women too much by insinuating that Garrod did not like women enough ("He spent much of his life at Oxford, unmarried, where he had rooms in Merton College for over fifty years"),[41] he shows, among other things, that Austen is presumptively a straight man's writer, putting admirers—from Wilde, to Swinburne, to Housman, to Forster, whose "I am a Jane Austenite" sounds like a coming-out statement—beyond consideration.[42]

This review of Austen's recent revaluations suggests several opportunities for further study. First, it is now a given that the novel "rose" to ideological prominence by the 1740s; but this essay shows that the work of "raising" the novel was still undone as late as 1940, when the curriculum at Oxbridge was being revised, and that the elevation of novel studies has a distinct relation to Austen. Second, in attempting to resist what are, to my mind, rather inflexible desire-driven models of "realistic" narrative that prevail today, this project also suggests that it may be worth our while to distinguish between the theory of the novel and the theory of narrative, and to historicize both. While it is widely assumed that novels are a branch of the police, this discussion suggests that it is not novels but rather the professionalization of novel studies which deployed methods of reading that guaranteed certain outcomes and devalued others. And third, for Austen study more specifically, this review shows how much we have to gain by bringing nonnormalizing Austenian readings back into view. For the denial and outrage of Kimball, Southam, and others notwithstanding, it has been not only Austen's detractors but her admirers, too, who have suspected that the "Passions" were (as Brontë put it) "entirely unknown" to her not because Austen was such a good girl but because in some secret, perhaps not fully definable, way, she was so bad.

## Notes

This essay first appeared in *boundary 2* 23 (1996) and is reprinted by permission of Duke University Press. 

1. David M. Halperin, *Saint Foucault: Towards a Gay Hagiography* (New York: Oxford University Press, 1995), 48. See also Paul Morrison's *Sexual Subjects* (New York: Oxford University Press, 1996).

2. *New York Times*, 22 April 1990, 36. Sedgwick discusses neoconservative attacks on her MLA paper in "Jane Austen and the Masturbating Girl," in *Tendencies* (Durham, N.C.: Duke University Press, 1993). I have found Sedgwick's remarks on self-evidence particularly suggestive.

3. See Southam 1987, 2:60.

4. Montague Summers, *The Galantry Show* (London: Cecil Woolf, 1980), 225.

5. Terry Castle's "Was Jane Austen Gay?" appeared as a review article of Deirdre Le Faye's new edition of Austen's letters in the *London Review of Books*, 3 August 1995. Her response, along with that of several other readers, appeared in the next issue, 24 August 1995. B. C. Southam's letter was published in the 7 September 1995 *LRB*. *Time* magazine reported on this "kerfuffle" in its 14 August 1995 issue; responses appeared in the 4 September 1995 issue.

6. My sense of Austen's cultural value owes much to John Guillory's *Cultural Capital* (Chicago: University of Chicago Press, 1993) in general, and more to Eric O. Clarke in particular, whose work on Shelley is profoundly suggestive. See "Shelley's Heart: Sexual Politics and Cultural Value," *Yale Journal of Criticism* 8 (spring 1995): 187–208. I am moreover grateful to Clarke for providing me with so many challenging suggestions for this essay.

7. The conflict rehearsed here about Austen not surprisingly recalls debates about the novel, too, whose narrative structures and agendas have been seen as repressive and "policing," or as resistant and theatrical. See, for example, D. A. Miller, *Novel and the Police* (Berkeley and Los Angeles: University of California Press, 1988), and Joseph Litvak, *Caught in the Act: Theatricality in the Nineteenth-Century Novel* (Berkeley and Los Angeles: University of California Press, 1992).

8. For a fuller discussion of the development of Austenian reception, see my "Austen Cults and Cultures," in *The Cambridge Companion to Jane Austen*, ed. Juliet McMaster and Edward Copeland (Cambridge: Cambridge University Press, 1997), 211–26.

9. Southam 1968, 1:95.

10. Allan Bloom, *Love and Friendship* (New York: Simon and Schuster, 1993), 191–208. Bloom, interestingly enough, attributes Austen's disciplinary lucidity precisely to her sexual detachment: "Perhaps her position as a novelist outside of the marriage game that is her subject matter permits her relative clarity and free-

dom from self-deception" (205). D. A. Miller, "The Late Jane Austen," *Raritan* 10 (1990): 55–79.

11. From "Miss Austen and Miss Mitford," *Blackwood's Edinburgh Magazine*, March 1870, reprinted in Southam 1968, 217.

12. Also: "Jane Austen was a complete and most sensible lady, but a very incomplete, and rather insensible (*not senseless*) woman" (Charlotte Brontë, letter to W. S. Williams, 12 April 1850, in Southam 1968, 128).

13. Lionel Trilling, *The Opposing Self* (New York: Viking Press, 1955), 209.

14. See D. H. Lawrence, "A Propos of Lady Chatterley's Lover," in Southam 1987, 2:107; George Sampson, "Jane Austen," *Bookman* 65, no. 388 (January 1924): 193.

15. H. W. Garrod's "Jane Austen: A Depreciation" was published in *Essays by Divers Hands: Transactions of the Royal Society of Literature* 8 (1928): 21–40; it has been reprinted in numerous other places. The version I have quoted is from William W. Heath, ed., *Discussions of Jane Austen* (Boston: Heath and Company, 1961), 32–40.

16. James's remarks, originally appearing in "The Lesson of Balzac" (1905) and reprinted in *The House of Fiction*, are included in Southam 1987, 2:230. Jonathan Freedman's *Professions of Taste: Henry James, British Aestheticism, and Commodity Culture* (Stanford: Stanford University Press, 1990) traces James's at first satirical response to aestheticism, especially as exemplified by Wilde, which then modulates into an attempt to create a purified, creative, and moral (because productive) aestheticism in his major fiction. Although Freedman is hesitant about engaging the erotic transgressiveness and especially the homoeroticism associated with aestheticism, his discussion of professionalism is quite relevant to my study. In attempting to wrest criticism from the hoi polloi and assign it to professionals, James is anticipating strategies that would later marginalize him, and James's own place in the genealogy of the novel is curiously unstable.

17. See Montague Summers, "Jane Austen: An Appreciation," *Transactions of the Royal Society of Literature* 36 (1918): 1–33. Summers's language of divine election is typical of all Janeites.

18. Henry Jenkins, *Textual Poachers: Television Fans and Participatory Culture* (New York: Routledge, 1992). Jenkins draws from Michel de Certeau's *Practice of Everyday Life* (Berkeley and Los Angeles: University of California Press, 1984) and from Pierre Bourdieu's *Distinction* (Cambridge: Harvard University Press, 1979) to show how high culturalists feel tainted by the adoption of their protocols for use with respect to low-culture objects and to suggest that fans transgress bourgeois structures of cultural valuation, which are bent on legitimizing their own objects and protocols of expertise.

19. Rudyard Kipling's "The Janeites" is included in *Debits and Credits* (1926). It was begun in 1922, finished in 1923, and first published in 1924, in a slightly different version from what appeared in the 1926 volume. All quotations are from *Debits and Credits*, ed. Sandra Kemp (Harmondsworth: Penguin, 1987), 119–40. Hereafter, this work is cited parenthetically as *DC*.

20. Frederic Harrison, letter to Thomas Hardy, 10 November 1913, cited in Southam 1987, 2:87–88.

21. According to Kent, H. F. Brett Smith, an Oxford tutor, served in World War I as an adviser in British hospitals. His special responsibility was the prescription of salubrious reading for the wounded, and he recommended Austen's novels to "severely shell-shocked" soldiers. I am much indebted to Kent's fine essay, "Learning History with, and from, Jane Austen," in *Jane Austen's Beginnings: The Juvenilia and Lady Susan*, ed. J. David Grey (Ann Arbor, Mich.: UMI Research Press, 1989), 59.

22. Miller, "The Late Jane Austen," 55.

23. W. J. Blyton's words are cited in the supplement to the *Oxford English Dictionary* (3:434), illustrating the word *Janeite*. The editors of the *OED* cite *English Language and Literature* 7 (1947) as their source, but I have been unable to locate this publication.

24. D. W. Harding, "Regulated Hatred: An Aspect of the Work of Jane Austen," in *Jane Austen: A Collection of Critical Essays*, ed. Ian Watt (Englewood Cliffs, N.J.: Prentice Hall, 1963), 166. Hereafter, this work is cited parenthetically as "RH." Harding's essay was originally delivered before the Literature Society of Manchester University on 3 March 1939 and was originally printed in *Scrutiny* 8 (1940): 346–62.

25. In some respects, Harding's characterization recollects Woolf's review of the Chapman edition, which also codes Janeites as dotty and superannuated men, "elderly gentlemen living in the neighbourhood of London, who resent any slight upon her genius as if it were an insult offered to the chastity of their aunts"; in "Jane Austen at Sixty," *Nation*, 15 December 1923, 433, and reprinted without these opening swipes at the Chapman edition in *The Common Reader* (London: Hogarth Press, 1925).

26. Harding singles out Eric Linklater's Janeite prime minister in *The Impregnable Women* (1938) and Beatrice Kean Seymour's *Jane Austen: Study for a Portrait* (London: M. Joseph, 1937), where she wrote, "In a society which has enthroned the machine-gun and carried it aloft even into the quiet heavens, there will always be men and women—Escapist or not, as you please—who will turn to her novels with an unending sense of relief and thankfulness."

27. F. R. Leavis, *The Great Tradition* (Garden City, N.Y.: Doubleday and Co., 1954), 19. Although the Austenian criticism of Queenie and F. R. Leavis surely differs profoundly from that of earlier, more belletristric Janeites, Leavis's animus sometimes prompts him to misrepresent Lord David's positions. In his *Jane Austen* (London: Cambridge University Press, 1935), which originated as a lecture at Cambridge, Lord David flatly states, "Jane Austen was profoundly moral" (32), and though Leavis would probably scorn the conception of morality that Lord David attributes to her, it is stretching things, indeed, to suggest that Lord David describes Austen's morality as aesthetic or sophisticated.

28. The brilliance of Mary Lascelles's *Jane Austen and Her Art* (London: Oxford University Press, 1939) I regard as exceptional to the argument I am making here in its formal emphasis, which is in keeping with American models of fictional analysis. Although Lascelles's study is indeed blissfully free of nastier gender- and class-based attacks, like those of Harding, Leavis, and Mudrick, she does have a professional ax to grind, opening her book by noting that Austen's "professed"

admirers indulge in biographical minutiae rather than engage in the work of sustained criticism.

29. Austen seems to have authorized this practice when she entertained her nieces and nephews by consenting, when asked, to tell them particulars about the careers of her characters subsequent to her novels' conclusions.

30. Edmund Wilson, "A Long Talk about Jane Austen," in *Classics and Commercials: A Literary Chronicle of the Forties* (New York: Farrar, Straus and Giroux, 1950), 196–203.

31. It is worth noting that Wilson's essay also argues that the homoerotic bond between Elinor and Marianne Dashwood in *Sense and Sensibility* is stronger than the heterosexual bond that yokes the sisters to their male lovers.

32. Marvin Mudrick, *Jane Austen: Irony as Defense and Discovery* (Princeton: Princeton University Press, 1952), 19. Hereafter, this work is cited parenthetically as *DD*.

33. As Mudrick himself acknowledges, this take on Emma's lesbianism is indebted to Edmund Wilson's "A Long Talk about Jane Austen."

34. Wayne Booth's essay first appeared in *Rhetoric of Fiction* (Chicago: University of Chicago Press, 1961), 243–66; it was reprinted in David Lodge, *Jane Austen: Emma, a Casebook* (London: Macmillan, 1991), 137–69. A generation of "New Critics" continued along the path Booth forged, claiming to discuss Emma's "growth" and "development" formally, but actually discussing narratives of gender and sexuality normatively.

35. According to Mudrick, Austen "converted her own personal limitations into the very form of the novel" (*DD*, 194).

36. Sedgwick, "Jane Austen and the Masturbating Girl," 125.

37. E. M. Forster, *Aspects of the Novel* (New York: Harcourt Brace Jovanovich, 1927), 67–82. In an excellent discussion of Forster's *Aspects*, Paul Morrison argues that Forster's remarks on narrative are much less emancipatory than what I suggest here. See "End Pleasure," *GLQ: A Journal of Lesbian and Gay Studies* 1 (1993): 53–78.

38. Leavis, *The Great Tradition*, 14–15 n. 6.

39. Susan Winnett pays particular attention to Trilling's 1950 essay, "Manners, Morals, and the Novel," in her *Terrible Sociability: The Text of Manners in Laclos, Goethe, and James* (Stanford: Stanford University Press, 1993), 27–32. While I admire Winnett's study, I think she may well inherit a view of Austen that Trilling and others handed down.

40. C. S. Lewis, "A Note on Jane Austen," originally published in *Essays in Criticism* (1954), 4:359–71, reprinted in Watt, *Jane Austen*, 34, 33.

41. Southam writes that "a clue" to Garrod's dislike of Austen lies in the fact that he was "a distinguished classical scholar who moved to English studies in the 1920s" (Southam 1987, 2:154 n. 13). Of course, many passionate Janeites answer to this description, so this "clue" explains nothing.

42. Forster, cited in Southam 1987, 2:154. Wilde writes from Reading Gaol in a letter of 6 April 1897, "Later on, there being hardly any novel in the prison library for the poor imprisoned fellows I live with, I think of presenting the library with about a dozen good novels. Stevenson's, some of Thackeray. . . . Jane Austen

(none here)." Wilde writes on 1 September 1890, "My dear Robbie, thank you for the cheque. Your letter is very maddening: nothing about yourself, and yet you know I love middle-class tragedies, and the little squabbles that build up family life in England. I have had delightful letters from you in the style of Jane Austen." According to biographer Richard Perceval Graves, A. E. Housman "enjoyed some of Hardy's novels, though he preferred Jane Austen." Evidently Housman's friend Arthur Platt, who held the chair in Greek at University College, London, "knew the novels of Jane Austen practically by heart." See *A. E. Housman: The Scholar-Poet* (New York: Charles Scribner's Sons, 1980), 84, and passim. Swinburne appears to have liked Austen as well, or at least he wrote Chatto (on 26 December 1882), asking him to send the "Steventon [*sic*] edition of Miss Austen."

2

# Jane Austen's Friendship

MARY ANN O'FARRELL

RECENTLY, taking up Valerie Grosvenor Myer's *Jane Austen: Obstinate Heart*, I found myself—when the opening chapter title asked "What Was She Like?"—turning to the chapter with a certain eagerness, as if expecting that it would fulfill its promise, and as if expecting that, having read it, I might know.[1] The chapter did not satisfy—how could it?—but in catching me in naive desire, it reminded me of my implication in the subject of this essay. To want to know what Jane Austen was like—to want to personify—is to want something in excess of what historicist contextualization or biographical detail might yield; such knowing demands a relation that includes me, that ultimately is about me. To wonder what Jane Austen really was like is speculatively and tentatively to initiate the structure of identification and complementarity and difference that is friendship. Would she have liked me? Was she like me? Would she have challenged me or scared me? shopped with me? found me too much? Would I have liked those things? Would she? Is it possible she was writing to me?

An answer to Myer's question that does begin to satisfy comes from Marianne Knight's account of Austen's visits, manuscripts in hand, to Marianne's older sisters: "I remember that when Aunt Jane came to us at Godmersham she used to bring the MS. of whatever novel she was writing with her, and would shut herself up with my elder sisters in one of the bedrooms to read them aloud. I and the younger ones used to hear peals of laughter through the door, and thought it very hard that we should be shut out from what was so delightful."[2] The scene Marianne describes is most easily readable as according with a certain fantasy: that being with Jane Austen must simply have been the most fun thing in the world. And yet, acting out friendship for this little sister and for themselves, Austen and the Knight girls also educate Marianne in the classic little-sister mix of resentment and desire. Peals of appealing laughter articulate for Marianne the intimacies of friendship, even as they sound friendship's hardness. Made by and demonstrable through a shutting out, Jane Austen's friendship, overheard, promises what friendship promises: the somatic exchanges and delights of private laughter, the protections of seclusion, the bonds of a self-conscious exclusivity. Responses to reading Jane Austen have often involved constructing her from fantasy as a kind of friend. Shut out alongside Marianne, Austen's desiring readers strain to hear her laughter or her voice, as from upstairs, but finally can know Austen only—as Marianne seems to know her in this recollection—by her effects. Even for someone alive when she was—someone just downstairs—Austen remains an absence (more fully, a space) at the center of that laughter, a desire that is the perceptible remnant of her invisible agency.

The material response to Austen that has meant the acquisition of purchasable goods which evoke her confuses Austen's effects (those consequences of her agency as author) with reproductions of what one could imagine to have been her property (her effects). Such items as "A Wallet of Jane Austen Writing Paper & Envelopes," "Jane Austen Card Games," the tchotchkes in the relevant pages of the *Past Times* catalog,[3] the home furnishings and food represented in Susan Watkins's *Jane Austen in Style*, are conjuring objects, goods that together articulate an oddly bounded and consumerist space at their center that is the supposititious and unconsumable Jane Austen, person (rather than the tantalizingly legible Jane Austen, text): the author-friend whose gift of stationery with her words already on it is vanity's marketable testimony to relationship, or whose recipe for white soup or negus (this one, at last, the most authentic) will tempt her forth, the spirit who raps at the call of Loo or Speculation on a table that serves equally for *objet*-shrines, for séances, or for Whist.[4] Popular culture's figurations conjure Jane Austens of their own: for the compilers of *Jane Austen's Little Advice Book*, Jane Austen is the sage friend whose epigrammatic remarks about "Worldly Things," about "Men and Women" and "The Human Condition," are just worldly enough not unduly to oppress;[5] for the producer of *Jane Austen Songs*, she is "a discerning musical amateur," available for children ("It is likely that Jane entertained her young nieces and nephews thus");[6] for readers of *Jane Austen in Style*, the helpful friend, trendy and *au fait*, with a gift for tasteful interior design.[7]

Implicating in their consumerism the conjured Austen of Regency materiality and masquerade, Jane Austen shopaholics make Austen a shopper as well as a commodity, speculating her into companionable existence in market and world. Speculation, too (the imaginist's occupation, this time, rather than the Jane Austen Card Game), informs Virginia Woolf's account of Austen's "personal obscurity." Considering Austen's retired life and early death, Woolf imagines Austen into another life: "Had she lived a few more years only, all that would have been altered. She would have stayed in London, dined out, lunched out, met famous people, made new friends, read, travelled, and carried back to the quiet country cottage a hoard of observations to feast upon at leisure."[8] The country cottage leisure, perhaps, and certainly the urban active leisure sound like those of Woolf herself, and it seems possible to imagine that, dining and lunching, maybe shopping, Woolf's virtual Austen might not have wandered unaccompanied, and would perhaps have counted Woolf among her new fit friends. Like Austen shoppers, like downstairs Marianne, like me, Woolf makes an Austen-friend of her desires, fantasizing relation in the space created by activity and circumstance. And yet, as Woolf conjures an Austen into her life, she is not conjuring wholly from herself but responding to the Austen of effects: lunching, dining, befriending, walking into town are products of the materialist Austen of the novels. (So, too, is Emma Thompson's Oscar night promise to stop at Austen's grave to report to her collaborator their movie's grosses, a response to Austen's notorious precision about finances.) If Austen is knowable only through her effects, those effects—goods and outcomes, both—have been most often understood as her novels, her letters, her juvenilia.

In thinking through some instances of the critical and popular fascination with Jane-Austen-our-friend, this essay turns sometimes to the novels (to Jane Austen's effects) in considering as well what is involved in construing authorship and readership as friendly activities. Talk of friendship often idealizes or reduces that complex and intense relation, describing it from outside its enclosure. Like Austen herself, those Austen critics who befriend her have tended—voluntarily or not—to work with or within a tougher and more difficult version of friendship than the culture generally allows, not censoring and denying friendship's difficulties but enacting (acting out) the edginess of its intimacies, its embarrassments and angers, tricky balancings and resentments. Examined alongside Austen, their imaginings contribute to an assay on the workings of friendship, as well as to a history of the cultural Jane Austen.

---

"A dislike so little just." Austen's *Emma* makes the question of Emma Woodhouse's dislike of the admirable Jane Fairfax into a challenge; even for Emma the question "might be a difficult question to answer" (167). The novel itself, immediately upon posing it, posits answers to the question, and these have been pursued by readers of the novel. Jane's elegant reserve, it suggests, so often contrasted with Emma's apparently more open temperament, makes her hard to know (Emma "could never get acquainted with her" [166]), hard to like, an icicle ("such coldness and reserve" [166]) in being hard to warm up to. And, though Emma benefits when their tempers are contrasted, Mr. Knightley suggests that she would not fare so well in a more serious comparison with Jane Fairfax: "Mr. Knightley had once told her it was because she saw in her the really accomplished young woman, which she wanted to be thought herself" (166). Jane is also dislikable by association; represented by Mrs. and Miss Bates, she cannot fail to irritate Emma. Jane's discretion is a constant frustration for Emma the newsgatherer and prevents even in possibility the exclusiveness that forms friendship out of gossip. Too, Jane Fairfax's appearance of "indifference whether she pleased or not" (166) must be painful for Emma—and not only by contrast—given the slippage between Emma's armor-vanity and her superattentiveness (learned at a valetudinarian father's beck) to the signs of peevishness and displeasure, a subtlety that, if not always accurate in its readings, is yet always on guard.

The plethora of answers to the question of why Emma so dislikes Jane Fairfax, seemingly an endless supply of justifications for Emma's feelings, are recognizable as overdetermination, but—as overdetermination—these explanations seem to collapse into the undetermined and unaccountable: Emma's dislike "so little just" is so excessively justified that explanations become indistinguishable, and Austen, poet of irrational dislike, ends in seeming most forcefully to establish that dislike (like its rival, affinity) is finally an eruption of the arbitrary.

And yet Emma's refusal of friendship with Jane Fairfax may be less an intrusion of the arbitrary than the product of the contingent structure which demands that friendship: "[I]t had been always imagined that they were to be so intimate" (166); the Highbury community thinks that they should be friends. The initial statement of Emma's dislike ("to have to pay civilities to a person she did not like through three long months!—") is also a statement of its genesis in obligation ("to be always doing more than she wished, and less than she ought!" [166]). Emma's dislike and withdrawal are her responses to the pressure of an expectation that she and Jane will be—because they ought to be—intimates. Explaining Emma's dislike of Jane, Mr. Knightley reveals that he needs it explained, and, doing so, exerts the pressure of *his* expectation in particular. As a response to Emma's statement that Jane is reserved, Mr. Knightley's "I always told you she was—a little" (171) shows the eagerness and insistence of his interest in the project of their friendship (he always told her) as much as it concedes to Emma the existence of a barrier to that project. And his pressure is endangering: Mr. Knightley's account of Emma's feelings overturns them and would (though it does not) teach her to mistrust herself. If Emma dislikes Jane because she "sees in her," as he suggests, a "really accomplished young woman," then Emma's plausible dislike of Jane becomes implausible ("what's not to like?") even as it becomes, implausibly, a covert admiration of her; Emma's dislike would be, then, no more than an indication of her liking.

If Emma dislikes the Jane Fairfax who is "so idolized and so cried up" (203), it is because she recognizes, quite rightly, that the injunction to like Jane and to be her friend is an implied correction. And, like the unhappy and well-behaved classmate wielded by ill-meaning parents as a weapon against their children, Jane Fairfax is made into an imperative categorically rejectable. If "it is natural to suppose" that Emma and Jane "should be intimate" and that they "should have taken to each other" (203), as Emma has learned to believe, the apparent naturalness of this supposition rests upon an unpleasant principle of complementarity. If Openness is enjoined to like Reserve, it is imagined to *want* it, and the apparent complementarity of the friendship one can see in advance of its existence ("those two should be friends") is revealed to be a one-sided supplementarity: the friend urged upon one is perceived as able to complete, to answer, to compensate. If this logic works in reverse—if Reserve lacks Openness—Openness cannot know this, and it seems impossible to see the corrective friend's lack as anything but the recessive form taken by what is in fact an excess and a compensation for what one *has* oneself.

At one moment in the novel, Emma and Jane Fairfax seem to fulfill one version of the collective fantasy that would impel them toward friendship. As one another's escorts into the dining room at Hartfield, "they followed the other ladies out of the room, arm in arm, with an appearance of goodwill highly becoming to the beauty and grace of each" (298). Arm in arm, Jane and Emma (a wholeness made by complementarity) are mutually dependent bodies making an attractive picture, gratification of a desire by now so familiar as to have become clichéd. If Hartfield—if Mr. Knightley—would see them together, this is because their friendship, despite the apparent high-mindedness that urges it, would become their persons as much as their world opines that it would become their characters; the arranged friendship is a public one, on view, and is certain to gratify only its arranger (the goodwill of Jane and Emma is suspiciously apparent), unless the arranged friends, finding themselves upstairs, also find something to laugh about there.

"Why do you like Miss Austen so very much?" Students in my Austen seminar unite in decrying a dislike so little just as Charlotte Brontë's of Jane Austen. But, if it is so little justified, Brontë's dislike is nevertheless well amplified. Her Austen is "shrewd and observant" (by contrast with George Sand, who is "sagacious and profound"),[9] unfeeling ("anything like warmth or enthusiasm; anything energetic, poignant, heartfelt, is utterly out of place in commending these works" [127]) and proud of it ("all such demonstration the authoress would have met with a well-bred sneer" [127–28]); for Brontë, Austen is superficial and pedestrian ("her business" is "with the human eyes, mouth, hands and feet" [128]), "sensible" (127) (damned with faint praise), disembodied ("the Passions are perfectly unknown to her" [128]), heartless ("what the blood rushes through . . . *this* Miss Austen ignores" [128]), and dismissable ("she cannot be great" [127]).

Brontë's responses to Austen are most directly responses to George Henry Lewes, written in two rapid letters to him (on 12 January and 18 January 1848) that follow upon his recommendation of Austen to Brontë, in letters now lost,[10] and upon his extravagant praise of Austen in a *Fraser's* review. A third letter, to William Smith Williams (reader for *Jane Eyre*'s publisher Smith and Elder), continues Brontë's comments on Austen, triggered this time by Williams's having sent her three Austen novels in a parcel of books he had chosen for her.[11] The loss of Lewes's letters means that their language is unavailable, which makes it possible only to speculate that as a chiding and guiding Mr. Knightley he fantasizes for Brontë, his contemporary, a textually articulated friendship with an earlier woman writer, fantasizes their friendship for himself. But his writings elsewhere indicate something about how Lewes may have seen Austen, and how he may have introduced her to Brontë. Commenting in 1847, for example, on what he believed to be Macaulay's citation of Austen as a "Prose Shakespeare," Lewes domesticates Austen, as he fantasizes for her an embodiment that is appealing and girlish: Shakespeare's "power of dramatic creation . . . [and] of constructing and animating character . . . may truly be said to find a younger sister in Miss Austen."[12] Not Judith, then, but Jane Austen Shakespeare is Lewes's elegant corrective to Charlotte Brontë, Jane Austen Shakespeare who is the really accomplished young woman so idolized by Lewes and so cried up, as accomplished as Emma-Brontë might have wanted to be thought herself. Lewes's recommendation, reiterated as often as Mr. Knightley's of Jane Fairfax (he always told her, in multiple letters and in published reviews), introduces Austen as Brontë's most becoming supplement ("One might gather from her works that she was personally attractive")[13] and thus announces Brontë's unattractive need: Currer Bell, he writes a few years after her death, "was utterly without a sense of humour."[14]

Brontë accepts Lewes's guidance, reading Austen for the first time at his suggestion, though she rejects his chiding (his defense of Austen, she writes him, has been "a strange lecture" [127]) by rejecting Austen. But Brontë's dislike of the admirable Austen, with its evident disruption of her complacency, is a dislike Austen herself would recognize. Brontë is petulant in her questioning (like Austen, yes, but why "so very much?" [126]), pointed and sarcastic ("have I not questioned the perfection of your darling?" [127]), and so unguardedly disturbed by the recommender's suggestion that her disagreement and distress arise, unbidden and irresistible, to overwhelm even correspondence not addressed to him. Of the "heresy" of her expressed dislike of Austen, Brontë writes to Williams but implicitly engages with Lewes: "If I said it to some people (Lewes for instance) they would directly accuse me of advocating exaggerated heroics, but I am not afraid of your falling into any such vulgar error" (128).

Flattering Williams, Brontë asks him to choose sides but, unable to contain herself, does so most unflatteringly; recommending Austen, "some people" will always be Lewes.

Like an Emma made mistrustful of her own perceptions—made briefly to imagine her dislike as liking—Brontë politely contemplates concession, when she writes to Lewes, and feigns interest in reforming herself: "If I ever do write another book, I think I will have nothing of what you call 'melodrama'; I *think* so but I am not sure; I *think* too I will endeavour to follow the counsel which shines out of Miss Austen's 'mild eyes'; 'to finish more, and be more subdued'; but neither am I sure of that."[15] Brontë is unable to sustain her repudiation of the expansively melodramatic in favor of a bounded realism, but her emphatic *think*ing signs her refusal to commit to the concessionary gesture. Brontë's account of Austen has been most notable for its portrayal of an Austen who has chosen containment in a well-regulated domesticity, and the strength of her rejection of Austen is its dismissal of Brontë's own small step toward all that would contain and subdue, all that would make mild. Austen's world, Austen's novel, is "a carefully fenced, highly-cultivated garden, with neat borders and delicate flowers," with "no open country, no fresh air, no blue hill, no bonny beck" (126). In contrasting Austen's confinement with her own open spaces—with the open country, fresh air, blue hill, and bonny beck she would want to claim for her own writing—Brontë spatializes openness and reserve, and Austen becomes a Jane Fairfax, if Brontë herself is not quite an Emma.

Brontë's dislike so little just works itself out vis-à-vis Austen in the way that some dislikes (but perhaps some likings, too) have a tendency to do—through the oppositional casting that will always determine that I am openness and she reserve.[16] This oppositionality is a way in which Brontë establishes, accepts, and perpetuates a relation to Jane Austen.[17] The friendship that is a rivalry is woven of contrasts and conditionals, and it is always represented as a proposition: if she is this, then I am that.

---

However obvious it has seemed to readers of *Pride and Prejudice* that Charlotte Lucas and Elizabeth Bennet are this and that, the novel makes clear that it is less obvious to themselves. Charlotte imagines, for example, that—despite Elizabeth's avowed dislike of Mr. Darcy—"all her friend's dislike would vanish, if she could suppose him to be in her power" (181). Doing so, Charlotte thinks that, at her core, Elizabeth acts from Charlotte's own prudential account of marriage, in which a husband is managed (sent gardening, kept out of a parlor) by a wife's power. For her part, Elizabeth imagines that—despite Charlotte's own words—Charlotte thinks about marriage as Elizabeth herself does, that Charlotte's engagement to a man like Mr. Collins would be "impossible!" (124), and that Charlotte would never act in accordance with her explicitly stated positions on happiness in marriage ("entirely a matter of chance" [23]). Their mutual Cole Porter fantasy of friendship as "just the perfect blendship" is dependent on simultaneous refusals of difference. If Elizabeth's blockage in acknowledging and accepting Charlotte's difference from herself poses a greater problem for the continuance of their friendship—Elizabeth's early persuasion that "no real confidence could ever subsist between them again" (128) seems a resentment cherished, though later relinquished—this is in part because her stubborn remakings of Charlotte are, apparently at least, the more hurtful because the more open; Charlotte's recastings of Elizabeth occur most often as thoughts and feelings reserved to herself. Elizabeth's betrayals of the friendship seem greater and more serious because she herself seems so in the novel dominated by her presence; the story is hers, and Charlotte is in its service.

Though Charlotte's serviceability to Elizabeth in their relationship is both voluntary and friendly, it respects Elizabeth's dominance as an object of interest. In egging Elizabeth on to make impertinent remarks to Mr. Darcy, Charlotte facilitates and participates in the fun of a friend's social triumph, and she means to do so as well, one suspects, in prompting Elizabeth to play and sing against Elizabeth's ostensible will; if Elizabeth's vanity has not, as Elizabeth claims it has not, "taken a musical turn" (24), it does turn toward the pleasures of display, and Charlotte sets her up and off nicely. Charlotte also serves in performing for the Bennets the social labor of engaging Mr. Collins, in life and in conversation; though this work furthers her "scheme" of diverting his attentions from them to herself (121), the Bennets do not know that this is so, and, despite their gratitude, seem not so very concerned about what they must presume is its tedium for her. But Elizabeth's constant recourse to Charlotte as retreat and as refuge from social exertions ("she returned to Charlotte Lucas" [90]; she "withdrew to Miss Lucas" [96]; she "owed her greatest relief to her friend Miss Lucas" [102]) makes Charlotte a value, their friendship a kind of home.

Still, their friendship seems tougher than this and sometimes more equable, articulated as the product of difference from its first appearance in the novel; while Elizabeth "safely" promises never to dance with the man who has mortified her, Charlotte wishes instead that "he had danced with Eliza" (20). At its best, their friendship seems textured (given character) by disagreement. Their discussion of how a woman should or should not show her feelings to a man—which means thinking about how or how well she can know those feelings given the constrictions of sociable interaction—is an impressive *process*, a complex working out of how Charlotte and Elizabeth each and together will cope with relegation (as to a place) and with regulation.

But something in their friendship demands the not-seeing that results in Elizabeth's inability to know that her impossibility is the possibility most available to Charlotte. "[T]he Lucases are very good sort of girls," says Mrs. Bennet, "I assure you. It is a pity they are not handsome! Not that *I* think Charlotte so *very* plain—but then she is our particular friend" (44). Discoursing on Charlotte's plainness, Mrs. Bennet embarrasses, this time, because she tells the truth, not only about Charlotte's looks but about their place in Bennet/Lucas, Elizabeth/Charlotte relations. The pity (Charlotte is not handsome) that inspires Mrs. Bennet to comment is not evinced by Elizabeth ("very pretty, and . . . very agreeable" [11]), whose feeling for her "particular friend" must mean ignoring (with a gracious "but then" inattentiveness) the evidence of Charlotte's plainness and the burdens that follow upon that plainness in a world where looks are a determinant of consequence. But in not seeing that about Charlotte which would make them unequally advantaged, "Mrs. Collins's pretty friend" Elizabeth (172) denies the circumstances that make Charlotte into Mrs. Collins. Elizabeth's ignorance (her capacity for ignoring) means not seeing something about Charlotte that makes a difference between them.

Elizabeth's entirely mistaken declaration that Charlotte would not behave as Charlotte finally does is explicable as a kind of forbidding; not seeing, Elizabeth would not allow, and it is a formidable and unseen Elizabeth whom Charlotte fears telling about her marriage plans and a forbidding Elizabeth whose adjective ("impossible!") functions as a negating imperative. Elizabeth models here friendship's own fascism, assisted in its work by friendship's somatic fixative, laughter: you know you don't mean that; "You make me laugh, Charlotte; but it is not sound. You know it is not sound, and that you would never act in this way yourself" (23). Fearing difference as a wound to friendship, and fearing its capacity to wound self, one friend coerces agreement by spells woven of personality and by means of what the other friend has already agreed will charm. Friendship's fantasy of perfect blendship proves illusory and imperfect, inevitably so, as blendship frightens with indifference and demands difference's self-assertions. But if difference began this Lucas/Bennet friendship, then it is perhaps less difference itself than the alluring fantasy of indifference that threatens it.[18]

"I am not romantic you know. I never was" (125). Some bit of vitriol released, Charlotte Lucas perhaps gets some relief from the strains of friendship in telling Elizabeth that she "never was" what Elizabeth's laughter encouraged only Elizabeth to think her. Telling Elizabeth what Elizabeth did not know, Charlotte insists on a recentering for herself, permitted (made) by Austen to disrupt the governing narrative in refusing—for herself and for the friendship—to know that the story is not hers.

Readers of Jane Austen have often felt disappointed by her, whether because of her marital endings or because of her reticences about them, because she supports a regime of manners and participates in the policing of bodies, because she seems to like or not to like children, because she is acerbic in her letters, or because she shocks one "unawares" with levity. This expressed disappointment is also readable sometimes as a kind of embarrassment that would deny and disavow her and itself; some sense of that embarrassed disappointment inheres as well in the strained readings by which, all Elizabeths here, some of us have tried to repudiate the ways in which our Austen is not sound by insisting on their impossibility. Thomas R. Edwards articulates these desires and disappointments as part of considering "the borderline of life and art," working with them in a way that grants friendship's charming power to Austen while reserving the power of separation to himself. Acknowledging the powerful fantasy of blendship, Edwards rejects its bland denegation (its not seeing) of Austen's particularity and of the sometimes cutting niceness of her perceptions in favor of the relief and recentering wrought by his friendly self-assertions.

In an essay that appeared in *Raritan*, Edwards establishes himself as a reader who is "[e]mbarrassed by Jane Austen,"[19] which is to say he understands himself (by his notion of embarrassment) as overtaken or overwhelmed by her. Edwards's concept of embarrassment, derived from "a Low Latin word that simply means 'a bar' " (62), is an obstruction or obstacle, a surrender to something outside the self. Though Edwards's embarrassment is not an explicitly somatized notion, embarrassment's bodily cognate—blushing—empiricizes the experience he describes of being in some sense *taken* in embarrassment, taken *with* that which embarrasses. That is, for Edwards embarrassment by Jane Austen is finally a kind of charm that overtakes ("the book is not *our* book, while reading it we submit to another mind, whose interests and purposes are not identical to ours" [79]); embarrassment by Jane Austen is a charm that—as fiction—misleads ("[w]e are asked in some way to credit and care about untruth, to trust an illusion we have good reason not to trust" [79]) and that endangers ("[s]uch fiction improves on life as we know it, and the danger is that it will improve life out of all recognition" [79]), but that—as the act of charming—is deeply relational in nature. The Austen who embarrasses (and whom one can imagine being embarrassed *by*) is implicated in the play of difference and indifference—of possession and separation—that is friendship, as she is implicated in the traumas and delights of reading imagined as a blending and an overtaking.

Much of Edwards's essay focuses on embarrassment *in* Jane Austen, but, though somewhat dismissive of them (moments when readers and characters share embarrassment are handled "more successfully" [74]), he is most interesting on those moments when the reader alone (when he himself) is embarrassed. One such instance is Austen's disparagement in *Persuasion* of Mrs. Musgrove's grief for her dead son; for Austen, the grief is manifest in "large fat sighings" produced by the "unbecoming conjunctions" of "personal size and mental sorrow" (68). Negotiating the unsettling embarrassments of his response, Edwards flirts with the "impossible!" that terrorizes Charlotte ("Perhaps she means only that such conjunctions are unbecoming in books" [74]), but this flirtation seems an excuse that lets him flirt more as if he means it with another and likelier reading. "If, however, she thinks that such conjunctions are unbecoming anywhere," he writes, "in life or art, as her sometimes quite heartless ridicule of real people in her letters might suggest, then my embarrassment is complete, my freedom as a reader has been intolerably abridged, and I don't know what to say except that I wish she hadn't said it, or that she had lived to revise the passage as she reportedly intended to do" (74). Edwards's strong response depends upon a more workaday understanding of embarrassment than he elsewhere articulates. If this sounds indeed like reading as an intolerable abridgment of freedom, it does not sound like the voluntary surrender that makes reading fiction, as he has suggested, "structurally an embarrassment" (79). Here, Austen's effects personify for Edwards an Austen with whom one might splutter and quarrel ("I don't know what to say," I wish you hadn't said it), the embarrassing friend whose behavior induces the briefest fantasy of her death (even if by wishing she had lived) and the contrary-to-fact rewriting of the world that would most literally rewrite the offense.

If Edwards ends by rejecting both his proffered accounts of embarrassment (the moments of embarrassment by Jane Austen are those times when "we most fully appreciate that a successful experience of any fiction is neither a docile submission to its illusion-making powers nor a literal-minded rejection of them" [79]), and if he rejects them in favor of a stabilized and balanced account of instability (embarrassed reading experiences instead are "a difficult and unstable negotiation with those powers, in which no final resolution of forces can occur" [79–80]), this balancing is at some cost. Achieving balance, Edwards loses some of the force of his socialization of reader relations with Jane Austen and some of the power he has forged in his relation to an embarrassing Jane Austen. If embarrassment itself, *chez* Edwards, means blendship and surrender, making embarrassment into a story makes it mean something else. Edwards's conception of Austen as sometimes an embarrassment understands the story as his (recenters the narrative on himself), effecting a separation even as it marks the site of a strong and seductive indifference. Seeing Jane Austen as an embarrassment means *seeing* her and doing so without recourse to a constraining impossibility; it entails disrupting the oppressive blendship by acknowledging the otherness of the friend and insists upon allowing Charlotte's plainness.

---

Considering the passages that some readers have thought of as intruding upon the "romantic climax" of Austen's *Emma*, Wayne Booth writes:

> The intrusions in no way diminish the portrait of the happy marriage to come, as we read in our roles as credulous participants in the conventional world of Hartfield and environs. But they provide us in our other roles, as readers who know we are reading a fiction, a climax to our friendship with a woman who lives very much in the world as we know it, who knows that *we* know that she has been presenting an idealized fiction, a woman whose gifts of imagination and wisdom far surpass Knightley's—and indeed yours and mine. In short, the most lasting demonstration of this novel, concerning men and women in the world, is that most of us, male and female, are as children compared with this one glorious human being, quite real on the page.[20]

The honors Wayne Booth bestows on the Jane Austen who has been a friend to him throughout his reading of *Emma* articulate a hierarchized friendship. The Jane Austen created by Booth's response to her is all-knowing (his "we" can only "make a stab at . . . correct inferences" [187], and, if we manage to know something, she knows we know it); she is untouchable, implacable (though she does so gently, she habitually "corrects our misreadings" [187] in his description of her); she is complete. Booth's Jane Austen as friend is somehow better (her "gifts of imagination and wisdom far surpass") so globally (surpassing "Knightley's . . . yours . . . mine") as not to need a particular object for her comparison; she is herself a superlative. The distanced product of a confusion of intimacy and authority, Booth's Austen is the person who abjects, who always gets to be the boss of you—the friend construed as mother. She *is* the mother (we "are as children" compared with her), imagined to be sufficient in her own resources, imagined to need placating, and no less desirable for all that.[21] Abstracted by her distributive capacities (better than all of us), Booth's Austen is not someone elected to friendship by the contingencies of affinity or of dislike, not someone to squabble or laugh with ("[y]ou know it is not sound"), not someone to complain to or about; she cannot be seen to need, and so she cannot be touching. The friend endowed with omniscience and omnipotence—made the all-giving or all-frightening mother of fantasy—is a friend deprived by means of such endowment.

When Edmund Bertram leaves Mansfield, in *Mansfield Park*, to be ordained with his friend Mr. Owens, Mary Crawford frets. Worried about the possible consequences of Edmund's time with the three "grown up" Miss Owens, she peppers Fanny Price with questions about Edmund's visit, his plans, his letters, and his friend's sisters. And when she does not receive from Fanny a conclusive answer to her question "Are they musical?" Mary babbles:

> "That is the first question, you know," said Miss Crawford, trying to appear gay and unconcerned, "which every woman who plays herself is sure to ask about another. But it is very foolish to ask questions about any young ladies—about any three sisters just grown up; for one knows, without being told, exactly what they are—all very accomplished and pleasing, and *one* very pretty. There is a beauty in every family.—It is a regular thing. Two play on the piano-forte, and one on the harp—and all sing—or would sing if they were taught—or sing all the better for not being taught—or something like it." (288)

Austen notes Fanny's calm (read—exaggeratedly—cold, heartless) response to Mary: "I know nothing of the Miss Owens." A friend might not answer the hysterical gaiety, the desperation and disintegration of Mary's question, as Fanny does, vacantly and "calmly." Untouched by Mary, Fanny misreads her and continues to give only grudging answers throughout the conversation ("Fanny felt obliged to speak"; she "could not bring herself to speak" [289]). Certainly Fanny has reason enough to be unsympathetic to Mary, whose feelings for Edmund are reciprocated, whether or not that reciprocation will lead to presumptive happiness in marriage. And Fanny has been made to witness and to participate in Edmund and Mary's courtship, her own feelings (at best) unregistered or (at worst) absorbed by the blank egotism of their infatuation. Though Fanny, too, of course has reason not to want to add the Miss Owens to her list of disturbing rivals, and though she is thought to be unable to "speak or write a falsehood" (411), she is certainly here ungenerous and unkind, and she is those things because unmoved by Mary ("Fanny did not love Miss Crawford" [147]), whose company—after all—she too has been seeking, and whose recognitions have brought her from serviceable isolation into the company of others. If Mary's friendliness to Fanny is, as a contemporary Fanny might say, only the signs of friendship, it is not so clear what friendship is without its signs, and Fanny deprives Mary even of these.[22] Fanny does not conceive of herself as unkind here (upright, perhaps, truthful) because she does not believe in Mary's feelings for Edmund ("The woman who could speak of him, and speak only of his appearance!" [417]) or believe in Mary's professed feelings for herself (" 'So very fond of me!' 'tis nonsense all. She loves nobody but herself and her brother" [424]). Like a reverse of Booth's Jane Austen, Fanny's Mary is complete and self-sufficient; refusing to pity Mary, "Fanny could have said a great deal, but it was safer to say nothing, and leave untouched all Miss Crawford's resources, her accomplishments, her spirits, her importance, her friends, lest it should betray her into any observations seemingly unhandsome" (199). Fanny's safe and unfriendly logic denies Mary the right or the capacity to have a need and leaves Mary, like all her resources, untouched by Fanny. If her pity is to be earned and only by those without resources, Fanny misunderstands that resources are husbanded and drawn on so that they may satisfy a prior or anticipated condition of insufficiency.

As readers have struggled to name the powerful and authoritative intimacy that is made in the course of reading Jane Austen, they have struggled also to name the overwhelming (some might say embarrassing) sense of inclusion and relation they produce and experience in the presence of her effects. One such reader, having rejected the name "Janeite" for herself, contemplated other options at the 1979 inaugural meeting of the Jane Austen Society of North America. Quizzed about alternatives by an anonymous "Talk of the Town" contributor to the *New Yorker*, Edith Uunila considers the alternatives before settling on one:

> "Austen fans" doesn't sound right either, does it? "Austen lovers"? I don't think so. "Austenites"? That's even worse. How about "friends of Jane Austen"? I've always thought of her that way. I read her when I'm sick or feeling sorry for myself. I read her when I'm trying to understand people, or the way the world is. Jane Austen *is* like a friend. I think that I can truly say that I am a friend of Jane's.[23]

The signs of friendship to which she refers—help in sickness or in self-pity, help in developing an appropriately worldly air—point in just one direction: this solacing and socializing Jane Austen is a friend to Uunila ("Jane Austen *is* like a friend"). In saying that Jane Austen is my friend, I might take possession of her (by friendship's deepest, sickest logic, since she is mine, implicitly she is not your friend), claiming her to claim associative status. Yet Uunila's final statement—the conclusion to which her careful review of options and evidence leads her—leaves her the possessed. Imagining myself a friend of Jane Austen's, I imagine *both* of us in need. If I can "truly" say I am a friend of hers, the intensification of that statement lies in my having proven myself, conjuring her with books and objects and syntactic echoes that I decide must satisfy her desire (I imagine it, too) for me. But that which "I think that I can truly say" I use my saying to make so. Making an Austen in need, I read her effects (her novels) as an appeal made with those peals of laughter from which no Marianne would be shut out. Like those of the orchestra or the library, the friends of Jane Austen construe her as an institution to be endowed, a space at the center of her effects and their desires. Fantasizing myself a friend of

Jane Austen's, I give myself in friendship to that space the better to ask things of it; and asking of an absent object, I desire possession and recognition for their own sake and for my own.

## Notes

1. Valerie Grosvenor Myer, *Jane Austen: Obstinate Heart* (New York: Arcade Publishing, 1997), 1–9.

2. Marianne Knight's recollection appears in Constance Hill, *Jane Austen: Her Homes and Her Friends* (1901; reprint, Folcroft: Folcroft Library Editions, 1977), 202. Quoted in Deborah Kaplan, *Jane Austen among Women* (Baltimore and London: Johns Hopkins University Press, 1992), 103. Biographical record continues to inscribe and to validate Marianne's sense of her outsider status; as the daughter of Austen's brother Edward (who had been adopted by the wealthy Knight family), Marianne was younger sister to Fanny Knight, most often honored in biographical prose (with a designation that fantasy suggests Marianne might have coveted) as Austen's favorite niece.

3. *Past Times'* Austen offerings vary from catalog to catalog and have included an "Emma Woodhouse Figurine" and the "Austen Sisters' Citrine Cross," as well as the Card Games. The figurine, indistinguishable from countless other china ladies, is made Emma Woodhouse not iconographically but by means of the catalog's designation, indication and invocation of the consumer magic produced by Austenian association. The Sisters' Cross, inaccurate as a reproduction, merely (catalog copy is careful to note) "recalls" crosses given to Jane and Cassandra Austen. But, as fantasy, the cross also recalls the sacred utility of the relic, while creating for Jane Austen's friend a relation of somatic connection through the material object. To wear something that the friend has worn (or to imagine that one is doing so) is to enjoy the mediation that negotiates an impossible meeting of body and body.

4. The Jane Austen writing paper was designed and produced for the National Portrait Gallery and made in the United Kingdom. The wallet itself explains what is inside: "Ten Folded, Letterheaded Sheets each featuring a Cameo Detail from A Portrait of JANE AUSTEN together with a Quotation: 'FOLLIES and NONSENSE, WHIMS and INCONSISTENCIES *DO DIVERT ME, I OWN*, and I LAUGH AT THEM WHENEVER I CAN." The Jane Austen Card Games, from the *Past Times* catalog, come with a rule book for "Round Games and Whist Tables . . . together with appropriate extracts from her writings."

5. Cathryn Michon and Pamela Norris, *Jane Austen's Little Advice Book* (New York: HarperCollins Publishers, 1996). Michon and Norris see Austen as paradoxical: "her image," they write, "(which seems to be that of bonnets and crinolines, tea and gentility) is sometimes completely at odds with her writings, which are always sly, often biting, and sometimes actually vicious . . . in an extremely entertaining way" (xii; ellipsis in the original), but, epigrammatized, Austen seems less paradoxical than rather simply cynical. Though Michon and Norris warn those of us who are "[s]erious students of Jane Austen" to, well, know we have "been

warned" (xiii) about their decontextualization and their humor (O.J. Simpson is *Persuasion*'s Wentworth, "making love, by breaking his mistress's head" [123]), they insist on their fidelity to Austen and their preservation of her, inviolate, by their presentation of her language in its immediacy, without acknowledging their framing of that language: "Rather than dissect her appeal yet again, we prefer to let her words stand for themselves" (xiii).

6. *Jane Austen Songs* is available as a *Past Times* CD. Liner notes by Jon Gillaspie, who produced the CD and who also plays fortepiano on it, indicate that the songs are "vocal works which Jane found attractive enough to purchase or, in the majority of cases, laboriously copy out for her long term enjoyment." Gillaspie's is a musical Jane Austen ("[h]er pianoforte lessons continued unusually late in life for a young lady at that period," perhaps because of the "complex" situation of Austen's "remaining unmarried"), and he has a particular sympathy for Austen in the "difficult period" when she lived unhappily in Bath: this time "was to be a musical wasteland for Jane and her collections contain no music published during the period 1801–06."

7. Susan Watkins, *Jane Austen in Style* (New York: Thames and Hudson, 1990). Its original title was *Jane Austen's Town and Country Style.*

8. Virginia Woolf, "Jane Austen," in *Jane Austen: A Collection of Critical Essays*, ed. Ian Watt (Englewood Cliffs, N.J.: Prentice Hall, 1963), 23.

9. Southam 1968, 126. Though, imagining that readers of Austen are the most likely readers of this essay, I make reference to Brontë's comments as they are reprinted in the Southam's edition, the comments also, of course, appear in fuller context in T. J. Wise and J. A. Symington, *The Lives, Friendships and Correspondence of the Brontë Family* (Oxford: Basil Blackwell, 1934), 2 vols. Page references to Brontë's letters as excerpted in Southam's collection appear in the text.

10. Rosemary Ashton, *G.H. Lewes: A Life* (Oxford: Clarendon Press, 1991), 66.

11. Juliet Barker reports that the books from Smith, Elder & Co. included *Sense and Sensibility, Pride and Prejudice*, and *Emma*. Brontë's letter to Williams is prompted by her having finished *Emma*. See Barker's *The Brontës* (New York: St. Martin's Griffin, 1996), 634–35, 948 n. 13.

12. Lewes's comments on Austen appeared in an unsigned review in the *Leader*, 22 November 1851. See Southam 1968, 130.

13. Lewes's "The Novels of Jane Austen" appeared in *Blackwood's Edinburgh Magazine*, July 1859. See Southam 1968, 148–66, 151.

14. Lewes, "The Novels of Jane Austen" in Southam 1968, 160.

15. Brontë's 12 January 1848 letter to Lewes, in Wise and Symington, *The Lives, Friendships and Correspondence of the Brontë Family*, 178–79.

16. Lewes contributes to an understanding of what he calls "the bias of opposition," that tendency by which a critic is "exasperated into an opposition" constructed to ensure that a work's "undeniable qualities" will pale beside its "undeniable defects." This bias, as Lewes writes and as Austen would know, develops in response to the "chorus of admirers" who cry up quality without attending to defect. Lewes discusses the oppositional bias in his 1872 essay "Dickens in Relation to Criticism," reprinted in *Literary Criticism of George Henry Lewes*, ed. Alice R.

Kaminsky (Lincoln: University of Nebraska Press, 1964), 94–105, 99–100. See D. A. Miller's use of Lewes's notion in *Narrative and Its Discontents: Problems of Closure in the Traditional Novel* (Princeton: Princeton University Press, 1981), 137, which brought the Lewes to my attention.

17. If Lewes may be understood to produce for Charlotte Brontë a relation to Jane Austen, those writings in which he compares George Eliot to Jane Austen make it possible to wonder what relation to Austen he manages for Eliot. Though praising Eliot, in "The Novels of Jane Austen," as Austen's "equal in truthfulness, dramatic ventriloquism, and humour, and greatly superior in culture, reach of mind, and depth of emotional sensibility," he also describes her in this way: as "Mr. George Eliot, a writer who seems to us inferior to Miss Austen in the art of telling a story, and generally in what we have called the 'economy of art.' . . ." See Southam 1968, 155–56. The model of friendship by which women are urged upon one another as corrective (and thus rivalrous) intimates—the Jane Fairfax problem—parallels a literary connection to Jane Austen sometimes visible in the texts of nineteenth-century women writers, whose mock-Austen moments (the first few of the "Great Temptation" chapters in Eliot's *The Mill on the Floss* and the early London scenes in Elizabeth Gaskell's *North and South* are two such) answer a demand for the Austenian by demonstrating that what a woman writer *might* do, she *would* not.

18. Singing Porter's anthem to friendship-as-blendship ("ours will still be hot") in an *I Love Lucy* episode, Lucy and Ethel discover that they are performing in the same dress. In a fit of anxiety about this sartorial indifference, they rip the dresses off one another, performing and reestablishing themselves as *together* by displaying their angry joy in separation.

19. Thomas R. Edwards, "Embarrassed by Jane Austen," *Raritan* 7, no. 1 (summer 1987): 62–80. Subsequent references will appear in the text.

20. Wayne C. Booth, *The Company We Keep: A Ethics of Fiction* (Berkeley and Los Angeles: University of California Press, 1988), 434. Subsequent references will appear in the text.

21. Booth's description of Austen as "glorious human being" comes at the conclusion of his discussion of ideological complaints about Austen's *Emma*—that it insists upon marriage, that Emma must learn to see the world "*as Knightley sees it*" (427; italics Booth's), that the novel reinforces "those deep seated sexist beliefs that are taught by most Western fiction until our century" (428–29). Booth takes these complaints seriously and concedes them, in some way, until he works his concessions into an account of the novel by which it is seen to "contain[] within itself the antidotes to its own potential poisons" (432). These antidotes are to be found in the discovery that, though characters are imperfect, a standard of perfection in the novel derives from "that great woman, the implied Jane Austen" (433) who is "quite real on the page" (434).

Booth resolves for himself the ideological problems of the novel by formalizing them: Austen "work[s] to incorporate her vision into a successful realization of a conventional form" (430); the novel has to end a certain way. Booth's own conclusion is readable as ideological (what isn't?), but it is more interestingly readable as formal, when formalism is understood to mean his argument has to end a certain way. Because he has learned from his Jane Austen to desire the whole and complete, the ordered and the clean—and because he loves Jane Austen—his argument about *Emma* is from the start determined to end in a vision and restoration of the author-mother-perfect-friend and must take whatever steps will lead to that restoration.

22. Fanny has earlier been more generous in bestowing the signs of her friendship. "[W]ithout loving her, without ever thinking like her, without any sense of obligation for being sought after now when nobody else was to be had; and deriving no higher pleasure from her conversation than occasional amusement, and *that* often at the expense of her judgment," Fanny "went to her every two or three days" (208). Untouched by Mary and unmoved by her in the discussion of Miss Owens, Fanny acts out an indifference acquired for purposes of display; "You know nothing and you care less, as people say," Mary notes. "Never did tone express indifference plainer" (288). But Fanny's well-spoken indifference (payback, perhaps, for the companion who had earlier remained "untouched and inattentive" in the face of "some tender ejaculation of Fanny's" about human and vegetative nature [208–9]) is the studied resolution of an irresistible restlessness: Fanny's visits to Mary and "the sort of intimacy which took place between them" are the product of "a kind of fascination" on Fanny's part (207–8). The hesitations and reluctances of Austen's language (a kind of / sort of relation between women) may name an erotic connection contained and dulled by the interposing figure of Edmund Bertram. For further discussion of Mary and Fanny, see Misty G. Anderson's " 'The Different Sorts of Friendship': Desire in *Mansfield Park*," in *Jane Austen and Discourses of Feminism*, ed. Devoney Looser (New York: St. Martin's Press, 1995), 167–83. Janet Todd allows her discussion of the "strangely threatening" nature of some friendships in Austen to trouble her notion that "social friendship" (which she finds most clearly exemplified in Austen's novels) "is a nurturing tie." See *Women's Friendship in Literature* (New York: Columbia University Press, 1980), 4–5, 246–301.

23. "Homage" in "Talk of the Town," *New Yorker*, 5 November 1979, 41–42. I thank Deidre Lynch for suggesting that I look at this passage, and I thank audiences at the University of Utah and the University of Colorado at Bolder, as well as participants in D. A. Miller's graduate seminar at Columbia University, for their stimulating responses to this essay.

# 3

## Sensibility by the Numbers: Austen's Work as Regency Popular Fiction

BARBARA M. BENEDICT

### Introduction

Charlotte Brontë's sneer at Jane Austen still resonates. "And what did I find [in *Pride and Prejudice*]?" she demanded in 1848. "An accurate daguerrotyped portrait of a commonplace face; a carefully fenced, highly cultivated garden." Brontë's contempt for Austen crystallizes the Romantic opposition to Regency fiction thirty years after the posthumous publication of *Northanger Abbey and Persuasion*. Compared to Scott's "big boom" and Brontë's sexual passion, Jane Austen's works were considered by Romantic advocates safely "delicate."[1] These judgments have swayed generations of critics into maintaining that Austen wrote refined novels that pleased conservative readers by steering clear of sentimentalism or rebellion. This pigeonholing of Austen as an author of high literature remains in effect.[2] Yet Austen wrote love stories at a time when novels that portrayed female emotion and the struggle of independent heroines against social convention were the popular rage. Moreover, the Romantic ideal of authorship as a sign of laudable originality was, in fact, only newly emerging, and doing so among a literary elite to which Austen did not belong. Poised between two aesthetics, Austen faced an audience that Brontë did not acknowledge. How did these original readers encounter Austen's work—as "literature" or as "fiction"? Since her novels plumb a popular tradition of love fiction, why did critics categorize her work as highbrow? What, indeed, is the relationship of this highbrow classification to Romantic ideals of authorship?

Scholars have noted Austen's close attention to the eddies of literary fashion in *Northanger Abbey*. But all her novels allude to popular texts. *Pride and Prejudice* condemns Mr. Collins for refusing to read novels. *Sense and Sensibility* and *Persuasion* mock would-be Romantics' enthusiasm for fashionable literature; *Emma* refers to Mr. Martin's reading of Knox's *Elegant Extracts* and plunders John Almon's *New Foundling Hospital for Wit*; *Mansfield Park* and *Northanger Abbey* both center on the thoughtless use of a trendy text, *Lovers' Vows* and *The Mysteries of Udolpho*, respectively.[3] Clearly, Austen was interested in the commercial circulation of literature.[4] Indeed, her intertextuality suggests that she conceived of her novels in the context of current fiction, as a part of popular literature, and designed her novels to reach the audiences who were reading contemporary novels. An examination of the venues for the kinds of books Austen was writing, their audiences, what the safely sellable formula of novels seemed to be, and what conditions encouraged the development of this formula clarifies Austen's fictional structure and her early reception, while suggesting why she has been labeled elite. These contexts show that Austen's novels, albeit written originally for her family and informed by high, as well as popular, literature, were constructed and presented to audiences in the mold of circulating fiction: as the episodic adventures of familiar, sympathetic heroines, designed for a rapid read.

These audiences were part of the wide readership that Scott, the Romantic poets, the Brontës, and like-minded artists desired to reach in the early nineteenth century. Austen's fiction, however, scarcely encourages Romantic taste in such readers. In her plots, motifs, and settings, Austen instead makes the most of the overlap between early novels now considered "high," like Richardson's *Sir Charles Grandison*, and new, "common" novels like the anonymous *Harriet and Her Cousin, or Prejudice Removed*, doing so just when middle-class Romantic authors were attempting to forge a profitable difference between them. Moreover, her narrative sophistication and irony suggested a stylistic compatibility between high literature and popular fiction that challenged—indeed, contradicted—Wordsworth's argument (outlined in the Preface to *Lyrical Ballads*) that a new literary language was required in order to reach the neglected, common audience. By her thematic and generic formulas, her style, and her method of publishing outside the contemporary critical coterie, Austen contradicted the Romantic claim that fine writing required extraordinary experience, extraordinary character, and a revolutionary ideology.[5] Her work seemed to devalue fiction writing, defining it not as the demonstration of original genius or innate talent that the Romantics claimed, but as a craft requiring only basic skill and education. In the Regency and the early Victorian period, Austen could be seen as hostile to the Romantics' attempts to make authorship an elite profession and so to distinguish themselves from the writers-for-pay employed by such publishers as the Minerva Press. By categorizing Austen herself as elite, however, this ambitious, middle-class literary coterie asserted that popular taste ran not to the familiar but to the sensational, which they provided. They thereby sought to consolidate a hold on literary production.

## How Regency Readers Encountered Novels

During the last decades of the eighteenth century and the first of the nineteenth, however, literary production in fact often entailed the formulaic reproduction not only of content but of form. The venues in which readers encountered novels like Austen's promoted the replication of these formulas: circulating libraries accessed by means of catalogs. These contexts worked to shape fiction and to outline the way to read it. The Regency library was a transitional arena permitting a rich interchange between rival literary ideals. Here, critical hierarchies vanish. Libraries juxtaposed current and classical, entertaining and technical, profiteering and pious texts. In catalogs and on shelves, Austen and Burney stand cheek-by-jowl with "high" and "low" works, genres, and authors; either readers brought their own preferences or prejudices with them, or proprietors directed their taste. Indeed, since books were arranged by format and size, as in the catalogs, in large libraries readers relied on assistants to find, even to choose, their selections (see fig. 1).[6] This jumble elided the emerging distinction between literature as a class commodity and as a popular entertainment. Austen's novels, like many others, finesse these distinctions by combining qualities currently successful in circulating novels—the topic of female education and marriage, attention to social ritual, sensitivity to female conduct and internal consciousness, an elite setting—with qualities borrowed from high literature: parody, moral seriousness, topicality. Depending on their "take," readers could categorize these works as circulating novels, moral fiction, or both.

Circulating libraries also violated cultural hierarchies. By acquiring private libraries, they helped to propel literature into the public arena and became a means for the public to sample the taste of the elite, yet their supply of fiction overwhelmed their supply of the poetry, moral philosophy, and drama that formed the traditional basis of literary collections.[7] This competition between kinds of literature did not escape public notice. For example, in a comic petition published in the *Bath Chronicle* of 25 January 1781, personified books in a circulating library plead with literary proprietors to replace novels with "serious literature."[8] But *The Use of Circulating Libraries Considered: With Instructions for Opening and Conducting A Library either upon a large or small Plan* (1797) suggests that of 1,500 books, 1,050 should be novels, and 130 romances, making fiction 80 percent of the holdings. Libraries also advertised for subscribers in the newspapers and allowed visitors use of their rooms if accompanied by members or for a fee, thus blurring the boundaries between selective and general membership.[9] They allowed class mixing—and the exercise of

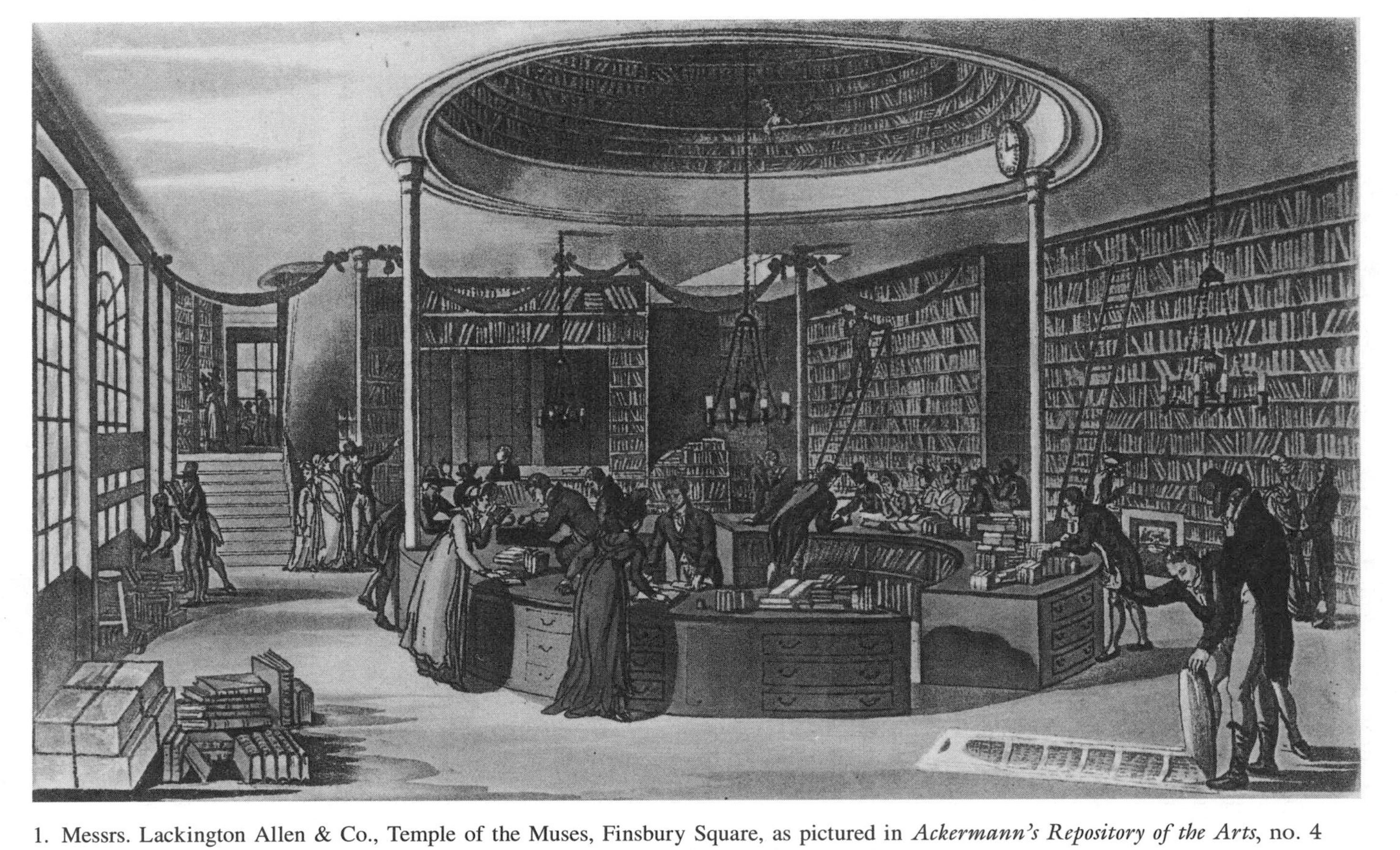

1. Messrs. Lackington Allen & Co., Temple of the Muses, Finsbury Square, as pictured in *Ackermann's Repository of the Arts*, no. 4 (1 April 1809). Courtesy of the Print Collection, Lewis Walpole Library, Yale University.

social skills not recommended by traditional literature, like flirting. Austen portrays this irony in *Pride and Prejudice* when she shows Lydia Bennet attending to men rather than books at Clarke's (30).

Yet circulating library audiences in the Regency could not escape class consciousness.[10] Libraries' location, contents, fees, and clientele gave them a class stamp. Subscriptions were based on income: the more clients paid, the more books they were permitted to borrow at a time, and the greater their access to new works.[11] The huge 1812 *Catalogue of N.L. Pannier's Foreign and English Circulating Library* in London provides a typical delineation of terms: "1st class: 2 guineas per annum, 10 volumes at a time in town and 15 in the country; 2nd class: 1£. 11s. 6d per annum, 6 volumes at a time in town and 9 in the country; 3rd class: 1£. 4s. per annum, 4 volumes at a time in town and 6 in the country."[12] Moreover, the catalog graciously promises that "[a]ny Lady or Gentlemen [*sic*] to whom it may not be convenient to take Books Quarterly, &c. may be accommodated Weekly or Monthly." By contrast, Harrod's Circulating Library in rural Stamford in 1790 featured over a thousand books, the majority novels. Its twelve-page catalog, which includes *Clarissa*, *Evelina*, *The Excursion*, *Castle of Otranto*, *Emma or Child of Sorrow*, and *Emily Montague*, omits all authorial names, yet devotes a whole page to selling medicines and miscellaneous goods such as boot blacking, musical instruments, and drawing implements.[13] This library serves as a general store for a regular clientele. The still less extensive and expensive Carnavon circulating library of Jones and Parry in 1835 asks only one pound annually.

Location also dictates taste. Whereas Pannier's served a faceless urban clientele, the Carnavon library set out to woo familiar customers by providing "Instructive, Entertaining, and Religious" books, and adding "New Popular Publications . . . as soon as published, according to the patronage."[14] Whereas Pannier's abounds with novels, Jones and Parry's twenty-two-page catalog includes Blair's *Sermons*, Young's *Night Thoughts*, Hester Chapone's *Letters*, *Rasselas*, works by Dodd, Doddridge, Franklin, Gregory, and many other religious and philosophical writers, along with plenty of history and three pages of biography.

In addition to prices, content, and location, the character of the proprietor, as Austen notes both in her letters and in *Sanditon*, determined the nature of a library. To entice clients, proprietors published sycophantic notes to the public in their catalogs. York's circulating library proprietor "W. STORRY Cannot suffer the present Opportunity to pass, without briefly expressing his grateful Acknowledgments for the liberal Support he has experienced from the Public; and at the same Time assures them that his utmost Endeavours shall be exerted to render his LIBRARY worthy of their future Patronage and Support."[15] Fisher's catalog is dedicated to subscribers with "sincerest gratitude. . . . He trusts that it will not be improper for him to say, that if his Library be, in any degree, worthy of general approbation, the public is obliged to his annual subscribers, who enable him to buy so great a variety of new books, on the most important subjects."[16] With such expressions of gratitude, proprietors attempted to kindle a personal relationship with their audiences that would resemble the bonds between old-fashioned booksellers and elite clients in the previous century.[17]

Circulating libraries expanded the uses of literacy. As John Bell explains, different readers subscribe for different reasons:

> There are gentlemen who wish to examine the merits of Books before they purchase them, and others whose convenience will not admit them to purchase many new Books;—*The British Museum* and other Libraries on [*sic*] public institutions, may contain every publication, but then the mode of accommodation to individuals, is on so confined a Plan, as to render it almost useless; and the application to private collections . . . may put friendship to the test. In order, therefore, . . . To facilitate the advantages of Literature—To enable every reader to form a proper judgment of Books before he becomes a purchaser of them . . . I submited [*sic*] the following plan. . . .[18]

Bell recognizes that readers encounter books in different ways, but he interprets these differences as demonstrations of readers' unique tastes and stresses that libraries, like the commissioned booksellers, can cater to individuals by allowing them to vet texts before borrowing or buying them. As a service rendered to a mass audience, however, this practice and venue encouraged all readers to sample books before purchasing them. Reading itself could become an act of casual impressionism acted out in a social milieu, rather than the private act of intellectual commitment that Romantic theory endorsed.

Libraries also could be seen as turning authors into suppliers of cheap commodities, and raising booksellers from mediators to managers of literary culture. To the Reverend Edward Mangin, formulaic fiction that panders to the lower and middle classes degrades literature, converting it into merchandise. He blames circulating fiction for freeing the writer to feed the audience's fantasies, and thus promoting an idle greed for pleasure. This commercialization alarms Mangin because, by removing literature from the purview of critics, it seems to leave one of the most influential arenas of cultural production to be regulated by market forces alone. This decentering of cultural creation was, in fact, already over a hundred years old, but in the light of the new Romantic ideal of the spiritual independence of authorship, circulating fiction, simultaneously old-fashioned and newfangled, embodied cultural corruption.[19] Novels were a site not only of public morality but also of commercial and cultural competition.

In attacking circulating libraries' violation of both traditional and emerging, elite literary values, Mangin inadvertently outlines what readers expected when they took out a novel. Circulating libraries marketed novelty—but novelty of a particular, predictable sort. As John Bell explains, libraries traditionally specialized in permanent rather than ephemeral printed materials since "[p]amphlets in general, have been excluded from the Catalogues of Circulating Libraries, with very great propriety, as they are generally of the Mushroom kind, and seldom enjoy a less precarious existence" (preface). In the Regency, however, libraries increasingly featured topical items. At the same time, inflation, and, in particular, the gouging price of 31s. 6d. charged for Scott's three-decker novels, eroded the power of traditional booksellers to purvey fiction and so increased the importance of libraries for readers.[20] In this context, the circulating library became the first arena openly to value the experience of literary novelty over proprietorship. Its customers borrowed rather than bought; the pleasure it afforded was thus unapologetically ephemeral.

At the same time, this novelty was itself formulaic, and the libraries' catalogs underscored this. Organizing readers' responses to circulating library fiction in highly significant ways, these catalogs show which familiar features of novels were valued by their contemporaries. They were themselves formulaic books that both retained their value and required constant updating. In 1817, when the Reverend E. W. Grinfield, M.A., minster of Laura Chapel in Bath attempts "the diffusion of Religious and Useful Knowledge amongst the Labouring Orders, by the means of cheap Circulating Libraries," he suggests that "[t]he first step towards the promotion of such an Institution is the *Publication of a General Catalogue*."[21] The London-based Earle, whose shilling catalog was published by John Nichols, stresses the importance of the catalog as an object of expenditure and a guide:

> The present Catalogue is printed different from any in London, it being the Practice of most Libraries to make their Catalogues appear as large as possible, for which Purpose, they particularize, and some even give short Accounts of the Books; whereas the one now offered exhibits at one View 90 different Books, except where there is a Collection, containing sundry Things. He trusts his Plan will be approved, as his Aim is to give Subscribers as little Trouble as possible—and it will be found as extensive as any in England. (Overleaf)

As Earle's boast demonstrates, each detail of a catalog conveys essential information to readers, although expensive ones prefer descriptive precision whereas economical ones value quantity. All catalogs, however, remind readers of the bargain circulating libraries provide. Most number each selection in vertical columns, listing the unitalicized title, the number of volumes, and the reference numeral, often printing at the far right the price of each work for those who might wish to buy it. This detail informs readers of the work's estimated value, serving discreetly to underscore the advantage of borrowing rather than buying the book. Since these values usually rest merely on the size of a book, they remain fairly constant: Mackenzie's short but trendy *Man of Feeling*, for example, as a single volume almost universally commands 2s. 6d., while three-volume novels cost upwards of 9s. Totting up the cost of all the books a reader might peruse in a year certainly evidences the value of a library subscription.

Unlike the auction catalogs that were printed for elite collections, the catalogs for circulating libraries ignore publication dates and often omit authors' names. A sequence of sale catalogs printed in the early nineteenth century suggests that this is a significant difference not merely of practice but of policy, and moreover a difference that echoes the struggle between the Regency reader's appetite for literature's replication and the Romantic idealization of original authorship. In 1801, Turner published a catalog for his library and bookshop using the conventional method of classification by format and alphabet, mixing genres and pricing books by their length and popularity. If within the catalog novels were attributed to specific authors, they sometimes cost more: item #271 *Castle of Athlin and Dunbayne*, attributed to "Mrs. Radcliffe," is valued at 3s. 6d.; also her accredited *The Italian* at three volumes costs 15s.; and her *Sicilian Romance* is 7s. for two volumes.[22] Turner follows these principles in his 1814 sale catalog. In 1817, however, his catalog of books for sale includes a penultimate section invitingly entitled "Novels," while in 1819 he cites several previously overlooked novelists for the first time by name and includes the dates of their editions, including as item #2597 "Mackenzie's Man of Feeling, *n.* bds. 2s.6d. 1815."[23] Interestingly, the brand-new edition of Mackenzie's novel with original boards commands the same price as an old, undated one, presumably in far worse condition. This suggests that novels, no matter how popular, did not accumulate value as classics in exactly the same way that famous editions of poetry and philosophy did. Clearly, the value of this novel lay for most readers in its role as the literary epitome of sentiment.

This practice of dating editions and thus advertising them as collectible objects continues in Turner's sale catalogs for 1823 and 1827. The circulating library catalogs' practice of omitting dates suggests that novelty was so desirable to library proprietors that they preferred not to devalue their stock by admitting damning information that might make a book seem outdated. It also implies, however, that readers were unlikely to care about which edition of a novel they were ordering.[24] Catalogs thus reveal the difference between the elite custom of collecting books as objects and the new reading classes' practice of collecting the experience of reading them.

Significantly, the volumes of a work are numbered individually, but since the listed prices serve for the entire work, any volumes subsequent to the first are not priced. This reveals that whereas for book collectors with vast houses like Austen's Mr. Darcy, who "cannot comprehend the neglect of a family library" (*Pride and Prejudice*, 38), a book's value lies in its entirety, for circulating library readers, mobile, space-short, or penny-pinched, each volume should be worth borrowing on its own merits.[25]

Packaging, like circulating library catalogs, also presented novels as interchangeable rather than unique. Despite their books' touted novelty and transience, the physical arrangement and presentation imposed by libraries gave their volumes a uniformity comparable to that of the books lining the shelves of gentlemen's libraries, where selections were bound in matching covers. Although printers, binders, booksellers, and proprietors altered the presentation of all books during the period from the eighteenth century to the end of the Regency, novels underwent a particularly significant makeover. Printed in octavo or duodecimo, small and portable, they were jacketed in marble, sky-blue, or rose-colored paper that advertised both their function as articles designed for feminized leisure and their similarity. Designed to appeal to the consumer's eye, this packaging imposes an external regularity on the novels constituting the fictional "library" and suggests a parallel internal uniformity of form and quality. Readers are encouraged to expect familiar contents.

Familiar titles reinforce this uniformity and provide readers with the clearest clue to these contents. The subtitular hint "A Novel" rarely appears in catalogs, so titles alone must serve to signal their genre or subgenre. Bell's catalog categorizes books by format (novels never appear in the large formats), and then genre, but whereas volumes in sections like "History and Antiquities," "Divinity," and "Voyages and Travels" are listed by author, the volumes in "Romances, Novels, and other Books of Entertainment" appear only by title. Although Storry's catalog lists its stock alphabetically under the author's name within format divisions, tales and novels as usual appear under their titles—including item #1047 *First Impressions; or, the Portrait* (4 vols., £1) and item #1663 *Musgrove (Eliza)* (2 vols., 6s.) (28, 42). Despite omitting the titles of its three hundred plays as "too tedious to mention," Harrod's lists all its novels by their titles. More scrupulous catalogs distinguish plays from novels by using parenthetical notes like "sent[imental] com[edy]" and "tragedy." Since many early catalogs mix all kinds of works—biography, travels, memoirs, novels, beauties (compendia of choice passages from the work of a particular author), poetry, biography, medicine, drama, periodicals, travels, dictionaries, and pictorial works—readers were expected to infer the genre of a work from its title. This lack of categorical differentiation separates circulating library catalogs from auction catalogs that categorize literature by genre; the former equate all kinds of reading as equally satisfying.

The similarity of novels' titles further underscores the similarity of their contents. These titles fall into a few, loose categories. Many are names that typecast protagonists, particularly women. While no Austen novel finds its way into Pannier's catalog, something entitled *Susan* appears at 2 vols. for 12s., and under "E" the evidently popular *Eliza Musgrove*, 2 vols., 4s. (#4549, 89; #590, 26). As Austen well knew, women's names, especially fashionable and familiar ones, seemed to survive endless repetition.[26] In *Northanger Abbey*, the narrator regularly plays with the associations of nomenclature, asserting Mr. Morland's respectability "though his name was Richard," explaining Tilney's forgiveness of Catherine as a sign of the sensibility of "a Henry," and tracing Tilney's ability to manufacture a Radcliffean fantasy to his intimate knowledge of "Julias and Louisas" (13, 94, 107). Ebers's 1816 catalog, for example, cites eight novels whose main title is *Julia*, and two more *Juliana* (117). Four *Emmas*, not even including Austen's or another published by Lane, appear here. These familiar names function for readers as a code for types of moralized sensibility.

The repetition of the titles within such lists also supplies readers with a context they could draw on to evaluate new novels. The publication of *First Impressions* may have prevented Austen from using that title, but the concept was already banal. In 1799, Earle's catalog lists as item #1687 "*Love at first sight*, by Gunning," five volumes for 17s. 6d.; as item #1687 "*Love at first sight, or miss Caroline Hamilton*," three volumes for 9s.; and as item #1689 "*Love at first sight, or the gay in a flutter*" for 3s. (39). This titular repetition suggests that originality was not an important criterion for publishers or readers. Ebers's library in 1809 lists, as item #11509, "*First Impressions, or Sketches from Art and Nature, animate and inanimate*, by J.P. Malcolm, Esq." at 16s., as well as #11070, "*Pride of Ancestry*," four volumes for £1.[27] In 1816, Ebers includes as item #5066 *Sense and Sensibility*, 3 volumes for 18s., and as item #4905 "——— and Prejudice, by a Lady, 3 vols. 18s." (169, 164). The latter appears beneath *Pride of Ancestry* at 4 vols. for £1 1s.[28] While such juxtapositions often, if not always, hint at topical echoes, titles only outline subgenre; they do not convey tone. Although readers relied primarily on the main title, since novels often lost their subtitles in catalogs, long repetitive titles added style, as well as emphasis. Many use these secondary clauses further to characterize their protagonists, for example, #5292 *Adultress (the), Aspasia, or the Dangers of vanity*, and *Alphonsine, or Maternal Affection* (5–6). A few titles describe a lurid incident: #169 *Atrocity of a Convent*, 3 vols., 15s. (4), or #95 *Annals of Suicide, or History of Self Murder* 3s. 6d. (3). The utter absence in the catalog of any clue signaling satire, sentimentalism, tragedy, or comedy suggests that for Regency readers, tone may have been less important than plot and unimportant compared to character, particularly the character of a female heroine.

The titles of Austen's first two published novels announce the novels' allegiance to one particular subgenre: romances about the education of heroines. In titling these books, Austen employs terms that were highly familiar to her audience and would immediately signal the central plots of her novels: "sense," "sensibility," "pride," and "prejudice." Indeed, she prunes away the subtitle that has become so typical of circulating fiction, and so prompts or licenses her publisher Thomas Edwards to exploit the densely packed terms by printing them repeatedly in the text. The first editions of both *Sense and Sensibility* and *Pride and Prejudice* repeat the title on each volume's opening page. *Sense and Sensibility* (London: Printed for the Author, . . . and published by T. Egerton, Whitehall, 1811) prints the title as a running head in each of its three volumes. *Pride and Prejudice* (London: T. Egerton, Military Library, Whitehall, 1813) not only prints the title "PRIDE AND PREJUDICE" on its half title page between double rules but includes a full title page that solicits the audience for Austen's previous novel: "PRIDE AND PREJUDICE: A Novel. In Three Volumes. By the AUTHOR OF 'SENSE AND SENSIBILITY.' " This both advertises the previous novel and reiterates its thematic category. *Sense and Sensibility* is a fictional exploration of sentimentalism; circulating readers remember this each time they open one of its volumes.

The importance of titles for quickly sending signals to readers was obvious to publishers.[29] The celebrated and successful William Lane of Lane's Circulating Library fused tout and tale in his humorous advertisement *A Tale Addressed to the Novel Readers of the Present Times.* A joking intertextual squib, serving simultaneously as advertisement and parody, this story opens:

> In a sequestered and romantic part of an interior county resided ELLEN, COUNTESS OF CASTLE HOWELL; a lady who united an excellent mind to an elegant person. She was reared, and had received instructions for her conduct through life from the protectress of ANNA, or the WELCH HEIRESS. And though she had a few JUVENILE INDISCRETIONS, yet her guardian angel, hovering around her, prevented her sharing the fate of the innocent AGNES DE COURCY.[30]

Suggesting how women's names and experiences were the topics of novels, Lane explains that "[h]er companions were PAULINE, A VICTIM OF THE HEART, and MADELINE, of the HOUSE OF MONTGOMERY. Her attendants LUCY, with the twins ELLEN AND JULIA, having been reared in the CASTLE OF WOLFENBACH, were, from some ERRORS OF EDUCATION, not the WOMEN THEY SHOULD BE" (3). The seven-page tale concludes by soliciting readers to visit Lane's Press: "The readers who are anxious to inquire earlier [than the year's probation Minerva demands] into the fates, and attendant circumstances, may be fully gratified by application to her Temple,—where, for the Entertainment, all these MYSTERIES" may be purchased (7). On the back page is the list of "JUST PUBLISHED" novels, including all twenty-six of those mentioned in the tale, and a list of twelve more "IN PRESS." The titles clearly told readers what subgenre of novel—Gothic or sentimental—they were.

## The Contextual Influence on Austen's Fiction

This principle of listing books by title alone began to change, however, when Romantic notions of authorship infiltrated libraries. The Reading circulating library established by George Lovejoy in 1832 explains meticulously that "[i]n the second part, from page 183 to 360, *Works of Fiction* are arranged separately in alphabetical order, under the *name* of the Author, and again under the *title* of the Book."[31] In this library, all of Austen's novels appear listed alphabetically under "Austen, Jane," with *Northanger Abbey and Persuasion* appearing under "N" (191). In this scholarly system of cataloging, Austen's novels are lifted from the traditional context of circulating fiction and appear as highbrow literature, the product not of a formula but of an individual sensibility. This represents them as Romantic products, texts for elite readers vetted by experienced critics.

As Lane's advertisement shows, however, for Regency writers and readers, circulating novels established their own literary context not through plaudits in critical reviews but through intertextuality. With a tonal flexibility difficult for modern audiences to grasp, these novels yoke self-consciousness and sentimentality. At the start of *Constantia; or, the Distressed Friend*, for example, Charles Easeby remarks to Sir Thomas Trevor, "If Fortune should ever throw us into a Train of Adventures (which you know had like to be the Case at our Departure from *France*) there could not possibly be found two Heroes better adapted to be the subject of a modern Novel. As it is, if I had *Oliver Goldsmith's Chinese* Habit . . . I should describe . . . [an] Allegory. . . ."[32] Novels depended on readers' knowledge of other novels, as Austen recognizes when she refers to Burney and Radcliffe in *Northanger Abbey*, her novel most explicitly addressed to the circulating library public, and when she sprinkles references to texts or heroines' names in vogue throughout her novels. In *Persuasion*, for example, a Louisa Musgrove, whose prototypical name resonates with fictional sensibility, charmingly injured (mainly in the head) by a fall, wins the heartbroken and poetic Captain Benwick. In contrast, the materially injured and bedridden Mrs. Smith exhibits fortitude, although Sir Walter Elliot scoffs, "a mere Mrs. Smith, an every day Mrs. Smith, of all people and of all names in the world, to be chosen," blithely overlooking his favorite Mrs. Clay's transparent name (158). Such a blend of metafictional satire and sentimental morality was not uncommon.

Moreover, novels themselves incorporated criticism of novels. *Female Sensibility; or, the History of Emma Pomfret*, published by Lane, opens much as *Northanger Abbey* does, by denying its own sentimental premise: "To the Reader: Whoever expects to find, in the following sheets, warm descriptions of Romantic adventures; improbable events . . . pompous acounts of bleeding heroes, and of sceptered tyrants, will be disappointed. This is an artless tale, told in an artless strain. The story is wrote only to the heart; and is plain, simple, and unaffected." Using two passages also quoted in *Northanger Abbey*—Thomson's "Delightful task! . . . To teach the young idea how to shoot," and "A maid in love . . . Sitting like patience on a monument, Smiling at grief"—the author argues that the events in this novel are "natural and familiar, and such as occur every day," and should thus inspire Aristotelian pity, not merely "respect."[33] These texts show that self-conscious theoretical realism used to sanction sentimentalism informs circulating fiction and informs the reader of how to read it.

Just as readers were accustomed to intertextual references and assertions of literary method, so they evidently welcomed direct addresses by the narrator. In *Female Friendship*, the narrator remarks encouragingly, "From what has been said, the readers will naturally expect two marriages;—nor will they be disappointed."[34] Austen uses the same ploy at the end of *Mansfield Park* when she "purposely abstain[s] from dates" to allow her readers to imagine the marriage that completes the novel's action (470). In *Northanger Abbey*, she leaves to the reader the exact chronicle of Henry Tilney's explanation of his father's perfidy to Catherine (247). Dependent on the reader's knowledge of fictional formulas, this technique places novels firmly within the circulating novel tradition, simultaneously flattering the reader, justifying the writer's structure, and demonstrating their bond. Again, the narrator of *Female Friendship* explains, "Having thus dispos'd of my principal personages, I must (after the example of my betters) likewise give some small account of the other characters mentioned in this trifling work" (2:261). In *Mansfield Park*, Austen uses the same formula to finish off the novel: "Let other pens dwell on guilt and misery. I quit such odious subjects as soon as I can, impatient to restore every body . . . to tolerable comfort, and to have done with all the rest" (461). Such outlines of the rules of novelistic structure direct authors how to fulfill the readers' expectations, and readers how to read the fictions.

Other rules concern the presentation of character. Like her fellow writers, Austen herself uses the formula of an opening informational chapter situating her families and heroines in their social context. *Female Friend-*

*ship: or the Innocent Sufferer* starts, for example, by describing the hero: "Sir Henry Summers was a man by nature formed sensible, open, and compassionate to the distresses of his fellow creatures, which he never looked on without pitying, nor was pity all he bestowed. . . . Yet notwithstanding he was thus endowed with every virtue that can truly form the amiable, generous, honest man; he had, in common with all human kind, his particularities . . ." (1:5). Austen parodies this sentimental formula in her juvenilia. *Jack & Alice: A Novel* begins with the pronouncement "Mr. Johnson was once upon a time about 53; in a twelvemonth afterwards he was 54 . . ." (*Minor Works*, 12). Imitating circulating fiction's practice of generic advertisement by the subtitle "A Novel," this squib runs through its main characters in a series of terse sentences: "Mr & Mrs Jones were both rather tall & very passionate, but were in other respects, good tempered, well behaved People. . . . Miss Simpson was pleasing in her person, in her Manners & in her Disposition; an unbounded ambition was her only fault. Her second sister Sukey was Envious, Spitefull & Malicious. Her person was short, fat & disagreable [*sic*]. Cecilia (the youngest) was perfectly handsome but too affected to be pleasing" (12–13). As Austen's mockery makes clear, this schematic characterization adumbrates the plot to come and relieves the reader from having to evaluate ambiguous characters.

In her mature work, Austen deliberately aims at a surprising plot and at complexity of characterization. Nonetheless, her novels open with this formula, albeit tonally modulated by her reading in high literature. *Emma*, for example, starts by defining the heroine's virtues, clarifying her situation, and hinting at the flaw that will provide the drama:

> Emma Woodhouse, handsome, clever, and rich, with a comfortable home and happy disposition, seemed to unite some of the best blessings of existence; and had lived nearly twenty-one years in the world with very little to distress or vex her.
>
> She was the youngest of the two daughters of a most affectionate, indulgent father, and had, in consequence of her sister's marriage, been mistress of his house from a very early period. (5)

*Sense and Sensibility* begins by defining the Dashwoods' situation; a similar pattern appears in *Mansfield Park*, *Northanger Abbey*, and *Persuasion*. Only *Pride and Prejudice* opens, after an ironic generality, in medias res and delays the narrative revelation of character. In general, Austen adheres to the formula of defining her characters by their social circumstances, and physical and moral traits.

Unlike the eighteenth-century practice of reading for detachable "beauties," the reading elicited by circulating fiction increasingly concentrates on plot and character development. In Ann Radcliffe's transitional novels, the two techniques often conflict, as her long, pictorial passages halt the plot and sometimes interfere with the characterization, but later works tend to jettison description in favor of incident.[35] This feature informs the circulating novel's structure. Incidents propel plot. Since libraries lent books by the volume rather than the work, multivolume formats proved most profitable, but readers were more likely to peruse multiple volumes if they were waiting for the resolution of a drama. Although single-, double-, and quadruple-volume works exist, by the early decades of the nineteenth century, the three-decker dominated, partly perhaps because of the notoriety that Scott's novels gained for this format from 1814 through the 1820s. The borrowing terms of libraries reflect and reinforce this formula, often lending customers volumes in multiples of three. Because circulating fiction was lent out this way, the structural device evolved of ending each volume, like an episode in a televised serial, with a "hook."

Earlier epistolary fictions, written, unlike Richardson's *Pamela*, from a retrospective viewpoint, contain no real urgency, since the reader knows from the first sentence the heroine's fate. Mrs. W. Burke's two-volume *Elliott: or, Vicissitudes of Early Life*, for example, contains climaxes, but the volumes are almost interchangeable—this is also true of Frances Brooke's *Julia Mandeville*.[36] The epistolary travelogue *The Portrait*, like Brooke's *Emily Montague*, interlards sentimental descriptions of the love affair of Miss Maria Bellmont and the brother of her epistolary friend Miss Harriot Marchmont with accounts of journeying through Russia.[37] These and similar novelistic devices offer readers select, sentimental beauties—pictorial descriptions or linguistic virtuosities to be lingeringly memorized—that do not culminate in a denouement. Since they proceed rhythmically and episodically, rather than progressively, they evoke and depend on a leisurely, impressionistic kind of reading.

This, however, was increasingly not the kind of reading that circulating novel clients enjoyed, charged as they were by the day. Moreover, novelists writing to appeal to such readers needed to provide a cumulative interest. Rather than supplying beauties to be lingeringly memorized, they designed obsolesence: plots to mesmerize audiences through three volumes and then to release them. Austen employs some the techniques of the earlier fiction while developing new strategies more suited to the new ways of reading. Rather than providing pictorial descriptions or linguistic virtuosity, she creates dramatic scenes. They abound in *Sense and Sensibility*: the moment when Willoughby rescues Marianne; when Elinor and Marianne discover that the gentleman approaching over the hills is Edward, not Willoughby; when Marianne confronts Willoughby at the London ball; and when Willoughby arrives at the stroke of midnight just as Marianne begins to recover in her sickbed above stairs. In her later works, Austen adapts this technique to the new formula of longer chapter, volume, and work lengths, indicating again her sensitivity to contemporary changes in taste. Moreover, her method of free indirect style, which relinquishes the narrative to the heroine, increases the drama and strengthens the identification with the heroine that readers coveted. These devices lead readers from one volume to the next.

Austen's overarching structure resembles Walter Scott's: a cumulative action segmented into a three-tiered novel, with patches of description and dramatic dialogue, and a climax at the end of each volume. The first volume of *Sense and Sensibility* concludes with the scene in which Elinor learns definitively of Lucy's engagement to Edward, when she views Lucy's miniature portrait of him and recognizes his hair ring. The final sentence—"After sitting with them a few minutes, the Miss Steeles returned to the Park, and Elinor was then at liberty to think and be wretched"—promises readers emotional descriptions as well as complications of plot in the next volume (135). Volume 2 repeats and intensifies this dynamic by recording (ironically) in its final paragraph Lucy's triumph: "Sir John . . . brought home such accounts of the favour [the Miss Steeles] were in, as must be universally striking. Mrs. Dashwood had never been so much pleased with any young women in her life, as she was with them; had given each of them a needle book, made by some emigrant; called Lucy by her christian name; and did not know whether she should ever be able to part with them" (254). In *Mansfield Park*, Austen combines this technique with metafictionality by concluding the first volume when Julia, erupting into a scene that itself depicts a dramatic rehearsal, "with a face all aghast, exlaimed, 'My father is come! He is in the hall at this moment' " (172). With acute irony, Austen not only imitates the dramatic structure of *Lovers' Vows* by concluding a volume with an abrupt pronouncement of disaster; she also imitates its plot. Just as the play turns on the shocking return of the missing protagonists, so the novel announces the sudden return of the absent patriarch. Austen's readers go to the next volume to learn what will happen, not merely to enjoy more dialogue and character.

## How Novels Were Read

Dramatic techniques complemented libraries' lending policies. Since novelty was a library's bread-and-butter, especially in London and fashionable watering places like Bath, proprietors urged patrons to read quickly. Turner's insisted that, "New novels must not be kept longer than a week, and new plays and pamphlets not longer than two days."[38] Pannier entreats readers in italics, "*It is requested that the Book lent may be returned immediately it is read.*" Readers competed for new publications. When he tries to borrow *Vensenshon, or Love's Mazes*, a romance hot off the press, Mangin himself notes that "the proprietor of a circulating library assured me, at the time of lending it, that he gave me the preference over fifteen expectants."[39] The more customers paid, the sooner they got to borrow fresh books.

Rapid reading entailed rough treatment. N. L. Pannier's Circulating Library catalog for 1812 warns grimly on its opening page, "N.B. Ladies and Gentlemen Subscribers are respectfully informed, that if any Book is written in, torn, or otherwise damaged, while in their possession, the same to be made good." Ebers in 1816 inscribed a new rule: "If a Book be written in, torn, or damaged, whilst in the Possession of a Subscriber, that Book, or the Set (if Part of one) to be paid for. *The very great injury caused by persons writing their remarks, and otherwise wilfully damaging, even the most valuable works, has determined the proprietor to introduce this rule*" (original italics; rule 5). Other proprietors complain of notes in the margins and of torn leaves. Even Mangin, fantasizing about the fate of his text, describes the history of a circulating library volume as physically battering: "It will . . . be turned over, thrown down, taken up again, cut open, read, and returned to the shop with the usual and flattering marks of having seen service; viz. a leaf or two torn out, scratches of pins, scoring of thumb-nails, and divers marginal illustrations, executed by means of a crow-quill, or a black-lead pencil."[40] Clearly, readers did not regard these books as valuable possessions worthy of care. Nonetheless, they did comment on the books themselves, suggesting that novels were read as part of a play or as a conversation between anonymous readers. They had an active life in readers' minds.

Although most of Austen's early readers indeed remained both anonymous and silent, the author did record some opinions about *Mansfield Park* and *Emma* that show the ways in which readers compared her novels with others in the popular genre. Most focus on particular characters: " 'We certainly do not think as a *whole*, [*Mansfield Park* is] equal to P. & P.—but it has many & great beauties,' " observes Francis William Austen, but rather than citing passages or scenes, he proceeds to specify his "favourite" personalities (*Minor Works*, 431). While Austen may well have prompted these remarks, they indicate contemporary standards of judgment echoed in the library catalogs and novels' titles that register the Romantic emphasis on character. Three kinds of responses dominate the record: emotional reaction, such as liking or hating; moral responses like admiration; and aesthetic evaluations of technique, signaled by words such as "pleasing," "enjoyable," and "natural." While neither exclusive nor contradictory, these differences in terminology do signal different criteria of value and distinguish distinct groups of readers. Since Austen's family tend to be well-educated and sophisticated readers, they often employ aesthetic terms. "My Eldest Brother—a warm admirer of it in general.—Delighted with the Portsmouth Scene" (432). "Mrs. James Austen, very much pleased. Enjoyed Mrs. Norris particularly, & the scene at Portsmouth. Thought Henry Crawford's going off with Mrs. Rushworth, very natural" (432). "Cassandra—thought it quite as clever, tho' not so brilliant, as P. & P.—Fond of Fanny.—Delighted much in Mr. Rushworth's stupidity" (432). Such aesthetic evaluations depend on the reader's own experience, for one class's realism is another's romance. Responses from Lady Gordon and Mrs. Pole, written after *Emma* had been published with its dedication to the Prince Regent, stress Austen's technique, differentiating her from other novelists by emphasizing the authenticity of her elitism: "In most novels you are amused for the time with a set of Ideal People whom you never think of afterwards or whom you the least expect to meet in common life, whereas in Miss A——s works, & especially in M P. you actually *live* with them, you fancy yourself one of the family" (435). Lady Gordon contrasts romantic fantasy with novelistic precision. Mrs. Pole more openly compares Austen to circulating library novelists:

> There is a particular satisfaction in reading all Miss A—s works—they are so evidently written by a Gentlewoman—most Novellists fail & betray themselves in attempting to describe familiar scenes in high Life, some little vulgarism escapes & shews that they are not experimentally acquainted with what they describe, but here it is quite different. Everything is natural, & the situations & incidents are told in a manner which clearly evinces the Writer to *belong* to the Society whose Manners she so ably delineates. (435)

These readers indicate that one trademark of the popular novel was a heady setting in high society.[41] Such a setting might feed the social fantasies of common readers, but evidently it offended inhabitants of this society themselves. Austen herself satirizes this feature in her burlesque "Plan of a Novel," which concludes by insisting that "[t]hroughout the whole work, Heroine to be in the most elegant Society & living in high style. The name of the work *not* to be *Emma*—but of the same sort as S & S. and P & P." (*Minor Works*, 430). She jokes that this planned novel's elite signature is to be reinforced by an abstract title, one that privileges the play of concepts and not the experience of the heroine. Here, Austen herself records the contemporary hostility between classes over control of the literary arena.

This difference between conceptual and characterological nomenclature distinguishes Austen's elite audience, including most of her family, from the audience for circulating fiction. Similarly, aesthetic criteria evaluating technique were not the most general standards of evaluation. Austen's middle-class acquaintance generally employ moral and emotional terms of criticism, focusing on the novel's piety and characters. "Mr. & Mrs. Cooke—very much pleased with [*Mansfield Park*]—particularly with the Manner in which the Clergy are treated.—Mr. Cooke called it 'the most sensible Novel he had ever read.'—Mrs. Cooke wished for a good Matronly Character" (433). Amidst the general moral applause, however, some readers indicated that the three criteria of aesthetic, moral, and emotional pleasure came into conflict: "Miss Sharpe—'I think [*Mansfield Park*] excellent—& of it's good sense & moral Tendency there can be no doubt.—Your Characters are drawn to the Life—so *very, very* natural & just—but as you beg me to be perfectly honest, I must confess I prefer P & P' " (434). Alethea Bigg shares Miss Sharpe's opinion: "I have read M P. & heard it very much talked of, very much praised, I like it myself & think it very good indeed, but as I never say what I do not think, I will add that although it is superior in a great many points in my opinion to the other two Works, I think it has not the Spirit of P & P., except perhaps the *Price* family at Portsmouth, & they are delightful in their way" (434). These responses register the division between the elite criteria of realism and morality and the primary lure of the novel as a genre of romantic fantasy. This division mirrors the social and conceptual divisions that segregated literature from circulating novels.

Central to these evaluations was comparison. Within Austen's circle, her books were compared to one another: "Miss Lloyd preferred [*Mansfield Park*] altogether to either of the others" (432); "Mrs. Augusta Bramstone—owned that she thought S & S.—and P. & P. downright nonsense, but expected to like M P. better, & having finished the 1st vol.—flattered herself she had got through the worst" (433); "Mrs. Carrick—All who think deeply & feel much will give the Preference to Mansfield Park" (434). Elite readers differentiated her novels from common circulating fiction primarily because they knew the author: after noting Austen's evident experience of high life, Mrs. Pole records the sophisticated speculation about the author, turning Austen's novel into a kind of roman à clef (435). Within the catalogs of circulating libraries, however, comparison worked to reinforce the charms of each composition, rather than to elevate one at the expense of another.[42] Novels trained readers in reading novels, through their intertextuality or their repetitions of tropes that with increasing efficiency induced the desired, sentimental responses. The characteristics of female heroines accumulated in the mind of the reader to form an ideal heroine, a composite Emma—the character parodied in Austen's "Plan of a Novel." This comparative, heroine-centered evaluation reflects the ways novels were presented: as exegeses of female virtue.

## Conclusion

Austen structures her fiction according to circulating novels' formulas and strategies. In libraries and their catalogs, these novels become part of a public literary collection featuring tales of love in elite settings, a happy ending in the form of a marriage, and the fulfillment of readerly expectations. In her plots, characterization, organization, and narrative strategies of intertextuality, tonal fluidity, and self-consciousness, Austen underscores her obedience to them. Libraries' practice of lending works by the volume required readers to read quickly. It also encouraged Austen to arrange for her plots to move rapidly to a climax at the end of each volume, while continuing to provide dramatic beauties for her readers to remember after they had returned the book. As Regency libraries simultaneously enforced and transgressed class distinctions through their rules for visitors, advertising, and fee schedules, Austen also gears her novels both to her upper-class audience and to the novel-reading public. Likewise, as these libraries profited from readers' identification with a central character, usually a heroine, so Austen wove her fictions around the ambiguities of such an identification with flawed protagonists. Readers approached Austen's novels expecting to read quickly through all their volumes, closing the last with a sense of identificatory triumph with a familiar character, not with an extraordinary Romantic hero.

Although, as a member of a book-loving family, Austen doubtless wished her readers to buy her books, they were as well adapted to the circulating as to the private library, for she wrote in a practical spirit as a sometime author, rather than as an ideologue. The conventions she borrowed from circulating novels, including intertextuality, tonal ambiguities, and the negotiation of moralism and fantasy, framed her works as both fiction and literature—depending on the reader's own context. To the professional writers forging an authorial identity of unique genius, this very adaptability made Austen an exemplar of a privileged mode of casual authorship. Austen's very lack of ideological rigor allowed her to become known as the author of high literature. Ironically, for Romantic critics and many of their successors, her very marketing strategies for popularity marginalized her as elite.

## Notes

References to book catalogs, after an initial documentary endnote, appear parenthetically in the text. My thanks to Deidre Lynch for her help in editing this article.

1. Charlotte Brontë, to George H. Lewes 1848: Southam 1968, 126.

2. Even while acknowledging that her low publication runs cannot be taken to indicate her readership since "many of the copies went to the circulating libraries," and while noting Lewes's observation that she is "very widely read," Southam maintains that, "[p]re-1870, Jane Austen was never thought of as a popular novelist." See Southam 1968, 24, 28. By stressing her refinement, Henry Austen's "Biographical Notice," printed in the 1818 edition of *Northanger Abbey* and *Persuasion*, and James Edward Austen-Leigh's 1870 *Memoir of Jane Austen* reinforced this assumption that Austen was an elite author. Influential criticism, especially from the 1970s, focused on Austen's formal irony and thus cemented her status as a highbrow writer. Modern movies that place Austen's work among a host of filmic depictions of love may, in fact, more closely mirror her original context.

3. For an examination of Austen's use of popular sources, see Barbara M. Benedict, "A Source for the Names in Austen's *Persuasion*," *Persuasions* 14 (16 December 1992): 68–69.

4. For examinations of the commercialization of printed culture in the eighteenth century, see particularly Richard D. Altick's groundbreaking *The English Common Reader: A Social History of the Mass Reading Public, 1800–1900* (Chicago: University of Chicago Press, 1957), esp. 59–77; and Terry Lovell, "Subjective Powers? Consumption, the Reading Public, and Domestic Woman in Early Eighteenth-Century England," in *The Consumption of Culture: Image, Object, Text*, ed. Ann Bermingham and John Brewer (London and New York: Routledge, 1995), 23–41.

5. Clifford Siskin's recent account of how Austen rejected the magazines as a forum for her fiction and chose John Murray as her publisher seems to me to reinforce the artificial distinction between "high" and "low" literary forms that, in fact, during the Regency seemed very unstable. See *The Work of Writing: Literature and Social Change in Britain, 1700–1830* (Baltimore: Johns Hopkins University Press, 1998).

6. Hilda M. Hamlyn, *Eighteenth-Century Circulating Libraries in England* (London: The Bibliographical Society, 1947), 216, 208–9.

7. In "From Promotion to Proscription: Arrangements for Reading and Eighteenth-Century Libraries," James Raven emphasizes the contested division between public and private space, and the anxiety surrounding public libraries in *The Practice and Representation of Reading in England*, ed. James Raven, Helen Small, and Naomi Tadmor (Cambridge: Cambridge University Press, 1996), 175–201.

8. Paul Kauffman, "The Community Library: A Chapter in English Social History," *Transactions of the American Philosophical Society*, n.s., 57 (Philadelphia: The American Philosophical Society, 1967), 6.

9. Hamlyn, *Eighteenth-Century Circulating Libraries*, 218–19.

10. Jan Fergus points out that price limited servants' reading in "Provincial Servants' Reading in the Eighteenth Century," in Raven, Small, and Tadmoor, *The Practice and Representation of Reading in England*, 202–25.

11. Charlotte A. Stewart-Murphy, *A History of British Circulating Libraries: The Book Labels and Ephemera of the Papantonio Collection* (Newtown, Pa.: Bird and Bull Press, 1992), 14–24.

12. *Catalogue of N. L. Pannier's Foreign and English Circulating Library*, No. 15 Leicester Place, Leicester Square (London, Cavendish Square: Juigné, 1812).

13. *A Catalogue of Harrod's* CIRCULATING LIBRARY, Comprising 700 NOVELS, &c. and 300 Plays (Stamford, 1790).

14. *A Catalogue of the Instructive, Entertaining, and Religious* CIRCULATING LIBRARY, at Jones and Parry's, Booksellers, Stationers, and Print-sellers (Carnavon: For the Proprietors, [1835]), overleaf title page.

15. *A Catalogue of W. Storry's General Circulating Library, Petergate, York.* Containing upwards of Ten Thousands Volumes of Valuable BOOKS, in the different classes of polite literature, which are LENT OUT TO BE READ By the Year, Quarter, or Single Book (Agreeable to the Conditions specified on the following Page), and to which ADDITIONS WILL BE MADE of every NEW BOOK of GENERAL ENTERTAINMENT as soon as published (W. Storry, 1809), overleaf.

16. *A Catalogue of R. Fisher's* CIRCULATING LIBRARY, in the High-Bridge, Newcastle (Newcastle upon Tyne, 1791), overleaf.

17. See Barbara M. Benedict, " 'Service to the Public': William Creech and Sentiment for Sale," *Eighteenth-Century Life*, n.s., 15, nos. 1 and 2 (February and May, 1991): 119–46.

18. *New* CATALOGUE OF BELL'S CIRCULATING LIBRARY, Consisting of about Fifty thousand Volumes (English, Italian, and French) . . . Including all the BOOKS that have been lately published: Which are Lent to Read . . . By John Bell (London, [1778]), preface.

19. Rev. Edward Mangin, M.A., *An Essay on Light Reading, As it may be supposed to influence Moral Conduct and Literary Taste* (London: James Carpenter, 1808). On authorship, see Mark Rose, *Authors and Owners: The Invention of Copyright* (Cambridge: Harvard University Press, 1993).

20. Lee Erickson, *The Economy of Literary Form: English Literature and the Industrialization of Publishing, 1800–1850* (Baltimore and London: Johns Hopkins University Press, 1996), 130–31.

21. Rev. E. W. Grinfield, M.A., minister of Laura Chapel, *REFLECTIONS* on The Influence of Infidelity and Profaneness upon Public Liberty; Being the Substance of Two Discourses, Preached at Laura Chapel, Bath, To which is Subjoined A Plan for the Formation of National Circulating Libraries, for the use of the Lower Orders of Society (Bath: Meyler and Son, the booksellers of Bath and Bristol, Messrs. Rivington et al., 1817), 31.

22. *Catalogue of Turner's Circulating Library. Market-Place, Beverley. Containing Many valuable Books, which are lent out to read by Subscription, or by the single Volume, agreeably to the Conditions on the following pages* (Beverley: M. Turner, 1801), 15–16.

23. *APPENDIX* to M. Turner's *CATALOGUE* of New and Second-hand Books for 1819: A Catalogue of Books, (Ancient and Modern) which will be sold for ready money, at the prices affixed. By M. Turner, Bookseller, Stationer, and Printer. Old Books bought or exchanged for New ones (Beverley: M. Turner, 1817), 11.

24. See, for example, "*A Catalogue of a Collection of Miscellaneous Literature*: consisting of Works Relating to the British Colonial Possessions, Classics, Antiquities, History, Bibliography, &c. in various languages, being principally Additions to that part of the Stock of Messrs. Ogle, Duncan, and Co." On Sale for Ready Money by Howell and Stewart (295 Holborn, London, 1828), which specifies

"Richardson's Sir Charles Grandison, 8 vols. 12mo, *neat* 18s. ib. 1776" (46). See also *Catalogue of a Very Valuable Collection of Books and Prints*, The Property of The Rev. W. Hildyard of Beverley (Beverley: J. Kemp, 1832), which includes "*the original Edition*" of *Tom Jones* (3) and "Scott's Novels and Tales, 35 vols. *beautifully bound in red morocco, gilt extra, gilt edges and plates*" (11). There were, however, ways of discovering from a circulating library catalog how old a book might be. Although the catalogs are organized alphabetically, the reference numbers in circulating library catalogs designate the order in which the book was purchased by the library. Thus although readers might know from proprietors, assistants, or other readers whether a book was new, they might also calculate its novelty from its catalog number, since higher numbers would indicate recent acquisitions.

25. Caroline Bingley also attempts to define herself as elite by mourning the smallness of her father's book collection (*Pride and Prejudice*, 38); see my argument that ways of reading define social identity in "Jane Austen and the Culture of Circulating Libraries: The Construction of Female Literacy," in *Revising Women: Eighteenth-Century "Women's Fiction" and Social Engagement*, ed. Paula R. Backscheider (Baltimore: Johns Hopkins University Press, 1999).

26. In " 'We shall . . . call it Waterloo Crescent': Jane Austen's Art of Naming," Susannah Fullerton emphasizes Austen's restricted use of names as a "structural means of portraying her world," indebted to her own experience, but this ignores the contemporary literary context (*Persuasions* 19 [16 December 1997]: 106).

27. "*A Catalogue of Ebers's New Circulating Library* 23 Old Bond-Street, Two Doors from Burlington-Gardens; consisting of ALL THE MOST APPROVED AUTHORS IN EVERY BRANCH OF LITERATURE, Ancient and Modern" (London: Reyell, Sons, and Wales, 1809), 82, 183.

28. *Catalogue of Ebers's British and Foreign Circulating Library* 27 Old Bond Street, consisting of The Most Approved Authors, Ancient and Modern (London: Whittingham and Rowland, 1816), 169.

29. Hamlyn, *Eighteenth-Century Circulating Libraries*, 204. She also observes that "[a] later innovation was a system of classes of subscription. . . . Lane's proposals of 1798 include five classes of subscription. . . . Although terms were in general rising, in London there was evidently no *controlled price*. In Bath, however, the libraries seem to have had an arrangement between themselves, a rise from 3s to 4s a quarter took place in the early 1770's, and from 1s. 6d to 2s a month at about the same time," probably because of their heavy reliance on visitors (211).

30. [William Lane], *A Tale Addressed to the Novel Readers of the Present Times* (London: Minerva Office, W. Lane, n.d. [1795]), 1.

31. "*A Catalogue of the books in the general subscription circulating library at Reading*, first established by Mr. George Lovejoy, in 1832; purchased by Miss Langley in 1884. And since then much enlarged and greatly extended" (Reading: Miss Langley, 1887), preface.

32. *Constantia; or, the Distressed Friend. A Novel* (London: W. Johnston, 1770), 15. Later, Sophia records a witty conversation concerning novels: Lady Modish remarks, "And we are to have a new *Paris* Edition of Captain *Whim*, neatly bound and gilt. We ought to have him lettered too, replied I—or I shall never be able to distinguish him from the Works of other Authors, I mean the Taylors . . ." (12).

33. *Female Sensibility; or, the History of Emma Pomfret. A Novel.* Founded on Facts (London: W. Lane, 1783), preface, 58.

34. *Female Friendship: or the Innocent Sufferer. A Novel,* 2 vols. (Dublin: J. Williams, J. Porter, and T. Walker, 1770), 2:260. Subsequent references will appear in the text.

35. See Barbara M. Benedict, "Pictures of Conformity: Sentiment and Structure in Ann Radcliffe's Style," *Philological Quarterly* 68, no. 3 (summer 1989): 363–77.

36. [Mrs. W. Burke], *Elliott; or, Vicissitudes of Early Life,* 2 vols., By a lady (London: British Library, etc., 1800).

37. *The Portrait. A Novel.* In Two Volumes (London: Printed for T. Hookham, At his Circulating Library, New Bond-Street, 1783).

38. *Catalogue of Turner's Circulating Library.* Market-Place, Beverley. Containing Many valuable Books, which are lent out to read by Subscription, or by the single Volume, agreeably to the Conditions on the following pages (Beverley: M. Turner, 1801), iv.

39. Mangin, *An Essay on Light Reading,* 85–86.

40. Ibid., 3.

41. See, for example, *The Tyranny of Love; or Memoirs of the Marchioness D'Aremberg* (London: C. Elliot, [1800]).

42. In *Making the Modern Reader: Cultural Mediation in Early Modern Literary Anthologies* (Princeton: Princeton University Press, 1996), I argue that this readerly dynamic of comparative evaluation also organizes responses to literature in the anthology.

# 4

## Austen's Earliest Readers and the Rise of the Janeites

WILLIAM GALPERIN

THE INITIAL RESPONSE to Jane Austen's fiction is perhaps best understood in the context of debates about the novel and its functions that antedate the publication of Austen's writings by nearly half a century, and in the course of which realistic practice, chiefly as a regulatory apparatus, emerged as an aesthetic desideratum for fiction, especially women's fiction. The debate was nicely, if lopsidedly, framed by Frances Burney in the preface to her first and most successful novel *Evelina* (1778), where, in the course of defending the novel as a respectable and worthy genre, Burney simultaneously concurred with the genre's severest critics in proposing to rescue the novel from its current depravity. Although asserting that the novel's reputation cannot be reckoned independently of the legitimating efforts of Fielding, Smollett, Richardson, Rousseau, and Johnson, Burney insists at the same time that both the fate of the novel and its much-needed recuperation rest with novelists like herself: novelists writing chiefly for women, whose responsibility it was to retrieve the genre from "the fantastic regions of Romance."[1] In place of the "Marvellous," which has had a deleterious effect on young women who, in reading novels, are imbued with foolish expectations that may likely lead to "injury," Burney urges both novelists and novels to seek "aid from sober Probability" (8). Burney, for her part, has already sought this aid, so that in the pages that follow, the contagion to which the novel has become tantamount has been stanched for the moment by characters "drawn . . . from nature" and by the novelist's depiction of "manners of the times" (7). For unlike "history" per se, which was commonly regarded as a genre devoted to accounts of the extraordinary in life, it will be the function of Evelina's "history" (a term used somewhat cheekily by Burney) to approximate and inculcate truth rather than fantasy.

Burney may have been among the first female writers to urge the claim of probability as a representational desideratum. But she was scarcely the last. Writing just seven years later in 1785, Clara Reeve took the bolder tack of describing and privileging the novel as a genre distinct from romance. Where "Romance," according to Reeve, is a heroic fable treating "fabulous persons and things," the novel "is a picture of real life and manners, and of the times in which it is written." Where romance "describes what never happened nor is likely to happen," the novel "gives a familiar relation of such things, as pass every day before our eyes, such as may happen to our friend, or to ourselves; and the perfection of it, is to represent every scene, in so easy and natural a manner, and to make them appear so probable, as to deceive us into a persuasion (at least while we are reading) that all is real, until we are affected by the joys or distresses, of the persons in the story, as if they were our own."[2]

In admitting to the absorptive dimension of the probabilistic novel, Reeve points with striking candor to a potential problem or contradiction regarding the novel as a genre distinct from romance. If the novel, as Reeve maintains, stands in opposition to romance, it does so as much by an appeal to the probable or natural as by resembling its counterpart. The novel, in other words, can oppose romance and the work of romance only by effectively assimilating romance through the mechanism of what, as Reeve describes it, is really naturalization. For in naturalization, as Roland Barthes has famously shown, the everyday or the "real" is more a means by which the reader is absorbed and variously deceived than a subject matter that, as Reeve suggests, is necessarily delimiting or even accurate.[3] Rather than serving as an index of what is really "out there" in the world, the probable, as Reeve conceives and endorses it, is actually a screen or overlay for what is still idealized. It is a typology, by which the joys or distresses of persons in the story appear "as if they were our own" precisely because they are *not* our own: because "what never happened nor is likely to happen" to the reader has, with an assist from probability, been given a temporary reprieve from appearing merely fabulous.

Reeve, needless to say, does not enter this contradiction as thoroughly as I have made out. However, it is equally clear that she is not very good at protecting the novel in its commitment to the probable from the imprecation of bad faith. Reeve would no doubt argue that such a charge is beside the point: that the suasive aspects of the novel, which require the overlay of what Burney terms "sober Probability," are there simply to counteract the more seductive aspects of romance, from which, as both she and Burney contend, young minds routinely receive bad, and sometimes fatal, influences.[4] Nevertheless, in arguing for a new institution of influence in place of an older and presumably more dangerous one, Reeve and Burney find themselves awkwardly suspended between making probability a representational goal and their more dubious assertion that the new novel, however probable and thereby seductive, is also distinct from its more improbable and seductive antecedent.

That fictions of probability or the everyday could be absorptive in spite of their rhetorical and ideological function, and thus instrumental, like their seductively romantic counterparts, in fostering certain "expectations" that fictions of probability were to "rectify" and subdue,[5] was not exactly lost on Burney's contemporaries, at least some of whom were alarmed by the apparent breach in regulation. We can cite as one example Richard Payne Knight, who not only agreed with Clara Reeve in his endorsement of naturalizing and regulatory practices but had recourse, more specifically, to narrative fiction by way of articulating his position regarding proper improvements of the landscape. Concurring with his colleague Uvedale Price that the newer English gardens did not do a good enough job in uniting a great man to his property—in this case, by failing to obscure, or to naturalize as effectively as possible, his imposition on and control of the landscape—Knight summoned the analogy of modern fictions that manage similarly to undo the work of naturalization in the very act of performing it. Such fictions, he complains, abandon their regulatory task of giving "useful knowledge and sound morality" in the way they "relate, in intelligible language, events of familiar life"—albeit ones that, as he cautions, are "not quite incredible, nor quite common."[6] Such a muddle, surely, is a far cry from the crude binary that (following Burney's preface) locates the probable or the "common" at one extreme and the "incredible" or the "marvellous" at the other. Nevertheless, in the very way that this binarism routinely issues in a collapsing of difference—if only for the purpose of rendering the probable more palatable and absorbing to the reader—the effective blurring of the probable and the merely possible in fictional prose, beyond putting Knight on the alert, necessarily introduces a horizon of possibility that, as Knight's own remarks suggest, is unique and noteworthy in being remarkably close at hand. The interchangeability of the probable and the possible does more than simply compromise the aims and the apparent ends of probability as Knight suggests; such an exchange refers to, or less determinately *recalls*, possibilities by which fictions of probability, no matter how regulatory their apparent function, are transformed willy-nilly into what another contemporary, Charlotte Smith, coyly termed romances of the real.[7]

Although Knight's observations were made before the appearance in print of any of Austen's fictions, his sense of the potential divergence of probabilistic fictions from their regulatory function, chiefly in the way that their "familiar" as such is sufficiently *different* or unaccountable to constitute something other than a scene of education, is echoed in many of the initial responses to Austen's writing by professional and lay readers alike. Indeed, it was not until the statements in the *Quarterly Review* by both Sir Walter Scott and, after him, Archishop Whately, that Austen's subscription to the moral imperatives of probabilistic writing, along with her concomitant tendency to distribute praise and blame to the delight of a knowing readership, increasingly became the norm in assessments of her achievement and, by turns, the realistic practice of which she, far more than either Burney or Edgeworth, was seen as the most important practitioner. Before that point, however, and even afterwards, Austen's writings were met with responses that, in addition to registering perplexity over the apparent failure of her works to serve a specifically articulated ideology or agenda, are by no means decided on what is at stake in her depictions of the "every day." In addition to constituting the *effet de réel* that Reeve essentially describes, the "every day" in Austen is frequently perceived as a site of surprise, amusement, and possibility, so that far from simply according with the conservative function of domestic fiction as Reeve defines and extols it, Austen's novels appear more to justify Knight's fears: both in their repeated failure to impress some readers with a specific moral or lesson and, more important, in the uncanny and, I would further argue, oppositional yield that her fictions continually wring from what Michel de Certeau, in his riposte to Foucault's panoptical worldview, would later call the practice of everyday life.

Over and against both Knight's strictures and the various retrospective assessments that continue to regard realistic practice, and Austen's writings especially, as armatures of a developing middle-class hegemony, the responses of Austen's earliest readers, along with the defensive observations of commentators like Knight, suggest that both realistic practice and the protocols of reading texts that are nominally probabilistic were neither as entrenched nor as ideologically hidebound at the moment of their inception as is customarily assumed. If anything, it was the constitutive *instability* of the middle or professionalized class that later adopted Austen as its own, far more than anything that the novelist's immediate audience was inclined to derive from her work, that was most instrumental in transforming Austen into a writer whose particular purchase on the real was increasingly a stay against confusion. Despite the various imperatives to probability that were current at the moment that Austen was developing as a novelist, it devolved upon a later generation of readers and critics to render Austen the fundamentally conservative novelist that Reeve so vividly outlines, and to convert the reality-effect that Reeve at once describes and prescribes into the real per se.

Like many of her contemporaries, including Austen's earliest respondents, Reeve was perfectly aware of the naturalizing work of the "novel" as a polemical institution. But to later readers, from George Henry Lewes to Kipling's fictional Janeites, the particular integrity and moral authority of Austen's representations of the everyday were important chiefly in the stability (in the face of potential disenfranchisement) that a rigorous adherence to the supposed lessons of Austen's real, with its apparent investment in the blamable or blameworthy, might well effect. Thus while the cultural work of Austen's novels was suspended, in its initial reception, between the positions adopted by Reeve and Knight, or between readings that were alternately and often simultaneously probabilistic and possibilistic in their measurement of Austen's reconstruction of gentry life, subsequent readers such as Lewes appear to justify Gary Kelly's assertion that Austen " 'predicted' the identity and the literary culture of the gentrified professional classes which came to dominate society and culture in Britain and elsewhere during the nineteenth century."[8] For the proleptic reach of Austen's works, particularly as a disciplinary apparatus, was in the end an accident of history. Although "partial" and "relative," as Kelly, Raymond Williams, and Nancy Armstrong have all contended,[9] the "real" of Austen's fiction only became "normal, natural and normative"[10] in retrospect and in disavowal of reading practices in the course of which that same real was—with an obvious assist from Austen—viewed as remarkably heterogeneous. In the pages that follow, then, I trace the various contests and related reading practices that predate the consolidation of the "conservative Austen." The peculiar and privileged anteriority of these contests to our received sense of Austen, I hope to show, is an important reminder not only of the multiple and surprising functions that Austen's writing performed to its immediate audience, but of the alternative possibilities, in literature as in life, to which Austen's readership was eminently disposed.

---

If for readers by midcentury, then, it was the function of Austen's novels to naturalize and legitimate a discourse of praise and especially blame in a largely normative or regulatory initiative, the more immediate *effect* of Austen's fictions was to interrupt the otherwise seamless link between realistic practice and social hegemony. The reviews and comments regarding Austen's earliest published works, *Sense and Sensibility* (1812) and *Pride and Prejudice* (1813), seem almost split at times between the obligation to credit these works with a didactic purpose (which their prescriptive titles encourage) and a nearly transgressive attention to particularity independent of either plot or instruction.[11] The two unsigned reviews of *Sense and Sensibility* in the *Critical Review* (February 1812) and the *British Critic* (May 1812) are suspended between commending the "benefits" that female readers in particular will derive from "these volumes" (40) and a less determinate sense of the "satisfaction" (40), "pleasure" (35), and "interest" (35) that owes to particular incidents and to the accuracy of their depiction. This view is echoed in the only known contemporary observation on the novel from beyond the Austen circle—that of Lady Bessborough—who, in a letter to a friend, recommended *Sense and Sensi-*

*bility*, which she found "amus[ing]" despite what she described as its "stupid" ending.[12] Assuming that Lady Bessborough's sense of an ending accords with a sense of plot—or with a trajectory that, to one degree or other, echoes the Richardsonian topos of "virtue rewarded"—Bessborough sounds a theme that is repeated by reviewers and lay readers alike: the interpellative or ideological work of an Austen text, insofar as it is achieved through story, is somehow at cross-purposes with other aspects and particulars in her work, notably the vignettes of incidental characters, which captivate by other means and to other, less immediately comprehensible, effects.

This pattern is particularly evident in the responses to *Pride and Prejudice*, which was more widely read than *Sense and Sensibility* and more variously appreciated. Nevertheless, in the unsigned notices of the novel in the two periodicals already mentioned, the disjunction of plot and character, or between a simple story of "no great variety" (as the *British Critic* [February 1813] opined) and the various elements whose depiction yielded "amusement and satisfaction," is again paramount (41–42). Both reviews stress the representative nature of scenes and characters, while remarking at the same time on the curiously exemplary nature of these same elements. The *Critical Review* (March 1813) lauds the portrayal of characters (not "one [of] . . . which appears flat") and the "delineation of domestic scenes" (47), and the *British Critic* singles out the "result" of the Miss Bennets' visit "to the town where officers are quartered" as being "exemplified in every provincial town in the kingdom" (42). While the last observation certainly implies a didactic function to Lydia Bennet's eventual flight with the young officer Wickham (which the *Critical Review* actually calls a "lesson" [46]), it attests, just as importantly, to the accuracy of the observation itself, subordinating any exemplum to the pleasure inherent in the novel's representation. The one other known review of *Pride and Prejudice* is less attuned to these virtues and consequently to their variance from plot. In fact, the notice in the *New Review* (April 1813) is given over entirely to plot summary. Ignoring virtually everyone and everything in *Pride and Prejudice* beyond its two main characters, the *New Review*'s account typically narrows the fiction to its particular didacticism or instruction—specifically, the praise and blame that are consistent with, even tantamount to, a "story" which, as the *British Critic* had already noted, lacks variety.[13]

This more conventional sense of *Pride and Prejudice*, which is tied to the interest generated by the novel's story and by the marriage plot, is registered in lay readings as well. Annabella Milbanke, soon to be Lady Byron, remarked that, while *Pride and Prejudice* was "not a crying book," the "interest" in the novel is "very strong, especially for Mr. Darcy."[14] The marriage plot, as Milbanke's notion of "interest" implies, constructs

Darcy as a highly desirable mate for the heroine so that the telos of their marriage, by which Elizabeth is eventually rewarded *and* re-warded, concomitantly serves the landed and paternalistic interests for which "Mr. Darcy" (not to mention his house) functions as an endorsement. Yet whether this aspect of the novel is consistent with the other interests to which Milbanke also attests—its rendering of the everyday ("no drownings, nor conflagrations, nor runaway horses") along with the "diver[sion]" that its less "aimiable," if "consistently supported," characters also furnish—is another matter.

In fact, the "diverting" aspects of the novel that Milbanke simultaneously commends are as she dubs them: they are *divergences* both from plot and from the interests that Darcy at once commands and serves. This view of the novel is reiterated by John William Ward, the earl of Dudley, who found *Pride and Prejudice* remarkable not for its hegemonic work but solely (or so it seems) for its representation of the obsequious, fawning Collins. "Have you had 'Pride and Prejudice,' " he wrote to Helen Darcy Stewart, "there is a parson in it quite admirable."[15] By "admirable" Ward differs here from later readers, who universally loathe Collins and the upward mobility he embarrassingly figures, in referring only to the fact that his character is admirably rendered—and with an acuity sufficient to deflect attention from the novel's story line. In a similar vein, Maria Edgeworth noted in a letter that she had been reading the novel while traveling, where she was interrupted only by "corn fields—broad wheeled wagons and gentlemen's fine seats."[16] Although such comments are, with specific reference to the novel, a little opaque, the peculiar contest of absorption and distraction seems as much a conflict between book and world as a tension stimulated by the experience of the text itself, which Edgeworth is plainly taken with yet reluctant to say more about.

A similar perplexity afflicts Jane Davy, the wife of Humphry Davy, who confessed her dislike of the novel to Sarah Ponsonby, one of the famed ladies of Llangollen. "Want of interest," she opines, "is the fault I can least excuse in works of mere amusement, and however natural the picture of vulgar minds and manners is there given, it is unrelieved by the agreeable contrast of more dignified and refined characters occasionally captivating attention."[17] Like Milbanke, Davy notes a tension in *Pride and Prejudice* between the interest provoked by admirable characters (among whom she undoubtedly means Darcy) and the distraction, the noncaptivating attention, provided by other characters, who are functionally opposed to them. However, unlike Milbanke, who is happily struck by the tension of "interest" and "diversion" in the text, Davy decries the novel's divergence from the more conventional task of instruction by "dignified" and "refined" example, which is the only proper end, she suggests, of natural or realistic writing.

There is little doubt that of all of Austen's novels *Pride and Prejudice* is the most interesting or persuasive in the way that Jane Davy recommends. Thus it is a measure of Austen's unorthodox and unsettling practice as a realist that Davy would be so put off by what is arguably her most successfully conservative work. Nor is it any less a sign of the errancy of Austen's representational technique, with its remarkable divergence from plot and from the particular interest that story sustains, that her succeeding—and ostensibly most didactic novel—*Mansfield Park* elicited, in the majority of recorded observations by contemporaries, a nearly opposite reaction.

There are no known reviews of *Mansfield Park*, which is a little surprising given both Austen's growing popularity and the fact that her novels were now being brought out in quick succession. Nevertheless, among the contemporary comments that have been recovered, including those by relatives and acquaintances of the author whose opinions Austen actively solicited, there is remarkable consensus regarding the source and nature of the novel's interest, which is the "natural[ness]" (as Austen's brother Frank put it [13]) of both characterization and depiction of incident.[18] Such appreciation of the novel's verisimilitude occasionally flattens into opinions, both pro and con, on the disposition of the novel's characters, notably Mrs. Norris. But among those who hazard a more developed opinion, generally by contrasting *Mansfield Park* with *Pride and Prejudice*, the novel's virtues center generally on the density and inscrutability of its real, which plainly lacks the embellishments of the earlier and (by most accounts) cleverer text. There are, of course, those in the Austen circle who prefer the new novel on account of its moral theme. Yet among the majority who admire it for other, less determinate, reasons, it is invariably the attention to the everyday aspects of "common life" (as Lady Gordon discerned [17]), or the accuracy of its representations—which, as Mrs. Pole noted, confirmed the author's "belong[ing] to the Society whose Manners she so ably delineates" (17)—that remains the novel's strength.

Furthermore, among contemporary readers in general, there is surprisingly little or no admiration of the very didacticism that Jane Davy, despite designating it a work of mere amusement, found insufficient evidence of in the more humorous *Pride and Prejudice*. Lady Vernon compared the novel favorably to one by Burney (it is unclear which), praising *Mansfield Park* as "not much of a novel," but "more the history of a family party in the country, very natural, and the characters well drawn."[19] Similarly, Anne Romilly, in extolling the novel's virtues to Maria Edgeworth, preferred it to Scott's *Waverley*, which she disliked for its being too much a novel and too concerned with its hero rather than with "general manners." Romilly goes on to say that a good novel "must . . . be true to life, which this is, with a good story vein of principle running thro' the whole." Although also lacking in this vein of principle, or, as Romilly elaborates it, in the "elevation of virtue" or "something beyond nature" that "gives the greatest charm to a novel," *Mansfield Park* remains, to its particular credit, "real natural every day life, and will amuse an idle hour very well in spite of its faults."[20] It appears, then, that Romilly admires *Mansfield Park* for its realism and for its story, which she characteristically attaches to its "principle" or moral point. However, as she details her position, it is clear not only that *Mansfield Park* satisfies almost exclusively on the grounds of verisimilitude, but more importantly that the novel's effect—or pleasure—consists in something quite apart from realism as Romilly wants it practiced.

Contemporary observations seem alert, then, to the tendency of Austen's fictions to frustrate expectations without also losing interest. According to these accounts, interest in Austen's writings is invariably directed to aspects of everyday life, which are successful in diverting attention from the didacticism ordinarily upheld by "story" in its distribution of praise and reward. Jane Davy may have complained about the relative dearth of exemplary characters in *Pride and Prejudice* from whose progress the reader might take instruction. But she could not resist commenting on the "power of new character," as she termed it, which is "ably displayed" and shown to particular advantage in "Mr. Bennet's indifference" that "in truth" is "not exaggeration."[21]

Whether such muted social criticism as Davy derives from the more diverting aspects of *Pride and Prejudice* attests to Austen's "oppositionality" in this instance is another issue and one that can be assessed only through a more detailed examination of the novel. Yet withal, we must remember that the defining condition of the everyday practice that de Certeau, once again, calls oppositional is its tactical or covert formation or its ability to elude a disciplinary regime. Such practices, then, are practices of the "weak," which, even on the part of those as privileged as some of Austen's female contemporaries, appear here to take the form of secret or guilty reading. And in this form, where the real routinely proves resistant and inscrutable to its moralistic appropriation, reading invariably contrasts with the relatively empowered modes of response that de Certeau (after Clausewitz) would term strategic, which follow other such practices in being more regulatory and openly repressive. Thus it may plausibly be argued that the reading practices to which Austen's writing was clearly available at its inception were in many ways a countermovement to more determinate practices, both aesthetic and social, that are almost never, on the evidence of much contemporary testimony, universally met.[22] And this becomes quite evident in the controversy that effectively develops in the responses to Austen's fourth and (in her lifetime) most successful work, *Emma*. Not only does *Emma* occasion the first truly comprehensive assessments of its author's novelistic career to date; it also provokes certain readers—notably Sir Walter Scott, who reviewed *Emma* anonymously but influentially in the *Quarterly Review* (March 1816)—to an assessment of domestic fiction and realistic practice generally, to which Austen's writing gives critical, if by no means consistent, testimony.

---

Unlike some of Austen's lay readers, who recognized her divergence from realistic practice as it had been prescribed and defined at the time, Walter Scott may well have been the first to install Austen as the realist par excellence. In addition to noting the recent development of a "class of fictions . . . which draws the characters and incidents introduced more immediately from the current of ordinary life than was permitted by the former rules of the novel" (59), Scott is remarkably candid in outlining and in privileging the present "rules" of the novel. These last demand a more faithful adherence to "probability," which had been previously "transgress[ed]" in favor of "possibility" (61), but which in the "[new] style of novel" is ably served by "presenting to the reader, instead of the splendid scenes of an imaginary world, a correct and striking representation of that which is daily taking place around him" (63).

In using "striking" to describe the daily life represented in fictions such as *Emma*, Scott comes very close to identifying the more diverting and transgressive aspects of Austen's real, especially when measured against the aims and expectations of realistic practice and its vitiation of what Scott calls "possibility." And Scott continues in this vein, explicitly crediting "the author of *Emma*" with "keeping close to common incidents, and to such characters as occupy the ordinary walks of life," as a result of which "she has produced sketches of such spirit and originality, that we never miss the excitation which depends upon a narrative of uncommon events, arising from the consideration of minds, manners, and sentiments, greatly above our own" (63–64).

With the admission of a notion such as "excitation," which is *apparently* a yield (albeit by different means) of Austen's uncanny attention to the "middling" walks of life (64), Scott again verges on the divergent effects of Austen's representational technique. Yet the hierarchy that Scott simultaneously invokes in alluding to the minds and manners "above our own" is not simply at cross-purposes with the more original, less determinate, aspects of Austen's practice as he construes them; it is perfectly consistent with the regulatory or deferential ends of a practice in fiction that works less by a fidelity to life than by a process of naturalization where, as Scott notes, representations are kept "close to common incidents" by a controlling *and controlled* authorial hand.

Thus it is equally a feature of Austen's fictions (and the realistic practice they embody) that they "inculcate" a "moral" which "applies equally" to the "paths" of what Scott somewhat patronizingly calls "common life" (64). At this point, then, Scott abandons the ground he had occupied in attending to the acuity of Austen's depiction of common life, to discuss her plots or what he calls the "narrative of all her novels" (64). And this proves to be a telling move. In generalizing Austen's plots into one narrative, Scott not only implicitly places plot or story at odds with other elements that constitute Austen's originality; he goes on, in effect, to widen the gap between the regulatory work of Austen's plots, which he endorses, and the uncanny possibility that haunts Austen's ostensibly probable world, by getting at least two of the three plots he discusses wrong.

Although Scott's description of the story of *Sense and Sensibility* merely reduces the novel to its basic, least essential, elements in observing that "[Marianne Dashwood] is turned wise by precept, example, and experience" (64), he significantly misrepresents the plot of *Pride and Prejudice*. In remarking that "after some essential services rendered to [Elizabeth's] family," Darcy becomes "encouraged to renew his addresses, and the novel ends happily" (65), Scott elides the fact that the Darcy-Elizabeth connection is effectively resolved with nearly a third of the novel left to go, and that the eventual happy ending owes largely to their joint containment of Lydia's sexuality. Nor does Scott fare much better with *Emma* when, in summarizing the narrative, he implies that the concealment of Frank's "affair" is plainly known to the reader—and, by implication, to the narrator—well in advance of its eventual disclosure.[23]

That these misrepresentations involve aspects of the two novels, specifically the transgressions of Frank and Lydia, that delimit and contest the hegemonic reach of their story lines is hardly surprising. After all, it is at least one function of plot in Austen to work, as Sandra Gilbert and Susan Gubar noted some time ago, as a cover story.[24] At the same time, it is no less a function of Austen's highly unorthodox practice that her cover stories, as Scott demonstrates, never adequately cover. This is because "the narrative of all her novels" is continually tried by the details of all her novels—what Scott, for his part, calls the "minute detail"—from which, he contends, "the faults of the author," and of *Emma* in particular, "arise" (67–68).

In the case of *Emma*, as Scott elaborates, these faults center largely on the depiction of Emma's father and Miss Bates: two characters, it is worth noting, whose own preoccupation with detail effectively recapitulates the work of Austen's real overall in bringing the narrative of *Emma* to a grinding halt. Moreover, in contrast with these faults, where the novel is reduced to details that are readable yet curiously ungoverned, the apparent virtues of "the author's novels" consist in an ordering of detail explicitly akin to a landscape improved according to *picturesque* principles. Thus Austen's novels bear "the *same* relation" to improbable or sensational fiction "that cornfields and cottages and meadows bear to the highly adorned grounds of a show mansion, or the rugged sublimities of a mountain landscape." They bear this relation thanks to their largely naturalizing and regulatory tendencies, where the "pleasure [of reading] is *nearly allied* with the experience of [one's] own social habits," allowing one to return from the act of reading (or from "promenading" as the picturesque analogy warrants) "without any chance of having his head *turned* by the recollection of the scene through which he has been wandering" (68, emphasis added).[25]

In attesting to the invisible, yet profoundly coercive, work of naturalization, Scott offers an anatomy of realism as much as he does a defense. Nevertheless, in so defending realistic practice, specifically Austen's, with the proviso that it be shorn somehow of its more troublesome complications, Scott does more than simply join with picturesque theory in making realism an armature of social hegemony; he simultaneously departs from many of Austen's other readers either in discrediting or in seeking to appropriate the more antithetical and recalcitrant aspects of her writing. This is not to say that other contemporaries are not similarly divided in their appreciation of the different registers and kinds of "interest" generated by Austen's works. It is just that virtually no other contemporary reader is as transparent as Scott in the effort to bend Austen's works—and the work of domestic fiction generally—to a purpose to which Austen's novels are, by Scott's *own* observations, simultaneously opposed.

Scott would later change his views regarding Austen, opening them to precisely the elements that he had touched on but had resisted in his initial appreciation. However, there were a good many readers and reviewers of *Emma* for whom no revision of this sort would be necessary. The *British Critic* (July 1816) commented approvingly on the novel's contracted space of "unity," adding that "we know not of one [novel] in which the author has sufficient art to give interest to the circle of a small village." In addition, the unsigned review singles out for special commendation the very details—"the valetudinarian father" and the "chattering village belles"—that Scott identified as among the novel's faults, yet whose approval here is clearly of a piece with the review's other observation that the novel is neither moralistic nor fantastic (71). This praise is echoed in virtually all the reviews of *Emma*, where the "interest" generated by plot and theme is almost always subordinated to the interest given to everyday particularity in the novel.

Nevertheless, one review in particular—that in the *Champion* (March 1816)—comes closest to articulating the oppositional yield that Scott sought either to transfigure or to discredit.[26] As with most reviews of *Emma*, the *Champion* begins by commending Austen's "skill" in "representing objects of an ordinary, and at the same time so familiar a nature" (469). Yet the review quickly expands to a more sustained articulation of the uncanny aspects of Austen's writing, where the familiar (as the initial observation already implies) is in a way distinct from the ordinary and thus a measure of a possibility or otherness strangely close at hand. Noting that the author presents "nature and society in very unornamented hues," the review resists crediting the novel for its naturalizing work, adding that the "force of nature" is "so strong" that "few can take up her work without finding a rational pleasure in the recognitions which cannot fail to flash upon them of the modes of thinking and feeling which experience every day presents in real life" (470).

In one sense, the *Champion* is simply crediting the verisimilitude in *Emma*, where there is virtually no break between book and world. Yet it is also clear that the power of verisimilitude—with its necessary structure of difference—admits a flash of recognition that transforms familiar experience into something seen and understood anew. Far from a strategy of containment, then, or one of naturalization, Austen's real—the "real life" to which her novel directs the reader—is (to borrow Scott's own image) a reality to which one is somehow wrenched or "turned" rather than merely reconciled.

The *Champion* describes this recognition as a "rational pleasure," which may well be a bit of damage control, given the uncanny pleasure of Austen's text as it is here described. Nevertheless, such reflection as the novel apparently encourages is also severely rational in a critical or counterhegemonic sense: both in the kinds of insights it furnishes the *Champion*'s reader—for example, the sense that the utterly compliant Mrs. John Knightley is "just perhaps what a wife ought to be . . . sufficiently sensible—not at all clever—of a small mind which the ties and duties of domestic life abundantly fill" (477)—as well as in its opposition to an aesthetic practice that would divest details of the ability either to stimulate change through "rational pleasure" or, as the case may be, to exemplify it in everyday life. Thus the reviewer in the *Champion* moves ultimately from the example of *Emma* to a theory of the novel, specifically the new novel, which the reviewer describes as "fictitious biography" in contrast with romance, which the review calls "fictitious history" (473).

In distinguishing the novel-as-biography from the novel-as-history, the *Champion* resorts, again, to a fairly common distinction in which the genre of history is aligned with the epic in its representation of great events and figures and in being removed from the practice of everyday life. But even as the *Champion* contrasts the domestic novel—as exemplified by *Emma*—with other representations taken up with events and actions that the majority of readers will never witness, much less initiate firsthand, it does not undervalue either what the domestic novel necessarily chooses for its subject matter or the ultimate importance of that subject matter for contemporary and future readers.

It is more, in fact, that the domestic novel figures a new and alternative history, which is important both in its attention to the significance of individual lives (no matter how ordinary or seemingly insignificant the life chronicled), and, more important, in the related implication that such attention will—in a flash of recognition—disclose the difference that a given person can and often does make. "To the historian's generalizing eye," contends the *Champion*,

> unobtrusive virtue presents few features of prominence or splendour;—but the novelist has the licence of ranging into the recesses of domestic life, and of distinguishing the actions of the mind, the temper, and the feelings. Surveyed in this microscopic detail, characters which, to a more sweeping observer, furnish only the uniform out-lines of virtue and worth, will always be found to exhibit sufficiently distinctive traits of mental and moral individuality, to answer all an author's objects of giving them a personal identity and relief. (473)

On the face of it, it appears that the *Champion* is making a typically humanistic connection between "historical" figures, whose "actions" are visible even in "a wide survey of events," and characters whose more internal actions are invisible to such a vantage, yet are by implication just as important. Nevertheless, the connection here between the agency of the common or ordinary person and the particular perspective in which that agency is effectively brought into palpable relief, propels the argument in a different direction altogether. For among other things, the writing of conventional history, as the *Champion* describes it, recapitulates the very practices, at once representational and social, that create order at the expense of detail and preserve hierarchies through the maintenance of deferential behavior.

By contrast, the domestic novel, and *Emma* in particular, resist this containment through a different kind of attention wherein individual action, far from the equivalent of great action, remains an activity whose particular effectiveness is not only invisible to and necessarily at odds with the "sweeping" survey, but inextricably connected to a covert or microscopic formation. Thus rather than leveling the distinction between great and ordinary action, the domestic novel ideally preserves their difference, and the relative prestige accorded each, in disclosing practices that other versions of art contain either by ignoring or by appropriating to more didactic and narratable ends. Or to put it another way: *Emma*—as a specimen of fictitious biography—represents the potentially oppositional practices of everyday life oppositionally.

The *Champion* may well be unique in its reasoned appreciation of the peculiar agency of Austen's characters and of her writing in general. However, it is no less representative in identifying the kind of work that, as other readers confirm, *Emma* succeeds in performing, if not always to their delight and gratification. Maria Edgeworth, to whom Austen actually sent a copy of *Emma*, managed to get through only the first volume and passed the remaining two volumes to a friend unread, warning that "there is no story in it, except that Miss Emma found that the man whom she designed for Harriets lover was an admirer of her own—& he was affronted at being refused by Emma & Harriet wore the willow—and smooth, thin water-gruel is according to Emma's father's opinion a very good thing & it is very difficult to make a cook understand what you mean by smooth thin water gruel."[27] The movement here from plot—specifically the marriage plot—to detail, which Edgeworth, despite ridiculing, cannot resist rehearsing with equal scrupulousness, is instructive. Her Miss Bates–like demonstration actively recapitulates the novel's attention to the detritus of everyday life and its sundry preoccupations, showing the impact that such a focus, although unappreciated in this instance, necessarily makes.

This decided, if unwanted, impact of the novel is also attested to in a letter to Edgeworth by her friend Anne Romilly, who after expressing sympathy with Lady Byron in the wake of her separation from Lord Byron, turns to the more mundane matters of *Emma* and another novel whose identity is unclear. "In the first [novel]," complains Romilly, there is so little to remember, and in the last so much one wishes to forget, that I am inclined not to write about them."[28] Compared to the Byron affair, the quotidian details of middling gentry life in Austen's work may well seem forgettable. Yet Romilly manages, by a logic of negation where the forgettable is sufficiently memorable to be forgettable, to affirm the unsettling aspect of this kind of text. While put off by *Emma* as she is by bad romance (as the other, unnamed work purports to be), Romilly nevertheless confirms *Emma*'s failure at the naturalizing processes for which Scott commends it, yet which both Romilly and her interlocutor have been challenged now by the apparent absence of.

Finally, Susan Ferrier, a novelist in her own right, remarks in a letter to a friend that she has "been reading 'Emma,' which is excellent; there is no story whatever, and the heroine is no better than other people; but the characters are all so true to life, and the style is so piquant, that it does not require the adventitious aids of mystery and adventure."[29] In centering on the piquancy of Austen's style, Ferrier seems to be referring to what another Austen contemporary, Thomas Moore, praised as the "effect" in *Emma* achieved by the "method of describing things."[30] With its necessary connection to a narrative independent of story, Ferrier's "piquancy of style" alludes to the narrative-in-description, or to the piquancy of detail in characters and in other elements, whose peculiar truth, as the *Champion* described it, is more a flash of pleasurable recognition.

There are, needless to say, other reviews of *Emma* that I have not touched on, along with other contemporary comments, including reactions to the novel that Austen solicited herself as she did those to *Mansfield Park*.[31] While some of these depart from the more telling observations that I have just examined, they do not vary sufficiently or substantially to warrant fuller treatment. The opinions that Austen solicited on her own range from the opinions of those who do not like the new novel as much as the previous novels; to the opinions of those who, like Scott, admire its naturalizing and moralizing tendencies; to those who join with the majority of respondents in either being put off by the many details (especially the particulars recounted by Miss Bates) and by the relative lack of incident in the text; to those who are struck by what Frank Austen, among his sister's most discerning readers, called its "peculiar air of Nature."[32] At all events, the majority of responses to *Emma* attest to a narrative practice whose "effect," for better or for worse, is as striking in its peculiar attention as it is often unsettling.

---

The joint publication of *Northanger Abbey and Persuasion* in 1818, shortly after Austen's untimely death in the summer of 1817, was met with responses freighted by a sense of loss and the concomitant obligation to put the author's accomplishment overall in a larger perspective, which were simultaneously served by the preemptive biographical note appended to the volumes by Henry Austen. Criticism, or any evaluative comment, is rarely rendered accurate and discriminating when it must accede to such apparently authoritative observations as those with which the novelist's brother concluded his brief essay: "One trait only remains to be touched on. It makes all others unimportant. She was thoroughly religious and devout; fearful of giving offence to God, and incapable of feeling it towards any fellow creature. On serious subjects she was well-instructed, both by reading and meditation, and her opinion accorded strictly with those of our Established Church" (6). While Austen's regard for her "fellow creatures" accords well with her regard for the activity of ordinary individuals as it had been noted by readers before, the deference by which her view of life was apparently directed made it difficult for readers and critics to credit the less determinate effects of her writing in the posthumously published works. And their response was hampered further by the disparate character of the novels under consideration. The *British Critic* (March 1818) did well under the circumstances in widening its notice to a general assessment of Austen's representational technique. But despite emphasizing Austen's preoccupation with everyday life—which the review insists must have been exclusively drawn from her experience—the *Critic* is suspended between a recognition of the uncanny power of Austen's verisimilitude, chiefly the "unaccountable pleasure" derived from her "simple imitation of [an] object," and the need to account or compensate for the notable absence of narrative in *Northanger Abbey* or, as the review puts it, for the unabstractable nature of that novel's contents (81–82).

*Blackwood's* (May 1818) fares somewhat better in underscoring the "singular," indeed alternative, "history" that the novels constitute, noting that "any one of her fictions" could "be realized in any town or village in England," so much "that we think we are reading the history of a people whom we have seen thousands of times" (267). And yet, the review notes, "with all this perfect commonness, both of incident and character, perhaps not one of her characters is to be found in any other book, portrayed at least in so lively and interesting a manner" (267). In recognizing that Austen's "history" is a matter not of "simple imitation" but of a heightened attention to the quotidian, or of an attention sufficiently microscopic to open the probable to a greater range and possibility, *Blackwood's* follows very much on the heels of the *Champion* in noting Austen's singularity as a realist. Furthermore, *Blackwood's* departs—predictably enough from observations made in the *Quarterly Review* by Scott and later Archbishop Whately—in noting both the absence of plot and the novels' failure to "display . . . religious sentiments and opinions" (268). Somewhat pressured by Henry's biographical notice, which it paraphrases at length, the review concludes by asserting that Austen's novels are indeed shaped by "the spirit of Christianity" (268). But this last is clearly an occasional imperative at odds with the more incisive conception of Austen's unconventional and uncanny realism.

Not so Richard Whately, whose anonymous review (January 1821) of the last published novels some three years after their initial appearance accords with that of his predecessor in the *Quarterly*, Walter Scott, in lauding their regulatory and naturalizing aspects. Beginning, then, by quoting Scott on the "new style of novel," Whately proceeds to an appreciation of the instructive elements in works such as Austen's, which follow "the general rules of probability" (88). Reluctant, unlike the *Champion*'s reviewer, to credit Austen's as an alternative history, which had focused on the hitherto unrecognized agents in the world, Whately subscribes to the customary hierarchy separating the writing of history from that of narrative fiction and credits Austen with providing an exemplary "mode[l] of real life" (88) capable of producing the "instruction which used to be available to the world . . . in moral essays" (92). Such emphasis on Austen's didacticism does more than simply divest both Austen and the "new style of novel" of the various effects wrought by a broadening or attenuation of everyday life and action. Indeed, it proves the basis of a still larger critique, wherein Whately is disposed not only to discredit novels that bear insufficient relation to what he dogmatically calls "the real" (93), but to describe as "dangerous" those novels that, as Richard Payne Knight had earlier feared, "differ from common life in little or nothing but the improbability of occurrences" (89).

Predicated on the assumption that novels that are all but probable will likely imbue people, especially women, with expectations that eventually lead to harm, Whately's criticism broaches, albeit by containment, that other structure of "difference," where ordinary life resists a merely probable constitution so as to produce a less determinate shock of pleasurable recognition. Although Whately would like his readers to believe that the "probable" and the "real" are synonyms, it is his purpose clearly to *render* them synonymous in a mutually restrictive and restricted formation, and to enlist Austen and the novel in that project.

Thus rather than being at odds with the probable, whose partiality is additionally served by story, the "distinctness of description" and the "minute fidelity of detail" in Austen are for Whately part and parcel of a rhetorical and naturalizing apparatus. Operating in conjunction with free indirect style, this apparatus gives Austen's "fiction the perfect appearance of reality" and thereby aids its work of "deception" (96). One might expect a moralist like Whately to be troubled by such manipulation. But plainly he has no problem either in reducing fiction to a moral tract or in assuming that its most important purpose is to distribute advice in the form of praise and blame. (Miss Bates, he typically notes, is a fool, whereas Knightley is an apogee of sense.) In fact, Whately differs from many twentieth-century readers, who emphasize this putative aspect of Austen's fiction as if it were a new and ethically motivated discovery, only in being *untroubled* by the hegemonic and deceptive ends of a writing that combines "in an eminent degree, instruction with amusement" (105).

Whately's judgments, however proleptic, stand in distinct contrast with the observations of many of his contemporaries. And they contrast as well with the subsequent observations of his predecessor and guide, Walter Scott, who in the wake of repeated readings of Austen's novels was increasingly struck (as Anne Romilly had been earlier) by their divergence from his novels. In a journal entry of 1826, Scott was moved, in remarking on the "want of story" in a novel by Lady Morgan, to thoughts of Austen, in this case *Pride and Prejudice*, which he admits to having read "at least" three times. Contrasting Austen's descriptions of the "involvements, and feelings, and characters of ordinary life" with his own representations in a genre that he gently disparages as the "Big Bow-wow" strain of fiction, Scott laments that Austen's "exquisite touch, which renders ordinary commonplace things and characters interesting, from the truth of the description and the sentiment, is denied to me."[33] Although these observations recapitulate those in the earlier review, Scott appears also to have abandoned the "picturesque" interpretation of Austen in favor of a less decidable (and more humbling) sense of her "interest." "Interesting," needless to say, is rather a labile term with indisputable connections to the work of naturalization. Yet, as the comparison with the overbearing Scott suggests, "interest" in Austen is no longer necessarily consistent with the kind of control with which it was earlier aligned.

This "argument" is continued in journal entries from March 1826 and September 1827. In the former Austen is compared favorably (along with Edgeworth and Ferrier) to Thomas Henry Lister, whose novel *Granby* Scott criticizes for being too authoritative in its omniscience and too concerted in "put[ting] the reader exactly up to the thoughts and sentiments of the parties." The "women," according to Scott, "do this better . . . far superior to anything Man vain Man has produced of the like nature."[34] Scott, again, is not completely discounting the suasive use of free indirect style or suggesting that women writers, including Austen, lack a specific aim or purpose. But he seems—despite lumping these various writers together—to be pointing to another kind of purpose served by putting fiction at the disposal of a reader rather than by putting a seemingly empowered reader at the disposal of an authoritative text.

The entry of September 1827 brings up the analogy of painting to describe Austen, much as Knight had earlier deployed the analogy of narrative to describe the operation of the picturesque. "There is a truth of painting in her writings," writes Scott, "which always delights me. They do not it is true get above the middle classes of Society. But there she is inimitable."[35] Scott's recourse here to what, I would again argue, is the picturesque and its particular commitment to "truth" is certainly understandable, especially given his observations twelve years earlier. But the analogy is notable in the way it stresses Austen's "inimitable" practice as a writer rather than her adherence to certain representational principles and conventions. This uniqueness is similarly reflected in Scott's refusal now to articulate the ends or purposes of Austen's writing beyond the capacity to "delight." For the more minimal, less determinate, assessment of Austen's effect, brought on by repeated readings of the novels, follows the responses of other readers in self-consciously separating delight from the control to which it is traditionally cobbled in aesthetic theory, and by which it is contained, in the doublet "teach and delight."

---

The reissue in 1833 of Austen's six novels in Richard Bentley's *The Standard Novels* not only marked Austen's formal inclusion in the canon of essential European fiction; it gave rise to reviews and assessments that are noteworthy both for their relative contemporaneity and for the fact that they are in the main considered opinions based, like Scott's, on multiple readings of the novels. Thus it is especially interesting to note the by-now-familiar themes that are sounded in these responses. The *Literary Gazette* (30 March 1833, 199) urged the "rising generation" to read Austen's novels for their "absolute historical pictures" of a way of life that was fast disappearing. As with previous efforts to reconfigure history writing through Austen's realistic practice, the *Gazette* typically directs its sense of history to the everyday—to "the delights of a tea-table" or the "animation of going down a country dance"—which, however anachronistic, are important nonetheless in recovering the significance of ordinary life and activity.

For the most part, this significance of the everyday depends, as the *Gazette* notes, on the uncanny effects of seeing the "common-place" as if for the first time or of seeing "our acquaintences" in what amounts to a more "entertaining" guise (5 January 1833, 9). But such significance also involves, as it did for the *Champion*'s reviewer, a particular intelligence that a heightened or "complete[ly] tru[e] . . . . reality" makes available (9). Thus while typically covered over by adjectives such as "amusing" or "interesting," whose vagueness overall is also consistent with the received sense of the nonprescriptive nature of Austen's fiction, such intelligence in Austen is by no means neutral or without point. Seemingly pointless observations, in fact—for example, that the "majority of [Austen's] actors are like those of real existence—silly, stupid, and ridiculous" (9)—are ultimately inflected in the *Gazette* by more specific observations such as the one regarding Mr. Weston and Miss Bates in *Emma*: two characters who (to my knowledge) never have occasion to address one other directly. "Mr. Weston," remarks the reviewer, "with his gossiping, universal good-nature, is a copy of a thousand; and those who have not a Miss Bates among their acquaintance, are not like ourselves, who have at least a dozen" (199). The numerical differences, which multiply endlessly those who, like Mr. Weston, live securely, blithely, and without risk or loneliness by circumstances of class and gender, place them in marked contrast with women who, by other circumstances, are familiar enough in their obsessive and alienated awareness of the world around them. Thus the *Gazette*'s coupling is also noteworthy in its implicit sympathy for Miss Bates and the dozen (at least) like her, whose precariousness and apparent deformation are all too common yet worthy of more focused attention.

The review is much less direct about these matters than I am in rehearsing them. Nevertheless, the union here of two relatively incidental characters—indeed two characters with a shared penchant for gossip (albeit to different ends)—follows Austen's own procedure in letting their "reality" perform a supplementary work of observation and explanation with particular attention to the arbitrariness of their respective fates. Nor is it only the unnaturalness of their fates that is at issue. The very otherness or defamiliarity on which the *Gazette*'s sense of the arbitrariness of things depends here is, by a similar logic, the basis as well for a sense of possibility, wherein "life as it is" (to quote another contemporary review of Austen) is no longer life as it must be or even as it may be. The uncanny effects of a reality seen and understood as perhaps never before accomplish two things, therefore: they imbue "reality" with a "charm" of otherness so as to distinguish it from a less readable, more naturalized, "prototype" (9); and they manage, in necessarily presenting a reality different from itself, to render what is "absolute" (199) and "true" (9), according to the *Literary Gazette*, "absolute" in the strictly etymological—and destabilizing—sense exploited by Austen's German contemporary, Friedrich Schlegel.[36]

It must be emphasized, again, that the yield of the *Literary Gazette*'s appreciation of Austen is, commensurate with Austen's own practice, a matter of inference whose indices (in the reviews at least) are the vague and indeterminate references to the "interest" and "amusement" of her novels and their particulars. Nor is every review of the Bentley editions as attuned to these aspects of Austen and to the kind of change they alternately demonstrate and urge. The *Examiner* (20 January 1833, 37) typically notes the "truth[ful] . . . delineation" of Austen's various characters and credits the author, who is synonymous here with her narrator, with having "thoroughly understood" them. Yet this "understanding" of human character, as the *Examiner* construes it, consists more with judgment or blame, which the review—in appropriating Austen's narrative authority—eagerly renews. Similarly, the *Printing Machine* (19 April 1834, 77–78), which actually describes Austen as a contemporary, follows Whately in crediting her with having performed an educative or regulatory function without having also written a conduct book. As in Whately's notice, the anonymous review praises the naturalizing work of Austen's novels, specifically her ability to "paint scenes" that are not only "familiar" to her but also "thoroughly English . . . in the really good sense of the word" (78).

The regulatory or nonoppositional view of Austen's achievement would hardly die out with what at the time were the merely competing views of these journals, and of the *Quarterly* before them to which the *Examiner* in fact recurs. Indeed, the largely conservative conceptions of both Austen's achievement and the motives behind her writing would by turns come to represent something of a consensus that not even feminist criticism in our time has succeeded in overturning. Thus it is instructive to remember and to stress that for earlier readers, including those who, though chronologically proximate to Austen, were able with the benefit of only some hindsight to read her with the special attention that her novels attract and display, Austen's writing was palpably at cross-purposes with the hegemonic ends of what we have come in retrospect to regard as realistic writing.

The *Atlas*, which like the *Literary Gazette* took special note of each of Bentley's reissues, recapitulates many of the responses to Austen in which her writing was found to be arresting or striking rather than merely directive. Noting, as did many contemporaries, that the "great characteristic of Miss Austen's tales is their domestic truth" (30 January 1833, 40), which greatly exceeds the imperatives of plot and suspense, the *Atlas* hints at the oppositional reading practices encouraged by Austen's writings. Minimizing her narrator's omniscience and emphasizing instead that Austen's characters are somehow left to "speak and act for themselves" (40), the *Atlas* typically concentrates on the effect of Austen's writing, which is lodged in a "charm" of "style" so subtle that the reader is not "soon made aware of the spell that fascinates him," or of the "irresistible *vraisemblance* that animates the whole" and only "gradually wins upon the feelings" (40). That the irresistible similitude of Austen's representations encouraged readings that were in turn resistant, or otherwise independent of narrative authority, is less contradictory than it sounds. In the absence of any specific judgment or position to which her representations apparently lead, a "*vraisemblance*" that only gradually wins upon the reader represents a sharply critical recognition that, however stimulated by the text, comes ultimately from a respondent who, as it were, "acts for herself."

Thus rather than confirming a suasive or naturalizing tendency in Austen, "irresistible *vraisemblance*" refers to an ability to "chronicl[e]" what the *Atlas* coyly terms "life as it is" (40). For with its particular if strangely provisional constitution now, "life as it is" is less a sign of complacency or of resignation on Austen's part than the result really of a joint labor, or agency, where the reproduction of Austen's "real" in the act of reading is alternately provoked, as well as recapitulated, by the readable and increasingly possible world that adorns her pages.

---

In a recent essay that seeks similarly to excavate an oppositional, or more precisely a "queer," tradition of reading and appreciating the fundamentally antinormative aspects of Austen's writing, Claudia L. Johnson recurs to Kipling's famous vignette of the "Janeites" who had served in a World War I artillery unit, and attends particularly to the obviously homosocial aspects of male bonding in Kipling's account, both in the present (a London Masonic Lodge) and in the past (an artillery unit from which the still smaller unit of Austen enthusiasts or "Janeites" were culled).[37] Johnson also notes an erotic register to these same-sex relations, whose covert or closeted disposition now, beyond implicitly identifying the dominant culture as "hostile" and homophobic, finds a sympathetic chord in Austen's fiction, where the courtship plot is no less a closet or cover story within which (and from which) alternative lifestyles and ideologies are sufficiently sustained to be readable and recoverable. Johnson is on particularly firm ground in claiming that for Kipling's Janeites, no less than for many of Austen's earliest readers, as we have seen, "the atemporal aspects of narration, descriptive details, catchy phrases, and, especially, characterization," stand variously in opposition to plot, with its heteronormative momentum, and thus constitute a countercurrent to the more conventional and hegemonic aspects of domestic fiction.

Yet even so, Kipling's Janeites are scarcely immune to generalizations regarding character, both pro and con, with which a more conservative or naturalized conception of Austenian verisimilitude ultimately became coextensive. For in the very way that Austen's characters are, as one "Janeite" puts it "just like people that you run across any day" (159), they are also stereotypes and thereby vulnerable to a level of prejudice or judgment that, beyond granting a provisional and legitimating status to the Janeite reader, reflects a protocol of reading which had long served the normative aims that Johnson, like many early readers, rightly understands Austen's fiction to oppose. I am not suggesting by any means, of course, that the Janeites are off-base in describing the Reverend Collins as "always on the make an' lookin' to marry money" (159) or General Tilney as a "swine" similarly "on the make" (159) or in their unwavering hatred of Lady Catherine De Bourgh. Rather I am simply observing their tendency not just to emphasize the blamable in Austen but to anchor their blame in an unerring verisimilitude in which these caricatures are suddenly real people against whom a moral or ethical stand is virtually imperative. And I stress this dynamic because the way with Austen that Kipling describes recurs ultimately to a way of reading her that, regardless of its antecedents, became increasingly common and increasingly possible only with the development of a readership that was on the whole less sophisticated about representational matters and in greater need of the peculiar authority or entitlement that a partnership with Austen's narrator apparently provided.

An especially salient instance of this Janeite way of reading is the 1852 essay on Austen that inaugurated *New Monthly Magazine*'s series on female novelists. Although B. C. Southam dubs this "the first considerable 'middle-brow' piece on Jane Austen" on the evidence of what he takes to be its introductory bent (131), the essay is striking in the way it reflects the more informed judgments of contemporary literary professionals like Lewes and Macaulay for whom Austen's characters are similarly "real" and thus actual people from whom tangible lessons about the conduct of life can be reliably derived. The fascination with Austen's verisimilitude was scarcely a Victorian invention. But where midcentury readers depart from their earlier counterparts is in the tendency to transform a reality-effect, which earlier readers understood to be more an intervention than a transcription, into a real world shorn of all naturalizing props or techniques. When the *New Monthly* observes that the "figures and scenes on Miss Austen's canvas" are "exquisitely real" so that what is "flat" and "insipid [in other hands]" is, "at her bidding, a sprightly, versatile, never-flagging chapter of realities" (138), and proceeds then to assemble among its list of "lifelike" characters the figures in her novels who are often closest to caricature and most vulnerable to judgment, the "everyday" as such has effectively moved from a mere locus of attention and appreciation in Austen to an aspect of the novel that, as the earliest proponents of probabilistic fiction had hoped, is immaculately folded into its regulatory operation.

But there is a difference now. Initially, as we have seen, regulation was perceived by Austen's contemporaries (and, I would further argue, the novelist herself) as predominantly a function of the "virtue rewarded" plot, to which everyday detail frequently proved a hindrance more than an aid. However by midcentury, the increasingly normative operation of Austen's fiction is lodged almost entirely in a disposition to judgment wherein *character*, especially blamable character, is sufficiently coextensive with the everyday that the quotidian is also the *means* now by which the reality of those under judgment and the validity of the judgments upon them in which readers are privileged to indulge are reciprocally authenticated. It is true, too, that the cautionary characters in Austen are invariably compared in these assessments with heroes and heroines who are meant to serve as role models—so that the *New Monthly*'s adduction of characters ranging from General Tilney and Walter Elliot to Mrs. Bennet, Mr. Collins, and Lady De Bourgh is typically counterpointed by observations of Anne Elliot as "self-sacrificing and noble-hearted" or of Captain Wentworth as "intelligent, spirited, and generously high-minded" (138). But this hardly diminishes the fact that the authority of Austen's fictions and the values they putatively uphold increasingly derive their sanction from a reality—the real people to whom both author and reader can jointly condescend in the act of blaming—that is rarely appealed to with the same urgency or enthusiasm with respect to characters who are merely praiseworthy.

George Henry Lewes, the most erudite and prolific defender of Austen's fiction at this time, who is perhaps best known for having provoked Charlotte Brontë into her infamous critique of Austen as a writer lacking passion, sentiment, and poetry, is also typical in his tendency both to locate and to defend Austen's "fidelity" to real life in her "truthful representation of character" (130). Although Lewes's observations bear more than a trace of an earlier way with Austen in appreciating the degree to which Austen's characters are "at once life-like and interesting" so that the "good people" in her fictions "are . . . good, without being goody" (153), the peculiar density and inscrutability of character, along with the "every-day life" on which it bears, inevitably gives way to an appreciation of Austen's "noodles" as so "accurately real" that "[t]hey become equal to actual experiences" (153). To show this, Lewes summons the examples of Mrs. Elton and Mrs. Norris, whose blamability is both proof of, and by turns synonymous with, the acuity of Austen's real. "We have," writes Lewes, "so personal a dislike to Mrs. Elton and Mrs. Norris that it would gratify our savage feeling to hear of some calamity befalling them" (153). Lewes is being hyperbolic here, both in the fantasies he admits to harboring and in the reality-effect whose force has presumably provoked them. Nevertheless, the key word in his assessment is not "character" or "truth" or "fidelity," but "personal." And this is so because the extension of Austen's fiction into "actual experience" is for Lewes, no less than for Kipling, a seduction whose interpellative reach is keyed directly to the status conferred in the ability to judge and ultimately to hate. It is often assumed, of course, that "Janeite" enthusiasm for Austen's novels reflects a nostalgia for and thus an endorsement of the gentrified world that she brings so vividly to life. Yet nothing could be further from the position of those figures from whom the term apparently derives. Unlike the disempowered but notably savvy readers who actually inhabited Austen's world, Kipling's "Janeites," with their rather pitiful aspirations to empowerment and enfranchisement, illustrate and deconstruct the protocols of reading that have over time mitigated our understanding and appreciation of the difference that the novels *and* the historical agent who produced them succeeded initially in making.

## Notes

1. *Evelina or the History of a Young Lady's Entrance into the World*, ed. Edward A. Bloom (Oxford: Oxford University Press, 1968), 7–8. All further references are to this edition of the novel and appear parenthetically in the text.

2. *The Progress of Romance and the History of Charoba, Queen of Aegypt* (Colchester, 1785), 111.

3. "L'Effet de Réel," *Communications* 11 (1968): 84–89.

4. Reeve, *The Progress of Romance*, 115.

5. Douglas Lane Patey, *Probability and Literary Form: Philosophic Theory and Literary Practice in the Augustan Age* (Cambridge: Cambridge University Press, 1984), 214.

6. *An Analytical Inquiry into Principles of Taste* (London, 1805), 445–47.

7. I am alluding, of course, to the title of Smith's 1787 novel, *The Romance of Real Life*.

8. *English Fiction of the Romantic Period 1789–1830* (London: Longman, 1989), 19.

9. See Armstrong, *Desire and Domestic Fiction: A Political History of the Novel* (New York: Oxford University Press, 1987), 135–60; and Williams, *The Country and the City* (New York: Oxford University Press, 1973), 108–19.

10. Kelly, *English Fiction*, 20.

11. Unless otherwise indicated, page references to the published reviews of Austen are to the texts of those reviews reprinted in Southam 1968. My recovery of additional contemporary response to Austen, both public and private, is indebted to information contained in David Gilson's comprehensive *A Bibliography of Jane Austen* (Oxford: Clarendon Press, 1982). For an earlier survey of some of these materials, which argues against the once prevailing notion that Austen was largely unknown to her contemporaries, see Charles Beecher Hogan, "Jane Austen and Her Early Public," *Review of English Studies*, n.s., 1 (1950): 39–54.

12. *Lord Granville Leveson Gower: Private Correspondence 1781–1821*, ed. Castalia Countess Granville (London: John Murray, 1917), 2:418.

13. Nicholas A. Joukovsky, "Another Unnoted Contemporary Review of Jane Austen," *Nineteenth-Century Fiction* 29 (1974–75): 336–38.

14. Malcolm Elwin, *Lord Byron's Wife* (New York: Harcourt, Brace and World, 1962), 159.

15. S. H. Romilly, *Letters to "Ivy" From the First Earl of Dudley* (London: Longmans, 1905), 194.

16. Maria Edgeworth, *Letters from England 1813–1844*, ed. Christina Colvin (Oxford: Clarendon Press, 1971), 46.

17. *The Hamwood Papers of The Ladies of Llangollen and Caroline Hamilton*, ed. G. H. Bell (London: Macmillan, 1931), 351.

18. References to the opinions of both *Mansfield Park* and *Emma* solicited by Austen herself (which she in turn transcribed) are to the text in *Plan of a Novel According to Hints from Various Quarters by Jane Austen with Opinions on "Mansfield Park" and "Emma" Collected and Transcribed by her and Other Documents* (Oxford: Clarendon Press, 1926). For an extended treatment of the "opinions" as an alternative to the "masculine literary culture" represented in the reviews of Austen's novels and as a precursor, accordingly, to a way of reading Austen that is recognizably "Janeite" in its communitarian aspects, particularly regarding the intimacy that readers feel with respect to certain characters, see Laura Fairchild Brodie, "Austen and the Common Reader: 'Opinions of *Mansfield Park*,' 'Opinions of *Emma*," and the Janeite Phenomenon," *Texas Studies in Language and Literature* 37 (1995): 54–71. While Brodie has some interesting things to say about Austen's rather novelistic transcription of her friends' opinions, the binarism of male and female protocols of reading seems to me exaggerated and is in fact contradicted in any number of published reviews as well as in occasional comments by female writers such as Edgeworth.

19. *The Journal of Mary Frampton, from the Year 1779, until the Year 1846*, ed. Harriet Mundy (London: Sampson Low, 1885), 226.

20. *Romilly-Edgeworth Letters 1813–1818*, ed. Samuel Henry Romilly (London: John Murray, 1936), 92.

21. *Hamwood Papers*, 351.

22. For the theory of oppositionality as essentially tactical rather than strategic or overt, see de Certeau, *The Practice of Everyday Life*, trans. Steven Rendall (Berkeley and Los Angeles: University of California Press, 1984). For an application of de Certeau's theories to narrative and reading practices, see Ross Chambers, *Room for Maneuver: Reading (the) Oppositional (in) Narrative* (Chicago: University of Chicago Press, 1991).

23. The implication that Frank's engagement is at least known to the narrator (if not to other characters as well) comes in the sequence of Scott's summary in which the "concealed affair" is among the earliest details he discloses. "While Emma is thus vainly engaged in forging wedlock-fetters for others, her friends have views of the same kind upon her, in favour of a son of Mr. Weston by a former marriage, who bears the name, lives under the patronage, and is to inherit the fortune of a rich uncle. Unfortunately Mr. Frank Churchill had already settled his affections on Miss Jane Fairfax, a young lady of reduced fortune; but as this was a concealed affair, Emma, when Mr. Churchill first appears on stage, has some thoughts of being in love with him herself" (66).

24 *The Madwoman in the Attic: The Woman Writer and the Nineteenth-Century Literary Imagination* (New Haven: Yale University Press, 1979), 146–83.

25. For a more detailed account of the relationship of the aesthetic of the picturesque to the naturalizing practices of realistic fiction that Austen, no less than Clara Reeve, was altogether mindful of, see my essay "The Picturesque, the Real, and the Consumption of Jane Austen," *The Wordsworth Circle* 28 (winter 1997): 19–27.

26. William S. Ward, "Three Hitherto Unnoted Contemporary Reviews of Jane Austen," *Nineteenth-Century Fiction* 26 (1971–72): 469–77.

27. Marilyn Butler, *Maria Edgeworth: A Literary Biography* (Oxford: Clarendon Press, 1972), 445.

28. *Romilly-Edgeworth Letters*, 143.

29. *Memoir and Correspondence of Susan Ferrier 1782–1854*, ed. John A. Doyle (London: John Murray, 1898), 128.

30. *The Letters of Thomas Moore*, ed. Wilfred S. Dowden (Oxford: Clarendon Press, 1964), 1:396.

31. For other reviews of *Emma*, see Southam 1968, 70–77, and Ward, "Three Hitherto Unnoted Contemporary Reviews," 474–77. Among the more opinionated contemporary comments that I do not treat are those of Mary Russell Mitford, whose letters to Sir William Elford, written in her midtwenties, use the occasion of Austen's most recent production (which she, unlike many others, knew to be by "Miss Austen") to display her own wit and erudition. Thus *Emma*, which Mitford deems the "best . . . of all her charming works," provokes comments on the pleasures of "reading and re-reading Bacon," whom Mitford compares to Shakespeare and prefers ultimately to both Addison and Johnson. There may well be a connection between the pleasure of Austen's text (as Mitford has experienced it) and the "liveliness of illustration" in Bacon "which brings everything before

our eyes." But there is, more important, a fascination here with a certain authoritative viewpoint evident in Bacon and apparently lacking in Austen, who provides only "amusement," which reflects Mitford's unresponsiveness to Austen's antithetical achievement. (A. G. L'Estrange, *The Life of Mary Russell Mitford* [London: Bentley, 1870], 1:331.)

32. *Plan of a Novel*, 19.

33. J. G. Lockhart, *Memoirs of Sir Walter Scott* (London: Macmillan, 1900), 4:476.

34. *The Journal of Sir Walter Scott*, ed. W.E.K. Anderson (Oxford: Clarendon Press, 1972), 121.

35. Ibid., 352.

36. For a discussion of the sense of "actual infinity"—as opposed to a sense of "infinite progressivity"—characteristic of Schlegelian Romanticism, see Philippe Lacoue-Labarthe and Jean-Luc Nancy, *The Literary Absolute: The Theory of Literature in German Romanticism*, trans. Philip Barnard and Cheryl Lester (Albany: State University of New York Press, 1988).

37. "The Divine Miss Jane: Jane Austen, Janeites, and the Discipline of Novel Studies," reprinted in this volume. References to Kipling's "The Janeites" are to the text in *Debits and Credits* (London: Macmillan, 1926), 147–76.

# 5

## Decadent Austen Entails: Forster, James, Firbank, and the "Queer Taste" of *Sanditon* (comp. 1817, publ. 1925)

CLARA TUITE

> There is no knowing how estates will go once they come to be entailed.
>
> *(Mrs. Bennet in* Pride and Prejudice*, 1813)*

> [I]t was her desire to create, not to reproduce.
>
> *(J. E. Austen-Leigh,* A Memoir of Jane Austen*, 1870)*

> She did leave lawful issue in the shape of a son; an' his name was . . . 'Enery James.
>
> *(Rudyard Kipling, "The Janeites," 1926)*

> . . . a queer high-flavoured fruit from overseas . . .
>
> *(Henry James on aestheticism, 1904)*

> I am a *spinster* sir, & by God's grace intend to stay so.
>
> *(Ronald Firbank to Carl Van Vechten)*

> [T]here is a queer taste . . . which is not easily defined: a double-flavoured taste—half-topography, half-romance.
>
> *(E. M. Forster on* Sanditon*, 1925)*

### Introduction

The entail that we as readers of Austen are most familiar with is the entail that makes such an unwelcome appearance in *Pride and Prejudice* (1813), the legal device that formalizes the customary practice of inheritance through the male line, and is as such the means by which the Bennet girls are to be turned out of their family home on the death of their father and his estate passed to the nearest living male relative, Mr. Collins. This concern with the entail marks *Pride and Prejudice* as a leading example of the country-house novel, that bourgeois realist genre initiated by Austen, which plots the transmission of landed family property and dissects the complicated crossings of class, gender, and generation ensuring that transmission. This country house of fiction—to adapt Henry James's trope of the "house of fiction"—is a genre that has generated its own fictions of transmission within canonical British literary culture and its own complicated crossings of inheritance in terms of class, gender, and generation. Its canon intersects with that of a group of high-modernist and queer, closeted, or nonreproductive authors: the tradition moves from Austen with *Pride and Prejudice* (1813), to James with *The Portrait of a Lady* (1881), to Forster's *Howards End* (1910) and *Maurice* (comp. 1913–14, publ. 1971), to Firbank's pastoral country-house romances, to Virginia Woolf's *Orlando* (1928) and *Between the Acts* (1941), to the novels of Ivy Compton-Burnett, where the country-house novel reaches a particularly late or decadent phase.

This essay seeks to map the intertextual crossings and "back-crossings" of a circuit of texts by the queer, closeted, or nonreproductive authors who find their place within this genre. The circuit I wish to map in terms of the question of literary entails focuses on three texts:

1. *Sanditon*, Austen's posthumously published and incomplete final novel, written in 1817, when Austen was dying from Addison's disease, and published in 1925, a *late* and canonically and generically disruptive text within the Austen oeuvre. *Sanditon* is a kind of illegitimate Janie-come-lately to the Austen canon, coming posthumously to claim its inheritance and its place and also threatening the purity of that canon as it had been established since the late nineteenth century. Fantasizing the complete dissolution of landed property under the sign and in the endlessly circulating forms of coastal real estate, and failing to redeem the landed estate from that fate, *Sanditon* departs dramatically from the conventions of the country-house genre as apotheosized through the Austen oeuvre. Elegiac, and written under the sign of the backward look, it is also strangely utopic and forward looking, suggesting new directions of style, possibilities of genre, and fantasies of female mobility and independence. Set in the eponymous coastal watering hole, *Sanditon* represents the contemporary fashion for watering holes and the real estate speculation that such a fashion occasions. Focusing on a family of "Invalides," the Parkers, who have sold their landed estate and come to live in Sanditon, the plot centers on the economic rivalry between Mr. Parker and his partner in real estate speculation, Lady Denham, a serial widow, and on another more complicated rivalry between Lady Denham and her nephew, Sir Edward, for the charge of the former's niece—or cousin-of-a-niece—and live-in companion.

2. E. M. Forster's 1925 iconoclastic review of *Sanditon*, which offers, as I shall argue, a kind of antidecadent reading of *Sanditon* and attributes

to it "a queer taste, which is not easily defined: a double-flavoured taste—half-topography, half-romance."[1]

3. Ronald Firbank's *Valmouth: A Romantic Novel* (1919), which I read as both a decadent rewrite, or "back-crossing," and precursor of this "queer taste" of *Sanditon*, in its guise as watering-hole romance.

This essay seeks to elaborate the pun in my title, which brings together different verbal and nominal meanings of the term "entail." I wish to suggest that a "Decadent" construction of Austen would *entail*, in the sense of *imply* or *involve*, a reading of the relations among Forster, James, Firbank, and what Forster refers to as the "queer taste" of *Sanditon*—it would entail a reading of the inheritance of Austen within the works of these writers. In one sense, *Sanditon* is the literary estate entailed upon Forster, James, and Firbank as practitioners of the genre of the Austenian country-house novel. So, in this sense, my essay seeks to ask—pace Mrs. Bennet—how Austen's literary estate will go once it is entailed to a set of queer nephews. In this sense, "Austen's decadent entails" are the writings of Austen's queer nephews, understood as lines of succession and transmission.

Within the English literary tradition, Austen, as the canonical female writer who establishes a tradition of domestic-realist and country-house novels, represents a figure who undermines the usual practice of the entail, which is to naturalize a homosocial institution of exclusively male-to-male transmission that operates by both exploiting and occluding the female body and its nominated functions of biological and cultural reproduction. The fact that the Austenian literary tradition works to undermine this practice raises the question of the stigmatic status of the female gender for male writers who inherit their generic tradition through the female line. By exploring how Forster and James in particular explicitly disavow Austen as a literary foremother, the essay seeks to raise questions about feminist, queer, and decadent genealogies of genre. It sets out to explore the phenomenon of "Janeiteism" by offering a genealogical critique—in the form of parodic recapitulation or inversion—of the property plots, breeding fictions, and family romances of Austen's canonical literary history.

## Canonizing Austen's Country House: Institutions, Genealogies and Critical Fictions of Influence

In imagining a "Decadent Austen" I seek to capitalize upon the historical coincidence of two phenomena of the 1890s of apparently contradictory impulses: on the one hand, the initiatory gestures of the canonical production of Austen, which are critically implicated in the beginnings of English heritage culture and in the rise of curricular English, and, on the other hand, the English Decadent movement.

Through its concerns with generational reproduction and the transmission of property, the Austenian genre of the country-house novel anticipates the heritage industry of the late nineteenth and early twentieth century. A key site for the reconceptualizing of property relations and of bourgeois female social mobility during a period of intense social change, the Austen country-house novel performed the critical cultural function during the Napoleonic period of lyricizing and naturalizing a Burkean ideology of social hierarchy that involved the recommendation of the culture of the aristocratic estate as a form of national culture. Later-nineteenth- and early-twentieth-century canonical constructions of Austen as a signifier of green England are continuous with this enterprise. The nationalizing, organicizing, and pastoralizing imperatives of the preservationist rhetoric that characterizes the later formations of national heritage culture—though usually identified with the late nineteenth and early twentieth centuries—are in fact already being produced by Austen's country-house texts in their formidable regeneration of aristocratic cultural and social capital at a time of intense social conflict. In this way, Austen's fictions can be seen to initiate the very forms of Romantic nationalism that are later consolidated within a literary institution and wider popular culture that reproduce the Austen text as a canonical form of the British novel and as a signifier of national culture.

"Janeiteism," or the Austen industry, might be said to have begun as a Victorian family enterprise in 1870, with the publication of *A Memoir of Jane Austen* by Austen's collateral heir and nephew James Edward Austen-Leigh. This cottage industry of the literary estate transforms aristocratic landed property into cultural capital, land into text; in this context, Austen's country-house fictions function to reproduce the green core of the English countryside as a commodifiable cultural romance.

Austen-Leigh's *Memoir* makes its canonizing bid for Aunt Jane under the sign of the extended family's claim to the products of the aunt's nonreproductive labors. "[I]t was her desire to create, not to reproduce,"[2] Austen-Leigh writes, putting the spotlight on a decisively nonreproductive writing woman, and heroicizing female writing as a form of labor that is distinct from and superior to the labor of reproduction. In literary history's subsequent symbolic ascription of maternity to Austen as the canonical "foremother" of the British realist novel, these two functions of creation and reproduction will be neatly sutured—and consideration of Austen's abstention from the plot of reproduction will be waived.

During the consolidation of the Austen literary estate by Austen's collateral heirs, the manuscript of *Sanditon* was kept under wraps. As an incomplete text that lacks, among other things, the generic marriage ending of Austen's other novels, it would clearly have been seen to interrupt the nicely packageable Austen oeuvre of the almost parodically formulaic heterosexual romance. Added to that, the attention the novel pays to sick, self-pampering, and nonreproductive bodies would certainly have appeared unseemly. Or it may have been that *Sanditon*'s painful association with Aunt Jane's sickbed made the heirs reluctant to publish, except that Austen's descendants otherwise put the sickbed of Aunt Jane to good symbolic use throughout the family memoirs. Never in fact actually a bed, but usually a makeshift sofa and sometimes a donkey, Austen's sickbed is a recurrent trope of revelation in the family memoirs and a recurrent elegiac topos of quite unusual pathos:

> My Grandmother herself was frequently on the sofa. . . . There was only one sofa in the room—and Aunt Jane laid upon 3 chairs which she arranged for herself—I think she had a pillow, but it never looked comfortable.[3]

The first edition of Austen-Leigh's memoir makes no mention of *Sanditon*; the second edition of 1871 presents carefully selected extracts and paraphrases with the disclaimer that "such an unfinished fragment cannot be presented to the public." *Sanditon* was at last published in 1925 by Oxford University Press as *Sanditon: Fragment of a Novel*, edited by R. W. Chapman, editor, bibliographer, and high-priest-critic of Austen throughout the heady high-Janeite decades of the 1920s to the 1950s. And it is this moment of first reception of this posthumously published piece that I shall consider shortly with reference to E. M. Forster's review.

Following in the wake of Austen-Leigh's 1870 *Memoir*, 1890 marks the initiatory gesture of the specifically *critical* canonization of Austen, with the publication of Goldwin Smith's *Life of Jane Austen* for the Macmillan Great Writers Series. Within the 1890s, the year 1895 is particularly important. It sees the first issue of the English heritage magazine *Country Life*; it is the founding year of the National Trust; and it is the year of the trials of the aesthete Oscar Wilde, an event that put "queer" into circulation as a signifier of male homosexual performativity.

One way of explaining this coincidence between literary Decadence and the canonization of Austen is in terms of the perverse logic of English nationalism: in this logic, official national history at its most reverential and nostalgic, in that form of national history known as heritage culture, is marked by a model of history as "entropic decline."[4] In these terms, then, triumphalist culture dialectically produces a model of history as a process of decline and decay: a parodic reproduction of the privileged figure of the Decadent aesthetic.

That romance of degeneration which marks both a culture of nationalist triumphalism *and* its decadent others is paradigmatically instantiated by such cultural forms as the green, country-house Austen of heterosexual romance and the Merchant-Ivory queer romance—the genre of choice for what the late Derek Jarman referred to as "Brideshead Recidivists."[5] In the late 1990s, through filmic adaptation, Austen's country-house novel has proven to be a particularly adaptable genre, translatable, by elite, academic, and popular cultures simultaneously, into a signifier of the national culture of the English countryside. Such popular filmic adaptations serve to rejuvenate the classics in the same way that Austen's country-house classics themselves served the cultural work of rejuvenating the landed classes: they represent their private property as belonging to everybody. (As Linda Colley claims, "[o]nly in Great Britain did it prove possible to float the idea that aristocratic property was in some magical and strictly intangible way the people's property also.")[6] As Mandy Merck pointed out in 1993, "the *Brideshead* genre [in which she includes the film adaptations of Forster's *Maurice* and Nigel Sackville-West's *Portrait of a Marriage*] now rivals the stately home as the leading heritage industry."[7] In 1995, Terry Castle's exceedingly mild and well-mannered attempt in the *London Review of Books* to make Austen over as one of the stately lezzos of England—eschewing what she calls "the vulgar case for Austen's homoeroticism"[8]—is rabidly resisted by New and Old Janeites alike, who have their own heritage line in anti-American and anti-lesbian-feminist literary property plots.

The phenomenon that Merck refers to as "the screen's predisposition to make homosexuality mean marriage," which takes the form of a making over of homosexual energies into figures of a compulsory and compulsorily reproductive heterosexuality, is a feature of British high culture across a number of cultural traditions and institutions—and not simply created by opportunistic popular media, as Merck's account would seem to suggest. Besides the cinema's period drama, these institutions include English masculine pastoral elegy (from Milton's *Lycidas* [1638] through Gray's *Elegy* [1751] to Shelley's *Adonais* [1821] to Tennyson's *In Memoriam* [1850] and Arnold's *Thyrsis* [1866]); georgic poetry, which revises the pastoral emphasis on nature, leisure, and eros with an emphasis on enculturation and cultivation, and which joins poetic to agricultural labor in the work of nation-foundation; the country-house novel, as a bourgeois and feminized historical displacement of both the pastoral and the georgic that shares those genres' preocccupation with natural, social, and economic modes of patrilineal reproduction; and the institutionalized Victorian Hellenisms of Oxford and Cambridge, disseminated through the work of Matthew Arnold, which capitalize on the pedagogical eros of pederastic figures of generation and tradition, such as influence and "inspiration."[9] The fictions of "influence" and transmission that operate in these genealogies of genre are decisively and heterosexually reproductive, but they also license models of male-to-male insemination. In this sense, conventional cultural models of male influence are made over into, and are complicitous with, the compulsory heterosexuality of breeding fictions, yet they rely on homoerotic models of influence and insemination.

This pedagogical and pederastic tradition, a largely Arnoldian tradition that has had enormous influence over Anglo-American literary-critical institutions of reading, is spectacularly reproduced and revised in Harold Bloom's *The Anxiety of Influence* (1973). Bloom's account of literary influence sets up an Oedipal (i.e., generational) struggle between a later poet and a precursor. It models literary intertextuality as a form of pederastic eros suspended on a generational power differential. Influence is the taste or style of the precursor poet that the "strong" latecomer poet has the power to adopt or imitate, or command, or—at the critical moment—*resist*. For the strong poet, who does resist, influence is to be understood not as being *under* the influence of the precursor but as being able to command and channel that influence. For the strong poet, the anxiety of influence necessitates overcoming that influence.

This anxiety of influence is strictly masculine, Oedipal, and homosocial. Its dialectic of insemination and repulsion (which licenses male-to-male influence yet permits the latecomer to achieve greatness only by rebuffing the precursor) is a generative trope of literary history and of canon-formation. As a grand narrative of literary influence within the canonical lyric tradition, Bloom's account offers a paradigmatic instantiation of the way in which the institution of literary studies is modeled at once on homosocial models of strength and heterosexual models of reproduction.[10]

Despite the fact that Bloom's model does not address in any explicit way the issue of female lines of literary transmission, its figure of "anxiety" can be interestingly engaged with reference to the anxiety of male authors who inherit from female precursors—and with reference, specifically, to the inheritance of male novel authors from Austen. For a larger English literary (largely poetic) tradition, one modeled on male-to-male insemination, Austen occupies an ambivalent position. For male authors, occupying a place in the Austenian tradition of the novel is similarly fraught. In historical terms, the canonization of Austen, and the anxiety this produces, coincide at the end of the nineteenth century with the advent of a newly institutionalized English studies, a discipline that is implicated in the development of women's education. This question of the stigmatic status of the canonical foremother is particularly important during the first half of the twentieth century, and in relation to Austen, for the novel genre itself is in this period canonized largely via the figure of its canonical foremother, Austen.

E. M. Forster and Henry James have long been identified as inheritors of the Great Tradition of the Austenian novel. In F. R. Leavis's *The Great Tradition* (1948), the first literary history to canonize the English novel genre itself within the generic hierarchy, Austen is referred to as "a major fact in the background of other great writers," a great triumvurate that includes Henry James. Leavis claims explicitly that passages of James's work "show [Austen's] clear influence."[11] An overlooked precursor to Leavis's account is Robert Liddell's *A Treatise on the Novel* (1947), which had similar canon-forming impulses, yet which did not itself become a canonical work of canon-formation as Leavis's text did. Liddell's account styles itself a "Genealogy" and pairs Austen and James throughout as examples of novelistic perfection.[12] One of the first readings of James in the tradition of the Austen novel is Harriet Waters Preston's 1903 review of *The Wings of the Dove*: "I do not think how anyone can see that Mr. James was ever very successful in the novel of English manners. . . . Mr. James is *maladif* if not morbid. The Trollopes and Austens love air and exercise."[13] Here, the very gesture of distinguishing James from Austen in fact produces a narrative of inheritance: the James novel represents not so much a departure from as a morbid, decadent production of the Austen tradition of the novel of English manners.

In his early critical writings from the mid-1870s James was one of the principal commentators who, following the appearance of Austen-Leigh's *Memoir*, actively promulgated the canonical status of Austen within the novel tradition.[14] In the early twentieth century, when the canonization of Austen and through her the novel genre operated largely by approximating Austen's novels to dramas (and this had long been a gesture in the familiar comparison of Austen with Shakespeare), the critical emphasis on the dramatic character of Austen's work developed largely as an effect of the influential Jamesian legacy of the "drama of consciousness" and the "scenic method."[15] In the work of the writers for *Scrutiny* and of the North American New Critics that, from the 1930s to the 1960s, takes Austen's "dramatic power" as axiomatic and as evidence paradoxically of the perfection of her form of the *novel*, James lurks as the master reader of Austen. Indeed, James becomes a trope of the supremely knowing and discriminating "critical" consciousness.[16] As a supremely knowing critical consciousness—sharpened by a particularly acute sense of cultural cringe—James became a particularly enabling historical precedent for later-twentieth-century New Critical North American critics in their interventions into the formation of the British canon.

So James is significant both as an inheritor of the genre of country-house novel and comedy of manners associated with Austen and as a producer—retrospectively—of the canonical Austen, at least as a critical fiction.

The identification of a line of descent from Austen to Forster is a staple of twentieth-century Forster criticism, even when the comparison is engaged only to be denied, as is the case with F. R. Leavis's reading of 1938.

Arguably the first critic to announce Forster's inheritance from Austen is Virginia Woolf, in a 1927 overview of Forster's career that interrogates at length Forster's claims to "stand firmly on his feet among the descendants of Jane Austen."[17] However, standing on one's feet among the descendants of Jane Austen was a fraught and compromised activity for Forster as for James. In Cyril Connolly's 1928 reading of Forster, for example, Austen as precursor is legible in the intertextual background, in a review that feminizes Forster as it cites the preponderance of old maids in Forster's fictions, and that plays upon the slippage between work and author in invocations of the "demure malice" of "the familiar spinster."[18] Clearly, for Forster, such reception complicates the question of inheritance from the female line. It is this anxiety of influence that I now wish to engage through a reading of Forster's review of *Sanditon* and the position it occupies within Forster's oeuvre.

## "Forster Country": Patrilineal Romance and Anxieties of Austen's Influence

*Sanditon* was published in 1925 when Austen was at the postwar prime of her interwar canonical positioning.[19] Following its publication, E. M. Forster published in the leftist weekly *Nation* (21 March 1925) a self-consciously iconoclastic review based on the general claim that *Sanditon* is "reminiscent." The review was later included in an anthology of occasional articles, essays, and reviews published in 1936 as *Abinger Harvest*, named after the "Abinger Pageant" that Forster produced with Ralph Vaughan Williams in 1934, in the village of Abinger where Forster had come to live in 1924 after he inherited the lease of Laura Lodge, or West Hackhurst, on the death of his paternal aunt, Laura Forster.

These two occasions for the appearance of Forster's review of *Sanditon* produce two different texts to be read: first, one of the earliest critical receptions of *Sanditon*; second, Forster's own text, an anthologized piece within *Abinger Harvest* that has a symbolic status as part of the "harvest" collected in an anthology that represents itself as textual retrospect and self-memorializing monument. The "harvest" is significant as a paradigmatic georgic trope of agricultural labor, as is the identification of the writer's labor with that of the farmer. To take the text of this second occasion first, we might locate Forster's extremely critical review of *Sanditon* as a text impaired by "reminiscence" under the sign of Forster's own activity of reminiscence. The form that this retrospection takes within *Abinger Harvest* is the masculine pastoral and georgic elegy and its crossing of homosocial and homoerotic romances of patriliny. This is a predominant form throughout Forster's writing, appearing in the country-house novel, such as *Howards End* and *Maurice*; domestic biography, in *Marianne Thornton* (1956); occasional and autobiographical writings, such as *Abinger Harvest*'s "The Last of Abinger" and "Abinger Pageant"; and posthumously published stories such as "Little Imber."

In the preface to *Abinger Harvest*, Forster writes, "I proceed to angle in the stream, and draw out of it objects ranging in date from a Greek toilet-case to a house which belonged to my great-grandfather" (*AH*, 5). These two "objects"—the Greek toilet-case and the great-grandfather's house, Battersea Rise—metonymize two sets of social relations that are problematically interimplicated within Forster's writing—Greek, homosexual, pederastic culture and aristocratic, dynastic, patrilineal transmission. This opening juxtaposition frames *Abinger Harvest*, then, in terms of a fantastic economy of male-to-male inheritance, which also features in texts such as "Little Imber" and *Maurice*. It announces the pervasive and problematic imbrication in Forster's work between homoeroticism on the one hand and homosociality and the patrilineal transmission of property on the other. The dedication of *Abinger Harvest* to Forster's male "friends in a younger generation" (6) also enacts the generic (pederastic) protocols of the pastoral tradition, since the "anthology," from the ancient Greek for a collection of flowers, as in the *Garland of Meleager* (ca. 140–ca. 70 B.C.), is the genre of tribute from the older to the younger male. Forster's identification with a specifically *masculine* homosexual style or performativity is implicated within an intense and overdetermining patrilineal and homosocial investment. Engaging fantasies of inheritance at the intersection of male homosexuality and homosociality, Forster's work demonstrates how within each of these social and cultural economies—homoerotic fantasy and conventional homosocial practices of patriliny—the primacy of male-to-male inheritance works to occlude heterosexual reproduction and the female body.

Forster's pastoral- and georgic-elegiac productions position him within that male, Oxbridge-educated literary elite which aligns itself with what British cultural historian Tom Nairn has referred to as the "pseudo-feudal hierarchy" of the traditional elite; its task is the creation of a myth-world that bolsters the ailing patrician body, the "myth of the organic community, located in the countryside and in the indeterminate past."[20] In these terms, the country-house novel genre enacts the class-specific bourgeois cultural work of renovating aristocratic culture and making it over into a national image. This function is enacted in both *Mansfield Park* and *Howards End*. In *Mansfield Park*, the threat that is announced by Edmund's removal of the bookcase from his father's study—a synecdoche for the library, which operates as metonym for culture—is the departure of the cultured classes from their scripted role. This scene in *Mansfield Park* prefigures a variation on this class allegory that Forster will include in *How-*

*ards End*, where the brutal death-by-bookcase of Leonard Bast works to preserve a bullying pre–World War I aristocracy against the encroachments of those members of the lower class who, like Leonard, attempt to improve themselves through education.

Forster's subscription to this entropic romance of the countryside is also dramatized by the "Abinger Pageant" of 1934, which was staged by Forster, with the collaboration of Ralph Vaughan Williams, as a protest against the supposed obliteration of the countryside and its culture by "urbanization" (that is, by "houses and bungalows, hotels, restaurants and flats, arterial roads, petrol pumps and pylons" [*AH*, 384]). Forster's active conservation efforts were rewarded by the official renaming of the country around Abinger Hammer as "Forster country."

Almost twenty years after "Abinger Pageant," and ten years after Forster was forced to move from Laura Lodge after its lease had expired, Forster paid posthumous tribute to his paternal great-aunt, Marianne Thornton, with *Marianne Thornton 1797–1887* (1956). This "domestic biography," like Forster's domestic comedies, involves what Michael Warner has recently termed "repronarrativity," "a relation to self that finds its proper temporality and fulfilment in generational transmission."[21] In Forster's work this "repronarrativity" is produced through romances of patriliny.

Elaborating what the program of the "Abinger Pageant" refers to as the "continuity of country life" (*AH* 370), *Abinger Harvest*, like *Marianne Thornton*, is predicated on the inheritance of material and cultural property through the female line. Both those texts feature the country house as a trope of the interrelation between material and cultural legacies. Forster's review of *Sanditon* itself offers no explicit reflections upon his own inheritance from Austen. However, the other individual offerings of the *Abinger Harvest* miscellany reflect explicitly upon the relationship between textual and material inheritance; the (masculine) acknowledgment of inheritance from the female line; and the status of the posthumous text and tribute. So, within this intertextual context, juxtaposed, too, to *Marianne Thornton*, "*Sanditon*" reads as a filial rejection and disavowal of the Austenian legacies of the domestic comedy and country-house genres.

This attempt at extricating male-to-male inheritance from the mediation of the female body is suggested in an interview of 1957 that neatly evokes both the critical consensus which viewed Forster as an heir to the Austen tradition and Forster's anxiety about this inheritance. Forster replies to the question "What did you learn from Jane Austen technically?" by saying, "I learnt the possibilities of domestic humour. I was more ambitious than she was, of course; I tried to hitch it onto other things."[22] Here, Forster comes closest to explicit acknowledgment of Austen as a predecessor—but also to a more explicit anxiety of influence.

Now that I have contextualized Forster's review in terms of its appearance as part of Forster's own activity of reminiscence and retrospection, I would like to discuss the review directly in terms of its critique of Austen's "reminiscence."

## Forster's Review of *Sanditon* as Antidecadent Critique

Evaluating *Sanditon* as "of small literary merit," Forster's review is a self-consciously iconoclastic reading, which elaborates its iconoclasm through the language of degeneration, offering a kind of antidecadent critique of the text:

> In 1817 [Miss Austen] had reached maturity, but she was also ill, and these are two factors we must bear in mind while we read. Are there signs of new development in Sanditon? Or is everything overshadowed by the advance of death? . . . The MS. (the editor tells us) is firmly written. Nevertheless, the fragment gives the effect of weakness, if only because it is reminiscent from first to last. . . . She writes out of what she has written, and anyone who has himself tried to write when feeling out of sorts will realize her state. The pen always finds life difficult to record; left to itself, it records the pen. The effort of creating was too much, and the numerous alterations in the MS. are never in the direction of vitality. Even the wit is reminiscent. . . . It is the old flavour, but how faint! Sometimes it is even stale, and we realize with pain that we are listening to a slightly tiresome spinster, who has talked too much in the past to be silent unaided. Sanditon is a sad little experience from this point of view . . . the book promises little vigour of character and. . . . [c]haracter-drawing, incident, and wit are on the decline. (*AH* 167–69)

Forster's diagnosis mobilizes the key terms of a contemporary language of degeneration—"weakness," "little vigour," "lack of vitality," "decline"—the most familiar and available contemporary version of which is the discourse of antidecadence or degeneracy—the stigmatized version of Decadence—that is elaborated by figures such as Cesare Lombroso and Max Nordau and, closer to home, Henry James, who in 1904 excoriated the aestheticism of the Italian Decadent writer D'Annunzio as "a queer, high-flavoured fruit from overseas."[23]

By labeling *Sanditon* "reminiscent," Forster also draws on an emerging Freudian terminology. Following the terms of Freud's 1914 distinction between criminal and hysteric subjects, Forster's reading figures Austen simultaneously as degenerate and as sick patient—object of pathos—suffering hysterically from reminiscences.[24]

Forster's reading stages the revelation of a sick, female body that produces a sick text as symptom, displacing the horror of the sick body onto the text. This reading labors to divest *Sanditon* of the Romantic mystique attached to the fragment,[25] a mystique that it implicitly reserves for male-authored texts and for male authors who die before their time. Forster's *Sanditon* is not the "precious" trace wrested from oblivion, as it is for Chapman and for a later editor of a manuscript facsimile, B. C. Southam;[26] it is a fragment as feminine detail that bears the burden of signifying female lack, in, and as, the horror of nothing to see.

Forster's iconoclastic reading dialectically produces *Sanditon* as a decadent text *through* antidecadent critique. Except that *Sanditon* is *not* for Forster a Decadent text, because the practice and privilege of Decadence is a masculine prerogative. Ill health is a privileged category only in the male homosexual aesthetic economy, just as the Romantic mystique of the fragment is a prerogative of male writers and masculine texts. Forster's review dialectically raises the question of whether *Sanditon* can be read as a Decadent text, only to answer this in the negative.

While Forster implicitly arrogates the privilege of Decadence as aestheticized gesture to male practitioners, other writings by Forster suggest a marked ambivalence to Decadence as a masculine homosexual practice. In this way, Forster's antidecadent reading of Austen can be seen to perform a complicated displacement, mediation, or triangulation of an ambivalent attack on this contemporary masculine aesthetic movement. Forster's ambivalence toward the fin de siècle registers not so much a fear of homosexual implication as a desire to avoid contamination by the *effeminacy* that marks this late-nineteenth-century style of homosexual performativity. It registers a stylistic preference for *masculine* homosexual performativity. Forster's antidecadent critique of Austen enacts the same kind of disavowal that has been attributed, by Richard Ellmann, to James's conspicuously absent acknowledgment of notable contemporary aesthetes and Decadents. However, while I think that a similar strategy is operating in Forster's review, I do not see this as a direct operation of the closet, in the way that it seems to have been for James; James and Forster were closeted in their personal lives in quite different ways, and, similarly, the operations of the closet work in their texts in different and mutually illuminating ways. For example, where, as Ellman points out, James makes his desire to distance himself from Decadent texts and authors quite explicit, Forster does not.[27]

Reading *Sanditon* as a symptomatic spectacle of femininity as decay, Forster withholds male-identified Decadence from Austen and attributes to her the female lowercase decadence of literal decay, thereby keeping male Decadence pure—that is to say, male-practiced—and preserving it from the taint of degeneration that would result from the identification of a woman writer as a Decadent practitioner.

Canonical Augustan misogynist tropes of female authorship, which pathologize the female-identified genre of the novel through images of female corporeality, as in the boudoir poems of Swift and Pope, are clearly legible in the intertextual background of Forster's attack on a canonical female author who herself parodied female-identified sentimental novels and used the generic precedent of Augustan misogynist satire to do so. Forster exposes the decaying female body behind Austen's drag of masculine Augustanism, unmasking a real woman in the bedroom—dying and *en déshabillé*. If Austen's "wit" has been her claim to honorary inclusion as Neoclassicist in the male Augustan satirical club of Swift, Pope, and Johnson, Forster's claim that "[e]ven the wit is reminiscent" discredits these honorary credentials by revealing Austen to be, not Decadent, but merely decadent, merely female.

## James, Forster, and the Austenian Country-House Closet

We might read both Forster's and James's depreciation of Austen in terms of the logic of the relationship between the homosexual son and his mother. Occupying privileged places both within the minicanon of gay male high culture and the mainstream canon of the bourgeois novel, both James and Forster manifest anxiety over their Austenian legacy. The relationship to Austen that this criticism of Forster and James articulates may be figured, to adapt Eve Kosofsky Sedgwick's formulation, as the attempt of the pampered boy to escape the omnipotent but unknowing mother. Sedgwick devises this formulation to account for the intended reader of closeted pieces of gay-male-authored literary production such as "the coming-out story that doesn't come out" (a category that for her includes Forster's short story "The Other Boat"). These productions feature "an incomplete address to the figure of the mother" that involves "the attribution of an extreme or even ultimate power to an auditor who is defined at the same time as a person who *can't know*."[28] As Sedgwick argues, the unknowing mother provides a kind of pretext for inhabiting the closet. The image of the unknowing mother, in this case, Austen as canonical foremother, elaborates a male anxiety toward an influential female predecessor that necessitates the construction of the mother / textual predecessor as inarticulate, weak, and sexually unknowing. Furthermore, it mediates an ambivalence toward the heterosexualizing imperatives of the country-house genre, which serves as a kind of generic closet for these writers, who were at various times in their careers and to varying degrees closeted homosexuals. In this sense, we might think of the country-house novel genre as a closet—both protective and stifling—for James and Forster.

The trope of "knowing" is particularly important for James's epistemophilic fictions, often predicated upon the figure of the knowing ingenue. It would seem to bear a direct relation to the investment in the unknowingness of the literary foremother that is suggested in James's famous critical account of Austen: "[S]ometimes, over her work basket, her tapestry flowers . . . [she] fell a-musing [and] lapsed . . . into wool gathering. . . . [H]er dropped stitches[,] . . . these precious moments, were afterwards picked up as little touches of human truth, little glimpses of steady vision, little master-strokes of imagination."[29] Those "dropped stitches" figure a slip in the foremother's canonical posture, the failure of the feminine slip to contain feminine seepage. As I suggested earlier, in his early critical writings from the mid-1870s, James contributed significantly to the canonization of the novel genre and of Austen within the novelistic tradition. This position changes, however, in later Jamesian texts such as this one, where Austen becomes an object of criticism and a figure who is more significant for her "lapses" of canonical stature, as she is in Forster's review of *Sanditon*.

The maternal figure also features in a critical depreciation of James by Forster, who claims that the former's protagonists "often have a mother in the background and a nameless disease"[30]—where "mother in the background" and "nameless disease" appear in apposition: placed together but lacking explicit connection, as though accidentally related. For Leavis, as we have seen, the background position *is* the canonical position of Austen. It is there that she becomes an acquiescent monument serving as site and screen and facilitator of masculine critical exchanges and narratives of influence.

Although I do not have space to discuss this here, the case of Forster's posthumously published *Maurice*, which Forster began in 1913 and circulated among friends, suggests a growing disillusionment with what we would now call the compulsory heterosexuality of the country-house novel genre. As early as 1911 Forster had expressed an awareness of the limitations of the marriage plot, as this diary entry indicates: "I have never tried to turn a man into a girl, as Proust did with Albertine, for this seemed derogatory to me as a writer."[31] This disillusionment was also registered in the fears of impotence that are recorded in Forster's 1925 diary entries: it was particularly pronounced, that is, at the time of the review of *Sanditon*. In this sense, if *Maurice* must be read as an attempt to make the traditional narrative form signify homosexuality, then "*Sanditon*" is not simply a manifestation of an anxiety of influence, a feeling of impotence at not being able to keep producing Austenian domestic comedy, but also the manifestation of an ambivalent response to the genre, a disavowal of and disidentification with the Austen inheritance of the domestic comedy and country-house genre that was entailed upon Forster by common critical consent. (By 1971, in a baleful review of *Maurice*, Cyril Connolly's feminizing reading of 1928 has hardened into the identification of Forster as "the Sacred Maiden Aunt of English Letters.")[32]

*Abinger Harvest*'s figurative harvest is a gathering of the fruit of literary labor. It resists the narrative in which Austen figures as the maternal origin of the novelistic domestic comedy of manners; it repudiates being "hitched" to Austen, repudiates the critical fiction of heterosexual breeding, and reduces the Austen text to the symptom of a sick, sterile, nonreproductive female body. It involves an anxiety of influence that disavows being in the drag of the feminized domestic novel genre, while remaining closeted within a genre of "domestic comedy" that Forster attempts to hitch onto an idealized homosexual patriliny.

If the georgic trope of harvest glosses the reprint as collection and consolidation of written produce, it simultaneously requires and denies its own textual dissemination and is simultaneously fecund and barren. In this sense, *Abinger Harvest* is vulnerable to the same charge that Forster makes against *Sanditon*, that "the pen [there] merely records the pen," and that it is reproductively barren, as mere "reprint" and collection of fragments. The misprisioning function within *Abinger Harvest* of Forster's "*Sanditon*"—with its rhetoric of debility and decline, its repudiation of the Austen novel's canonical status as the green core of green England—is to shore up *Abinger*'s invocation of the georgic rhetoric of harvest. *Abinger Harvest* is a fertility token invoked to ward off the threat of feminine contamination of the late Austen's reminiscence, sterility, and decline.

## *Valmouth: A Romantic Novel* (1919) and the "Queer Taste" of *Sanditon*

> I could no more write a romance than an epic poem. I could not sit seriously down to write a serious romance under any other motive than to save my life.
>
> (Austen, *Letters*)[33]

If E. M. Forster would squirm at being identified with "spinster fancies" or at being dubbed the "Sacred Maiden Aunt of English Letters," it is precisely this title that the belated twentieth-century 1890s aesthete and Decadent Ronald Firbank—who declared, "I am a *spinster* sir, & by God's grace intend to stay so"—would happily kill for.

If Forster's antidecadent reading of *Sanditon* is a lost opportunity, raising the question as to whether *Sanditon* is a Decadent text only to foreclose the possibility, Firbank's *Valmouth: A Romantic Novel* allows the production and reception of the Decadent *Sanditon* that Forster forecloses, imbibing and spectacularly distilling what Forster stigmatizes as *Sanditon*'s "queer taste . . . which is not easily defined: a double-flavoured taste—half topography, half romance."

This final section of my essay charts something of the "queer" generic pedigree of romance from the foremother whose "desire it was to create, not reproduce," to her illegitimate son, or favored nephew, who writes himself spinster. Firbank's *Valmouth*, then, is the third codicil to this decadent Austen entail.

Written after *Sanditon*, but published before it in 1919, *Valmouth* is both the successor and precursor of—decadent flashback and flashforward to—*Sanditon*. To the extent that the relation between these two texts frustrates conventional (patri)linear breeding fictions of influence,[34] this relation is not a reversal of priority but a reversal of conventional filial wisdom, with *Sanditon* as both precursor of and latecomer to *Valmouth*.

This is a subversion of the law of primogeniture according to which inheritance descends lineally but can never ascend, the law of patriliny that is so emphatically and indelibly written into Forster's narratives. *Property* cannot travel backward and always travels forward through the economic law of entail that attempts infinite projection, forestalling and deferring the moment of the outcome, the moment of cashing in. However, the speculative Victorian *techne* of genetic engineering can and often must travel backward. This occurs in the genetic practice of "back-crossing,"[35] a mid-nineteenth-century Mendelian biological *techne* of botanical husbandry by which the composition of the forebear is only legible in retrospect through the composition of the later generation: breeding as confirmation of the hypothesis of probability, which works by activating the recessive genes.

By way of recasting genetics as a genealogy of genre, in the reading of *Valmouth* and *Sanditon* that follows I wish to use "back-crossing" as a generic and intertextual model for a reading practice in which the backward look opens out and makes legible the recessed generic tendencies of earlier texts.

The genealogical relation between *Valmouth* and *Sanditon* can be tracked using back-crossing as a principle of intertextuality, a technology of reading that makes legible the recessive generic affiliations, tendencies, and "tastes" of the *Sanditon* fragment *as* a romance, and as a romance that, as historical latecomer to the oeuvre, and in its spectacular departure from the compulsory plot of heterosexual romance of Austen's completed domestic realist novels, interrupts and impairs the canonized cultural romance in which the Austen novel figures *as* realistic heterosexual romance. Such a reading charts something of the "queer" pedigree from the woman who did not want to reproduce to her spinster son/nephew.

I take my cue for this account of the relationship between *Sanditon* and *Valmouth* from Brigid Brophy, who argues for the pervasive influence of Austen upon Firbank throughout his oeuvre and for, in particular, the intertextual relationship between *Sanditon* and *Valmouth* as watering-hole fictions, in a stylistic reading that capitalizes on the fact that the two oeuvres intersect at Bath—that paradigmatic site of morbid utopia—as a scene of figurative and literal production.[36] I wish to take Brophy's reading further, in terms of its implications for conventional literary history, by elaborating it with reference to the rhetorical structure of the metaleptic prolepsis, a move from the past back to the present, which effects the coincidence of the "queer taste" (the "double-flavoured taste [of] half-topography, half-romance") in terms of which *Valmouth* produces a Decadent *Sanditon*.

Whereas Forster's tenacious sense of the chronological, patrimonial, repronarrative line demands that he disavow a filial relation to Austen, *Valmouth* turns the fact that *Sanditon* can only ever be read anachronistically, always at least one hundred years too late, into a utopic possibility that allows the transfusion of Firbank's own self-consciously belated imitation of 1890s Decadence. Just as one contemporary reader exclaimed oxymoronically of *Valmouth* that "this is the real decadence"[37]—the real thing, that is, twenty years after the conventional flowering of real English Decadence—then we might also exclaim that *Valmouth* produces the real "queer taste" of *Sanditon*. This is a form of intertextual, nonfilial, nonreproductive reception and production: a form of decadent reproduction that we could name "degenerative evolution"[38] from Austen to Firbank and Firbank to Austen.

*Valmouth* is a decadent sequela to *Sanditon* and offers a genealogy and decadent sequela for both its feminine and masculine homosexualities: the bisexual sailor, Dick Thoroughfare, referred to as Corydon, is a decadent sequela to *Sanditon*'s "family of helpless Invalides" (409)—a group that includes a male hypochondriac who refuses to eat toast because it "hurts the coats of the stomach." The West Indian, Mrs. Yaj, the bagnio operator and masseuse, whose mysterious paddles and vibrating instruments treat women exclusively, in order to "restore [them] to all de world's delights,"[39] is a displaced version of *Sanditon*'s elegant serial widow, Lady Denham, who hotly competes with her nephew for her own niece—or niece-of-a-cousin, to be precise—and for the business and bodies of young, sickly West Indian girls, to whom she sells ass's milk.

*Valmouth* materializes both the sexual ambiguities of *Sanditon* and its colonial occlusions. Impinging upon this watering hole at the edge of the empire in both texts is the colonial other, the West Indian woman, *Sanditon*'s "sickly" Miss Lambe on the one hand and, on the other, *Valmouth*'s Mrs. Yajnavalkya, the curer of sick women who "like[s] to relieve my own sex": part of the "queer taste" of *Sanditon* that *Valmouth* regurgitates or redistills occurs through colonial reflux. *Valmouth* allows for a speculative rereading of *Sanditon*, opening out the figure of the black woman who is a spectral presence in *Sanditon*, suggesting the specter of slavery.

*Iconoclasm*, as Ronald Paulson suggests, referring to its original Puritan meaning, is "a breaking that either leaves the idol broken or reconstitutes it as a common utensil."[40] If Forster's iconoclasm leaves the Austen idol broken, Firbank reconstitutes that idol as a common utensil—and I think that the common utensil that the iconoclasted Austen would be is the wooden spoon—the *pedagogical* wooden spoon.[41] Firbank turns that scene of correction and instruction which features in the critical account of an Augustan, satirical Austen, as well as in the critical account of a Romantic, improving Austen, into a scenario of flagellation: hence Mrs. Yaj, administratrix of remedies and beatings and—on "Vibro day" (*V*, 411)—good vibrations. Firbank also does this by writing in as anti-marriage ending what in *Sanditon* is recuperable as the *incomplete* ending.

*Sanditon* does this iconoclastic work for the Austen oeuvre in its renunciation of correction for reminiscence, and in the departure from the heterosexual romance plot, in the pursuit of a romance between a rich widow and real estate speculator, Lady Denham, and a niece-of-a-cousin, Clara Brereton. According to the reluctant paraphrase of Austen's great-nephew, James Edward Austen-Leigh, Lady Denham is "a rich vulgar widow."[42] Might the vulgar Lady Denham, then, also be, to quote Terry Castle again, "the vulgar case for Austen's homoeroticism"? I believe she might.

As early as 1964, B. C. Southam suggests that "[t]he relationship between Lady Denham and her niece [*sic*] is open to speculation."[43] Interestingly, however, he does not offer any speculation. Indeed, in 1995 Southam makes an appearance in the *LRB* expressly to close down such speculations, in response to Terry Castle's daring to give a name to what there might be to speculate about in relation to correspondence between Austen and her favorite niece, Fanny Knight.[44] So, while Southam does not offer any speculation, I would speculate about the aunt-and-niece romance plot that is legible in *Sanditon* in the following terms.

*Sanditon* features a bizarre love triangle among an older woman, a younger woman, and a younger man, from whom the older woman wants to keep the younger woman. Lady Denham is a perverse twist on *Persuasion*'s Lady Russell, Austen's other older woman who has the power of persuasion and "influence" over a young woman, and who has "prejudices on the side of ancestry." Lady Denham is Austen's fantasy of a woman wielding not only the masculine power of "exchange" but the power to refuse to exchange: "She had chosen Clara, a Niece— . . . Clara had returned with her—and . . . not a syllable was breathed of any change, or exchange" (379). Whereas Edward Denham represents what Southam elsewhere refers to as an outdated "Afro-Gothicism," the "neo-Gothicism" of Lady Denham[45]—her nephew's rival for a younger woman—is one of elegant lesbian vampirism. Addicted to the sentimental novels that he is fed on the sly by the son of the circulating librarianess, Edward Denham represents an outdated, Lovelacean libertinism. Lady Denham, on the other hand, boldly anticipates the nineteenth-century elegant lesbian neo-Gothic of Balzac's *The Girl with the Golden Eyes* (written 1834–35), Le Fanu's *Carmilla* (1871–72), and Henry James's *The Bostonians* (1886).[46] This neo-Gothic lesbian vampirism involves the romance of the older woman with power, influence, and money at her disposal—the older woman as inappropriate and unnatural maternal supplement. We might employ the term "seaside Gothic" or "watering-hole Gothic" here to refer to Lady Denham's double depredations upon coastal real estate and young, defenseless, unmarried women.

In one way, *Sanditon* is a dystopia of Gothic decadence. Symbolically, women are conventionally excluded from Decadence because they are locked into the reproductive cycle. Lady Denham and her milch asses, with which she treats sick young women, counter this exclusion through a vampiric parody of maternity.

In place of a discernible heterosexual courtship plot, Lady Denham represents the new Gothic plot of wealthy lesbian vampirism, as she sucks her male partners dry in order to bequeath to the female favorite, who "secured a very strong hold in [her] regard" (335). It is in these ways, then, that Lady Denham is crucial to what Forster refers to as "*Sanditon*'s "queer taste . . . [its] double-flavoured taste—half-topography, half-romance." Topography and romance are linked in *Sanditon* through the figure of the female Speculator. Lady Denham departs from the role of mediator of male-to-male transfer of property, departs from the reproductive plot in which the married woman figures as the stabilizing sign of male property. This new form of romance marks a departure from the overscripted romance of Austen's previous novels, where the impetus for the generic marriage ending is upward social mobility for the appropriate kind of female subject. *Sanditon* instead sees a battle for female primogeniture, on the part of the serial widow who diverts funds from husbands to the upkeep of a niece.

However, in the patriarchal economy, the relationship between the childless serial widow and a niece who is on the fringes of the aristocratic kinship system, with shrinking claims upon the patronage of the family, is marked as one without any value. In keeping with the terms of that economy, this "rich vulgar widow, who cared for the prosperity of Sanditon only so far as it might increase the value of her own property,"[47] ought to be diverting the winnings that she gains from her serial loss of husbands to her nephew—she ought, that is, to be associated with an economy of patrilineal retrenchment, of the sort that features in *Mansfield Park* and *Persuasion*. Lady Denham should use her money for the improvement of the whole, by bestowing it on a male relative. And the niece-of-a-cousin, Clara Brereton, should be cut out, in the interests of retrenchment and consolidation. What happens instead in the text is that the female energies which should be recouped for the patriliny are diverted to themselves, or at least that is the way the narrative moves in its realization of the widow's desire.

It is because of this plot that "the marriage market" ceases to determine the representation of female subjectivity in Austen's work. And, to extend and complicate a claim made by D. A. Miller, it is not simply that in *Sanditon* Austen is "bored" with the marriage plot, that she "withdraws affect."[48] It is rather that something more is demanded: Austen *produces* affect for a different kind of romance. The text is marked not by celibate abstention from a romance plot but by the redirection of energy and affect to a romance of female primogeniture.

If the absence of a marriage ending in *Sanditon* can be ascribed to its incomplete status, Firbank for his part completes *Valmouth* by deliberately interrupting the marriage. The groom fails to turn up for the wedding, because he is most probably otherwise engaged with a passing homosexual interest, and the bride goes off before the ceremony in search of a butterfly that has attracted her attention. The butterfly in *Valmouth* literalizes the "queer taste" in *Sanditon* which consists in that text's perverse drive to avoid any serious truck with the marriage plot. A classical symbol of the ephemerality of mortal life, the butterfly has specifically homosexual resonances of ephemerality as a symbol of recreational, nonreproductive sex and the death of the paternal line. It is in these ways, then, I would suggest, that *Valmouth* works to foreground the decadent, "queer taste" of *Sanditon*, that *Sanditon* is simultaneously received and produced by *Valmouth*, a self-consciously, anachronistically, "Decadent" novella, written at the end of the 1910s. *Valmouth* is a decadent sequela to *Sanditon*, whose "family of helpless Invalides"—male hypochondriacs—are the forebears of the homosexual butterfly.

What Forster identifies as a monstrous departure from the canonical Austen in the "queer taste" or "double-flavoured taste" of "half topography" and "half-romance" is the nonheterosexual romance that cuts at the nexus of property and reproduction and revises their usual standing in the Austen romance. It is the lesbian seaside romance: a fantasy of female primogeniture by the sea without any return to the estate as the rural core of green England—the seaside real estate business is only "half-topography."

*Sanditon*'s Lady Denham offers an elegant lesbian neo-Gothic that anticipates *The Bostonians* (1886), the work of Austen's legitimate son, Henry James, her "lawful issue" and Sedgwick's paradigmatic connoisseur of the closet. This suggests another intertextual confrontation as back-crossing, here between mother and lawful, first son. It suggests, too, this line of inquiry: if the James fiction is paradigmatically queer—or of the closet—what does that say about its mother, the Austen novel? How is Austen as canonical foremother to blame, or to be congratulated? One way of answering this might be to say, along with Mrs. Bennet, that there is no knowing how literary estates will go once they come to be entailed.

## Notes

I would like to thank Judith Barbour, Susan Conley, and Deidre Lynch for their extremely helpful suggestions in the preparation of this essay.

1. E. M. Forster, "Sanditon," in *Abinger Harvest* (1936; Harmondsworth: Penguin, 1967), 169. Subsequent references to this work, hereafter abbreviated as *AH*, will be to this edition and will occur within parentheses in the text.
2. *Memoir of Jane Austen* (1871; Oxford: Clarendon, 1951), 157.
3. Caroline Austen, *My Aunt Jane Austen: A Memoir* (comp. 1872; London: Jane Austen Society, 1952), 13.
4. This term was coined by the British cultural historian Patrick Wright, in *On Living in an Old Country: The National Past in Contemporary Culture* (London: Verso, 1985), 70 ff.
5. Derek Jarman, *Dancing Ledge* (London: Quartet, 1984), 14.
6. See *Britons: Forging the Nation 1707–1837* (New Haven: Yale University Press, 1992), 177.
7. Mandy Merck, "Portrait of a Marriage?" in *Perversions: Deviant Readings* (London: Virago, 1993), 101–20, 112.
8. Terry Castle, "Sister-Sister," *London Review of Books*, 3 August 1995, 6.
9. On inspiration as a pederastic plot, and for terms such as "spiritual procreancy," see Linda Dowling, *Hellenism and Homosexuality in Victorian Oxford* (Ithaca, N.Y.: Cornell University Press, 1994), 83, xv.
10. On the fraught institutional and definitional relations among male homosociality, heterosexuality, and homosexuality in Western culture and English literature, see Eve Kosofsky Sedgwick's *Between Men: English Literature and Male Homosocial Desire* (New York: Columbia University Press, 1985).
11. F. R. Leavis, *The Great Tradition: George Eliot, Henry James, Joseph Conrad* (1948; Harmondsworth: Penguin, 1972), 13, 148.
12. Robert Liddell, *A Treatise on the Novel* (London: Jonathan Cape, 1947), 13, 19.
13. Quoted in *Henry James: The Critical Heritage*, ed. Roger Gard (London: Routledge & Kegan Paul, 1968), 332–33.
14. For James's explicit canon-forming gestures on behalf of Austen and the novel genre, see his 1876 reading of *Daniel Deronda*, which invokes as a model

"the exquisite art of Thackeray and Miss Austen and Hawthorne," or his 1877 inventory of "the leading English novelists," which lists in order: "Miss Austen and Sir Walter Scott, Dickens, Thackeray, Hawthorne and George Eliot." See *Theory of Fiction: Henry James*, ed. James E. Miller (Lincoln: University of Nebraska Press, 1972), 131, 154.

15. See preface to *Roderick Hudson* (1907) and *Notebooks* (1896).

16. James is a ubiquitous presence, for example, in Wayne C. Booth's *The Rhetoric of Fiction* (Chicago: University of Chicago Press, 1961).

17. For Virginia Woolf's reading, see "The Novels of E. M. Forster" (November 1927), in *Collected Essays* (London: Hogarth Press, 1980), 1:344. For other critical breeding fictions that trace a line of descent from Austen to Forster, see Ian Watt, introduction to *Jane Austen: A Collection of Critical Essays* (Englewood Cliffs, N.J.: Prentice Hall, 1963), 9; Malcolm Bradbury, introduction to *Forster: A Collection of Critical Essays* (Englewood Cliffs, N.J.: Prentice Hall, 1966), 2; John Colmer, *E. M. Forster: the Personal Voice* (London: Routledge and Kegan Paul, 1975), 18; Norman Page, "The Great Tradition Revisited," in *Jane Austen's Achievement*, ed. Juliet McMaster (London: Macmillan, 1976), 58 ff.; and, more recently, Shelly Dorsey, "Austen, Forster, and Economics," *Persuasions* 12 (1990): 54–59. Leavis opts for "D. H. Lawrence rather than Jane Austen" in his essay "E. M. Forster," *Scrutiny* 7 (September 1938): 185–202.

18. See Cyril Connolly, notice, *New Statesman* (1928), reprinted in *E. M. Forster: The Critical Heritage*, ed. Philip Gardner (London: Routledge & Kegan Paul, 1973), 340.

19. On Austen's cultural importance between the wars, see Deidre Lynch's magisterial essay, "At Home with Jane Austen," in *Cultural Institutions of the Novel*, ed. Deidre Lynch and William B. Warner (Durham, N.C.: Duke University Press, 1996), 159–92.

20. Tom Nairn, "The English Literary Intelligentsia," in *Bananas*, ed. Emma Tennant (London: Quartet, 1977), 59.

21. "Introduction: Fear of a Queer Planet," *Social Text* 29 (1991): 7.

22. E. M. Forster, interview by P. N. Furbank and F.J.H. Haskell, in *Writers at Work: The "Paris Review" Interviews*, ed. M. Cowley (London: Secker & Warburg, 1958), 32.

23. Henry James, "Gabriele D'Annunzio" (1904), in *Selected Literary Criticism*, ed. Morris Shapira (Harmondsworth: Penguin, 1968), 310.

24. "Hysterics suffer mainly from reminiscences": Sigmund Freud and Josef Breuer, *Studies in Hysteria*, trans. James Strachey, ed. Angela Richards (Harmondsworth: Penguin, 1986), 58. The distinction between criminal and hysteric subjects is formulated in "On Narcissism, an Introduction" (1914), in *The Standard Edition of the Complete Psychological Works of Sigmund Freud*, ed. James Strachey, 24 vols. (London: Hogarth Press, 1953–74), 14:88–89, and "Psycho-analysis and the Establishment of Facts in Legal Proceedings," in *Standard Edition* 9:99–114.

25. On the status of the fragment as a Romantic myth of textual production, see Marjorie Levinson, *The Romantic Fragment Poem: A Critique of Form* (Chapel Hill: University of North Carolina Press, 1986).

26. See the introduction to B. C. Southam's edition of *Sanditon* (Oxford: Clarendon, 1975), reproduced in facsimile from the manuscript in the possession

of King's College, Cambridge, and published in the bicentenary year of Austen's birth, which is a self-conscious response to Forster's iconoclastic "*Sanditon.*"

27. See Richard Ellmann, "Henry James among the Aesthetes," *a long the riverrun: Selected Essays* (London: Hamish Hamilton, 1988), 132–50.

28. *Epistemology of the Closet* (Berkeley and Los Angeles: University of California Press, 1990), 248. As Sedgwick suggests, "[i]f this topos hasn't been a feature of gay male criticism and theory, as it richly has of literary production, that is for an all too persuasive reason: the reinforcement it might seem to offer to unthinking linkages between (homo)sexuality and (feminine) gender, and its apparent high congruence with the homophobic insistence . . . that mothers are to be 'blamed' for—always unknowingly—causing their sons' homosexuality" (249).

29. James, *The Question of Our Speech* (1905; New York: Haskell House, 1972), 63.

30. "How he hates naming anything," Forster adds in a footnote. "Extracts from Forster's Commonplace Book," appendix A in *Aspects of the Novel* (London: Edward Arnold, 1927), 169.

31. From *Locked Journal*, 16 June 1911, quoted in Nicola Beauman, *Morgan: A Biography of E. M. Forster* (New York: Alfred Knopf, 1993), 336.

32. See Cyril Connolly, "Corydon in Croydon" (1971), in Gardner, *Critical Heritage*, 459. Norman Page compares Austen and Forster as "two celibate chroniclers of domestic experience in the home counties," in McMaster, *Jane Austen's Achievement*, 58, and Pete Hamill writes in 1965 of Forster as the "prim nanny of the novel" (Gardner, *Critical Heritage*, 425).

33. *Jane Austen's Letters to her Sister Cassandra and Others*, ed. R. W. Chapman (London: Oxford University Press, 1952), 452.

34. To the extent that *Sanditon* forfeits a claim to citation as a "source," as in source studies that authorize borrowing rights from predecessor to successor. For source studies and borrowing rights, see Barbara Johnson, "Les Fleurs du mal arme: Some Reflections on Intertextuality," in *Lyric Poetry: Beyond New Criticism*, ed. Chaviva Hosek and Patricia Parker (Ithaca, N.Y.: Cornell University Press, 1985), 264.

35. On genetic back-crossing, see H. Kalmus, *Genetics* (Harmondsworth: Penguin, 1954), 56.

36. Brigid Brophy, *Prancing Novelist: In Praise of Ronald Firbank* (London: Macmillan, 1973), 479. This text is brimming with examples of intertextual sympathies and revisions between Austen and Firbank.

37. Quoted in ibid., 102.

38. Degenerative evolution is the subject of the fin de siècle scientific text Jean Demoor et al., *Evolution by Atrophy in Biology and Sociology*, trans. Mrs. Chalmers Mitchell (London: Kegan Paul, 1899).

39. Ronald Firbank, *Valmouth* (1919), *The Complete Firbank* (London: Picador, 1988), 396. All subsequent references to this work, hereafter abbreviated as *V*, will be to this edition and will occur within parentheses in the text.

40. Ronald Paulson, *Breaking and Remaking: Aesthetic Practice in England, 1700–1820* (New Brunswick, N.J.: Rutgers University Press, 1989), 5.

41. I am referring here to the canonical reading of the didactic Austen, which Eve Kosofsky Sedgwick has referred to as the "Girl Being Taught a Lesson" school

of Austen criticism. See her brilliant essay, "Jane Austen and the Masturbating Girl," *Critical Inquiry* 17 (1991): 833.

42. Austen-Leigh, *Memoir*, 195.

43. B. C. Southam, *Jane Austen's Literary Manuscripts: A Study of the Novelist's Development through the Surviving Papers* (London: Oxford University Press, 1964), 119.

44. "Sister-Sister," review of *Jane Austen's Letters*, ed. Deirdre Le Faye, *London Review of Books*, 3 August 1995, 6; for Southam's letter, see *LRB*, 7 September 1995, 4. Terry Castle had already replied to a barrage of letters in response to her review in a letter of her own, *LRB*, 24 August 1995, where she claims that "[n]owhere in my essay did I state that Jane Austen was a lesbian [but that the relationship with her sister] had its unconscious homoerotic dimensions" (4), and asserts, "Surely literary critics writing in the *London Review* are still allowed to speculate about such things" (4).

45. B. C. Southam, "*Sanditon*: the Seventh Novel," in McMaster, *Jane Austen's Achievement*, 8–9.

46. Camille Paglia suggests that the power struggle between a rich lesbian and an egotistical ladies' man for a feminine girl in *The Bostonians* comes from *The Girl with the Golden Eyes* (see *Sexual Personae: Art and Decadence from Nefertiti to Emily Dickinson* [New Haven: Yale University Press, 1990], 610); but it also comes from *Sanditon*, in the competition between Sir Edward and Lady Denham for Clara Brereton, and between Clara and Sir Edward for Lady Denham's money.

47. Austen-Leigh, *Memoir*, 195.

48. "The Late Jane Austen," *Raritan* 10 (1990): 77–78.

# 6

## The Virago Jane Austen

KATIE TRUMPENER

*In Memory of Carol Kay (1947–1998)*

> An invitation to give the Peter le Neve Foster lecture on *Women Writers* to the Royal Society of Arts . . . I felt pleased, & competent. Agnes Paston, saying in vehement Norfolk What about ME? sprang into my mind. Other emergences were Murasaki & Mme de la Fayette; question of why women aren't composers germane. Sévigné, Court society servile, at best pug's parlour. Jane Austen & Flaubert. *J'attends le coit de ces beaux volatiles.* J.A. under no such compulsion. Her simple theme. Boy meets girl. Girl gets Boy. George Sand. George Eliot. Odd that she should have been taken as a man—except that at that date so many male writers could have been taken as old women—but AM I SURE?
>
> Mrs. Radclyffe [*sic*], Mrs Browning, Ctina Rossetti. Colette. Virginia Woolf.
>
> Womanly qualities: nice calculation, neat stitches, industry. But also a particular freedom and intensity. . . .
>
> N.B. Should I—yes, I must—read Selma Lagerlov [sic]?. . .
>
> We jointly cleaned the refrigerator.
>
> *(Sylvia Townsend Warner, Diary entry, 5 September 1958)*[1]

### The Great Jane Austen of Mythology

In Elizabeth Taylor's *A Game of Hide and Seek* (1951), Harriet Claridge is painfully in love with Vesey Macmillan. Their mothers are old friends, militant suffragettes who endured prison and hunger strikes together. In contrast, Harriet's own life feels hapless and indecisive. Vesey, too, is so evasive and elusive that Harriet eventually marries Charles Jephcott instead. Fifteen years later, Vesey turns up again and lures Harriet to the brink of an affair. Harriet and Charles find themselves newly uncertain of one another.

> Down in the drawing-room, Charles and Harriet sat without speaking. The wireless usefully filled the gap. Charles read *Persuasion*—his favourite book, to which Harriet imagined he resorted when wounded. . . .
>
> At irregular intervals, he turned pages; once or twice he glanced at the fire, but never at his wife. Harriet sat very still, and wary. . . . When Charles turned a page, her eyelids lowered, her mouth tightened. She wondered if he were reading the chapter on women's constancy; for the book became a reproach all by itself.
>
> "What a novel to choose!" Charles thought. "Only the happy in love should ever read it. It is unbearable to have expression given to our painful solitariness, to rake up the dead leaves in our hearts, when *we* have nothing that can follow (no heaven dawning beautifully in Union Street), except in dreams, as perhaps Jane Austen herself never had but on the page she wrote."
>
> "What is wrong, Charles?" Harriet suddenly asked. She felt that he would never speak; that he would punish her for years and years, in silence. "What are you thinking about?"
>
> He snapped the book together in one hand as if shutting her out from his experience there.[2]

Charles tries to block out the worries of the present by taking refuge in silent reading, and in the apparently ordered world of a familiar Austen novel. Instead the book intensifies the couple's sense of estrangement, evoking meditations terrifying in their fear and sadness. Taylor's own novel subtly mirrors *Persuasion*'s famous autumnal mood, plot of love belatedly revived, and reflections on lost youth. For Taylor, and for other twentieth-century women novelists, Austen's influence pervades both the consciousness and the deep structure of their writing.[3] They are in particular preoccupied with the "darker" Jane Austen of *Mansfield Park* and *Persuasion*, responding as much to the sense those novels display of narrowly averted social tragedy as to their interest in female agency.[4]

As *A Game of Hide and Seek* dramatizes, these novelists write in the wake, and sometimes in the shadow, of the militant feminism of the suffrage movement, and this too shapes the form of their novels, their mandate as writers, and their relationship to Austen. In the 1890s, Charlotte Yonge and George Saintsbury had pointed to Austen to argue for the superiority of traditional womanly values over new, belligerent feminist demands.[5] For all her independence of spirit, Saintsbury insisted, Elizabeth Bennet has "nothing offensive, nothing *viraginous*, nothing for the 'New Woman' about her"—and neither, implicitly, did Austen herself.[6] The New Woman in H. G. Wells's *Ann Veronica* (1909), however, develops an increasingly complex view of Austen as she realizes the difficulty of female emancipation. Leaving home, she borrows money from an older man to pursue a college degree in biology; the man initially presents himself as her "friend" and benefactor but eventually tries to rape her, with the justification that he is already "keeping" her. Ann Veronica is appalled but also ashamed of her own naïveté.

> "This is what comes of being a young woman up to date. By Jove! I'm beginning to have my doubts about freedom! . . . The young women of Jane Austen's time didn't get into this sort of scrape! At least—one thinks so . . . I wonder if some of them did—and it didn't get reported. Aunt Jane had her quiet moments. Most of them didn't, anyhow. They were properly brought up, and sat still and straight, and took the luck fate brought them as gentlewomen should. And they had an idea of what men were like behind all their nicety. They knew they were all Bogey in disguise. I didn't! I didn't! . . ."
>
> For a time her mind ran on daintiness and its defensive restraints as though it was the one desirable thing. That world of fine printed cambrics and escorted maidens, of delicate secondary meanings and refined allusiveness, presented itself to her imagination with the brightness of a lost paradise, as indeed for many women it is a lost paradise.
>
> ". . . If I had been quite quiet and white and dignified, wouldn't it have been different? Would he have dared? . . ."
>
> For some creditable moments in her life Ann Veronica was utterly disgusted with herself; she was wrung with a passionate and belated desire to move gently, to speak softly and ambiguously—to be, in effect, prim.

But her struggles for emancipation and meditations on Austen do not end here. She joins the militant suffrage movement, storms the House of Commons, insists on being arrested, and learns that life in prison is foul and lonely. Irritated by her fellow suffragists, she falls into "a phase of violent reaction against the suffrage movement." Her own "wild raid for independence," she decides, was self-centered, "Pride and Pride and Pride." In her cell, she finds self-knowledge and repentence, like Elizabeth Bennet and Emma Woodhouse before her—and therefore thinks about Austen again. " 'You've got to be a decent citizen. . . . The wrappered life—discipline! One comes to that at last. I begin to understand Jane Austen and chintz covers and decency and refinement and all the rest of it. One puts gloves on one's greedy fingers.' "[7] During her earlier crisis, Ann Veronica, like Yonge and Saintsbury before her, looked to Austen for a protective decorum, a historical retreat. Now, instead, Austen embodies a self-imposed moral code, a personal ethic that ought to underlie political action. By the end of the book, Ann Veronica has run away with a married man, an act that to Austen would have seemed irresponsible and immoral, worthy only of a Lydia Bennet. Yet she acts from deep inward conviction, and eventually the world comes around.

A modern feminist who follows Austen, then, need not end up prim. Austen was championed by suffrage leaders like Millicent Fawcett.[8] Rebecca West, too, found Austen "very marked" and "quite conscious" in her feminism, especially in her analysis of "the institutions of society regarding women."[9] To W. H. Auden, Austen was an icy materialist, if "not an unshockable blue-stocking."

> You could not shock her more than she shocks me:
> Beside her Joyce seems innocent as grass.
> It makes me most uncomfortable to see
> An English spinster of the middle class
> Describe the amorous effect of "brass,"
> Reveal so frankly and with such sobriety
> The economic basis of society.[10]

For Elizabeth Bowen, Austen is interested not only in social dynamics but in more fundamental, unsettling issues of power. At "the heart of the mannered Regency," Austen creates "a muted Elizabethan world of her own. On the polite plane, violence has its equivalent."[11]

Throughout the nineteenth century, Austen's delineation of social life in Highbury and Meryton (and the work of Mary Mitford, John Galt, and Elizabeth Gaskell) inspired annalistic novels and novel cycles, alternately satirical and nostalgic, about village or suburban communities.[12] Some meditated critically on the nature of local attachments and historical change.[13] Others were more straightforwardly traditionalist and isolationist. By the early twentieth century, Austen was generally read as a complacent, if witty, conservative, a miniaturist who "liked everything to be tidy and pleasant and comfortable about her."[14] As Deidre Lynch has argued, this view of Austen shaped a snug, smug mode of depicting domestic life in "Little England."[15]

Yet an important counterreception read her as a hardheaded realist. "I have often thought of writing an article on the coarseness of J.A.," writes Virginia Woolf. "The people who talk of her as if she were a niminy piminy spinster always annoy me. But I suppose I should annoy them."[16] Neither quaint nor comfortable, Woolf's Austen is "a limited, tart, rather conventional woman for all her genius," yet so severely "impersonal" in her satire that she "remains for ever . . . inscrutable."[17] In "Jane Austen Practising" (1922), Woolf evokes Austen's "accumulating" reputation over the "past ten or twenty years" as "stifling" layers of "quilts and blankets" that need throwing off. Turning the novelist into "the great Jane Austen of mythology," the Janeites have piled "up the quilts and counterpanes until the comfort becomes oppressive." Luckily, Austen's own work demystifies itself; already her juvenilia echo with "penetrating laughter."[18]

West too called for an end to "this comic patronage of Jane Austen"—to the view that she is "limited in range," ignorant of passion, or lacking in a "sense of the fundamental things of life." For West, Austen exemplifies her Enlightenment moment. Her "determination not to be confused by emotion, and to examine each phenomenon of the day briskly and on its merits, was never a sign of limitation. It is a sign that she lived in the same world as Hume and Gibbon." Yet Austen is also capable of deep feeling; her novels reflect long personal experience of loneliness and despair. Behind *Sense and Sensibility* is "a face graven with weeping." And "through the lattice-work of her neat sentences, joined together with the bright nails of craftsmanship, painted with the gay varnish of wit . . . you will see women haggard with desire or triumphant with love, whose delicate reactions to men make the heroines of all our later novelists seem merely to turn signs, 'Stop' or 'Go' toward the advancing male."[19] In an earlier essay of the mid-1920s, on the other hand, West reads Austen against Ivan Pavlov's *Conditioned Reflexes*; Austen's approach to human behavior is experimental and protomodernist.[20] For West, Austen's power as a social chronicler derives at once from her attention to the inculcation of conditioned, "automatic" social responses and from her psychologically differentiated studies of romantic longing and sexual sublimation, as forces that both challenge and bow to convention.

Over the last twenty-five years, scholars have continued to debate Austen's relationship to the feminist controversies (as to other social movements) of her time. At the same time, and in parallel to these scholarly controversies and reconstructions, the reprinting program of Virago Modern Classics has implicitly argued for an earlier, powerfully feminist reappraisal of Austen, in the body of modern and modernist fiction written by women.[21]

The Virago Modern Classics, this essay will argue, actually contain a double reception of Austen. The novels and critical essays of key "Virago" novelists suggest a complex engagement with Austen's legacy, as with the question of a female literary tradition. So too, over the last two decades, as they have worked to spark public interest in forgotten female modernists, the Virago editors (and the contemporary women critics and novelists commissioned to write introductions to individual reprints) also worked implicitly to establish Austen as the mother of "their" viragos. The Virago novelists and the Virago editors, this essay suggests, evoke Austen—and pose the larger question of a female literary tradition—in subtly different terms. Its own effort is to juxtapose and counterpoint these two discussions. Thus it reexamines Sheila Kaye-Smith and G. B. Stern's *Talking of Jane Austen* (1944), for instance, in light both of the authors' own novelistic oeuvres (partially reprinted by Virago) and of Edmund Wilson's reaction to their readings. At the same time, it offers sustained readings of E. M. Delafield's *The Optimist* (1922) and F. M. Mayor's *The Rector's Daughter* (1924), two closely related novels that offer modern rewritings of and modern commentaries on *Mansfield Park* and *Persuasion*.

In the 1890s, the reissue of Austen's novels attracted many new readers and catalyzed a new wave of interest in her work.[22] The resurrection of feminist literary culture at the same time created an equally important shift in the way that Austen was read and understood. Women writers of the period, to be sure, disagree about the nature and significance of Austen's legacy, as about her relationship to the social order she describes. For some, Austen works to uphold the social, moral, and sexual codes of her age, and her position is incompatible with the modern struggle for gender equality and sexual emancipation. Yet for others, Austen remains exemplary—and emancipatory—both as a stylist and as a moralist. To them, Austen's politics are clearest in the brief but powerful moments in which she evokes the social and economic plight of women, chronicling the sufferings of impoverished widows and poor dependents, honoring the forbearance of the maiden aunt, or linking the labors of governesses to the sufferings of the slave trade. And she shows later women novelists how to forge a new style, subject matter, and ethical position for themselves.

## Virago Modern Classics and the Problem of a Women's Literary Tradition

At the beginning of Angela Carter's *Several Perceptions* (1968), a self-styled "barbarian" and dropout singles out *Mansfield Park* (and the Gospel of John) to set alight in the university library. His act expresses hostility both toward his girlfriend (an English literature student who composes "endless essays concerning Jane Austen's moral universe") and also toward Austen's putatively small-minded, coercive moral world.[23]

Less than a decade after such attacks on Austen and on the canon, feminists began trying to reconstitute new, female countercanons, often recentered on Austen. In 1978, Virago Press began publishing its Virago Modern Classics reprint series. Still ongoing, the series presently numbers over three hundred titles (most late nineteenth and early twentieth century novels written by British women); its financial and critical success has galvanized many other "canon-breaking" reprint efforts, feminist and otherwise. In tracing the lineages of contemporary feminist writing, the series has revolutionized scholarly understanding of modern British fiction and society. Read together, the Modern Classics raise fascinating questions about the reach and breadth of modernism. "Classic" modernist techniques and preoccupations flourish in women's writing until after World War II; they touch works, furthermore, whose primary sensibility remains realist rather than avant-garde. If the series involves an ongoing search for formal innovation among women novelists, its other aim (according to the publishers' statement printed on the last page of most volumes) is "to demonstrate the existence of a female tradition in fiction which is both enriching and enjoyable. The Leavisite notion of the 'Great Tradition,' and the narrow, academic definition of a 'classic,' has meant the neglect of a large number of interesting secondary works of fiction."

Both in its discoveries of a distinctly female modernism and in its attempts to "demonstrate a female tradition in fiction," the Virago Modern Classics show the implicit influence of Woolf, pathbreaking both in the stylistic innovations of her novels and in the cumulative attempt of her essays and fiction to rethink the place of earlier women writers. In *A Room of One's Own* (1928), famously, Woolf confronts the question of the relationship between "women and fiction" by rehearsing—and discarding—the obvious response: "a few remarks about Fanny Burney; a few more about Jane Austen; a tribute to the Brontës and a sketch of Haworth Parsonage under snow; some witticisms if possible about Miss Mitford; a respectful allusion to George Eliot; a reference to Mrs. Gaskell and one would have done."[24] Instead, Woolf describes the material conditions and economic autonomy necessary for the development of women's writing, while tracing lines of filiation from early modern women diarists, playwrights, and poets, through eighteenth-century female novelists, to "the four famous names"(67). Without their female forerunners, Austen, the Brontës, and Eliot

> could no more have written than Shakespeare could have written without Marlowe, or Marlowe without Chaucer. . . . For masterpieces are not single and solitary births; they are the outcome of many years of thinking in common, of thinking by the body of the people, so that the experience of the mass is behind the single voice. Jane Austen should have laid a wreath upon the grave of Fanny Burney, and George Eliot done homage to the robust shade of Eliza Carter—the valiant old woman who tied a bell to her bedstead in order that she might wake early and learn Greek. (66)

What is possible aesthetically for any particular (woman) writer depends at once on the preconditions created by her tradition, the lineage of the women authors who come before—and on her own personal socioeconomic circumstances. As her readers had known since the publication of J. E. Austen-Leigh's *Memoir* in 1870, Austen lacked a room of her own to write in; forced instead to write in the sitting room, she listened for the creaking door that signaled the approach of visitors, a "piece of blotting paper" (67) poised to conceal her manuscript. So would *Pride and Prejudice* "have been a better novel if Jane Austen had not thought it necessary to hide her manuscript from visitors?" (68). No, Woolf decides. Austen presents an almost unique case among women writers; her works manifest an innate fearlessness and sense of freedom, despite the "narrowness" (68) of her circumstances and the social constraints on gentlewomen, despite the fact that she "never travelled . . . never drove through London in an omnibus or had luncheon in a shop by herself"(69).

Austen hovers as a central—perhaps *the* central—figure in Woolf's account. Yet her oeuvre calls into question Woolf's tenets about literary history. Clearly indebted to the female novel writing that has gone before her, Austen will herself become a standard by which twentieth-century women writers measure themselves. At the same time, Austen's most important legacy to the writers of posterity is her sense of artistic autonomy, her ability to turn to advantage the underdeveloped state of the women's literary tradition, her triumph in shaping a distinctive style. Where other nineteenth-century women writers struggled to adapt male prose style, she "laughed at it and devised a perfectly natural, shapely sentence proper for her own use and never departed from it" (77). So too in Woolf's own day, women writers inspired by Austen's example "broke" (81) her sentence and style to find their own means of expression, and found their own forms of modernism. For Woolf, Austen stands both in the midst and outside of an extended (if fragmentary) tradition of women's literature. Austen depends on, yet plays with, and breaks with, that tradition. Her legacy lies both in the influence of her style and subject, and in the courage of her iconoclastic example; her descendants, in turn, both learn from and break with her.

Fifty years later Austen (along with, to a lesser degree, the Brontës and Eliot) remains central to the way Virago editors reconstruct the modern female literary tradition.[25] Yet their invocation of Austen tends to be less dialectical, more instrumental, and more affirmative than Woolf's, just as their view of literary history tends to be less erudite, more foreshortened, and more catholic. Woolf presents Austen as a paradoxical yet pivotal figure for a female tradition. The Virago editors use Austen rather as a fixed point of orientation, as they work to construct a new map of literary history. Indeed, although they explicitly envision the Modern Classics as a counterweight to F. R. Leavis's narrow canon of British writers who form "the great tradition," their use of Austen inadvertently bears a strong resemblance to Leavis's own.[26]

"Jane Austen is one of the truly great writers, and herself a major fact in the background of other great writers," argues Leavis in *The Great Tradition*. Despite her own "indebtedness to others," she provides

> an exceptionally illuminating study of the nature of originality, and she exemplifies beautifully the relations of "the individual talent" to tradition. . . . She not only makes tradition for those coming after, but her achievement has for us a retroactive effect: as we look back beyond her we see in what goes before, and see because of her, potentialities and significances brought out in such a way

> that, for us, she creates the tradition we see leading down to her. . . . Jane Austen, in fact, is the inaugurator of the great tradition of the English novel.[27]

So too in the introductions and afterwords of the Virago Modern Classics, Austen appears consistently as a figure who gives coherence to a tradition. Looming as a "major fact in the background of other writers," she apparently defines their relationship to their literary legacy, influencing their style, characterization, plotting, and worldview. Elizabeth Taylor "loved and revered" Austen and, like her, "confined herself to writing in a relatively enclosed scene," animated by rounded characters.[28] Ada Leverson's satirical novel trilogy *The Little Ottleys* (1908–16) is "unmistakably descended from Jane Austen," with an admixture of Oscar Wilde.[29] E. H. Young's *Jenny Wren* (1932) and *The Curate's Wife* (1934) follow *Sense and Sensibility* in counterpointing the sentimental educations of two sisters.[30] Mrs. Humphry Ward's *Marcella* (1894) includes characters modeled on those of *Mansfield Park* and *Emma*; Jane and Mary Findlater's *Crossriggs* (1908) consciously follows *Emma* in its characterization and plot, despite substantial differences between the Findlaters' Scotland and Austen's Hampshire.[31]

At times, the claim of Austen's influence is proffered as a marketing device. The cover blurb for *The Semi-Attached Couple and The Semi-Detached House* (1859–60) bills Emily Eden as a "true if minor successor of Jane Austen."[32] The introduction to Harriet Martineau's *Deerbrook* (1839) cites a contemporary review comparing it to Austen and situates its publication "at a rather bleak time in women's fiction, in the period between Jane Austen and the eruption of the brilliant writing of the Brontës and George Eliot."[33] Again, the back-cover blurb reproduces this point in simplified form, promising the reader entry into "the world of Jane Austen and the Brontës." Other critics offer more intricate meditations on Austen's legacy. Bel Mooney's afterword to Young's *Chatterton Square* (1947) evokes Austen's "miniaturism" not to praise her technique but to evoke the complexity and tragic undertones of her social vision. "Beneath the small strokes of delicate brush-work, and underpinning E. H. Young's stories of West Country provincial life, are the perennial darker issues which flow also through Jane Austen's drawing rooms: the threat of war, deceit, the inevitability of loss, human disappointment, blindness and misery."[34] Jane Marcus's introduction to West's *The Judge* (1922) echoes *A Room of One's Own*; galvanized by the renewed, public struggle for women's rights, female modernists introduce a new political urgency into the tradition of socially critical writing by women.

> The seventeen-year-old suffragette is the natural daughter of the English nineteenth century novel as it was shaped by women's hands. Jane Austen, George Eliot and Charlotte Brontë would recognise in her their own heroines, pitched

> headlong into history. . . . Those who have wished Jane Austen at Waterloo or Charlotte Brontë out of Haworth Parsonage find their literary daughter, Rebecca West, on the barricades.[35]

Mooney's Young reclaims Austen for modern life by highlighting her pessimistic undertones. Marcus's West updates Austen—and Eliot and Brontë—by giving her heroine a heightened, distinctly twentieth-century sense of historical agency.

## The Spinster in the Parlor

When Sylvia Townsend Warner meditates on the famous women writers of history, she associates them both with "a particular freedom and intensity" and with the cleaning of the refrigerator, domestic industry at its most mundane. Likewise, when the Virago novelists consider the Austen legacy and the female tradition she is seen to anchor, they are preoccupied both with the agency she allows her characters and with the way Austen's own experience—immersion in family life; domestic routine; spinsterhood—darkened or limited her worldview.

To some novelists, indeed, Austen's world is not only circumscribed but potentially entrapping for her readers. The male narrator of Margaret Kennedy's elliptical Regency novel *Troy Chimneys* (1953) tries to persuade the heroine to admire "my favorites: *Emma* and *Mansfield Park.*" Such novels, she retorts,

> kept her continually in the parlour, where she was obliged, in any case, to spend her life. A most entertaining parlour, she allowed, but:
>
> "That lady's greatest admirer will always be men, I believe. For, when they have had enough of the parlour, they may walk out, you know, and we cannot."[36]

In 1950, Kennedy published a short Austen biography. Yet her own novel is modeled rather on Henry Mackenzie's *The Man of Feeling* (1771) and James Hogg's *Confessions of a Justified Sinner* (1824), with their virtuoso play of narrative voice. Austen, in contrast, is associated with a women's novel of manners whose constricted sense of locale circumscribes consciousness.

So too, for the semiautobiographical narrator of Catherine Carswell's *The Camomile* (1922), Austen—and that "eternal trio" of Austen, the Brontës, and Eliot—represents a mode of literature divorced from life's more expansive possibilities.

> Except for a few nice little poems thrown off at intervals, or stories for children . . . or letters like Madame de Sévigné's, is there any womanly sphere in literature? There's the eternal trio of course—Jane Austen, the Brontës, and George

> Eliot (the last I don't really like, though I think she was a writer and had to write or be annulled as a human being). But I admit that for me, when I'm reading anything serious, to know that the author is a woman who sat in her petticoat and her hairpins, leaving life aside to put words on paper, puts me off like anything.[37]

If contemporary readers were fascinated by Austen writing in the sitting room, Carswell resists this claustrophobic image of the writer's life. Friend of D. H. Lawrence and biographer of Robert Burns—writers who refused conventional sexual morality—Carswell wrote two novels describing women's parallel struggles for social, aesthetic, and sexual freedom. The manifesto-like title of the first, *Open the Door!* (1920), might be read as exhorting the reader to take flight not only from Nora's Doll's House but from Austen's parlor.[38]

In diary entries of the 1930s and 1940s, Antonia White associates the female literary tradition—Austen, the Brontës, Eliot—with the subordination of women, and with sexual repression as much as with emancipation.

> Nov. 30, 1937. . . . And it is very clear that a great part of my unconscious preoccupation is with the idea of myself as a mutilated man. . . . Also in serious work, the idea that to be an artist involves suppression of sexual life. Not borne out in fact by male artists. In women you might make out a case for it, narrowing it down to writers. Jane Austen and the Brontes. I *suppose* George Eliot had a sexual life; Georges [*sic*] Sand certainly did. Interesting all these except Jane Austen took men's names. Jane Austen the only one that wrote *as a woman* . . and was the most perfect *artist*, though by no means the most moving or profound writer. But *she* writes as an *unmarried woman*—the sharpness of the girl, or the wistfulness or shrewishness of the spinster. She makes marriage the climax of all her heroines' careers and I can think of no married couple in her works that she does not gibe at. To fail to get married is to be disastrously humiliated; yet marriage itself is ludicrous. . . .[39]

Excluded from the married state, Austen can view it with a quizzical, if wistful eye. Yet she continues to present marriage as the goal of women's lives. Male writers criticize social constraints in light of their own sexual or intellectual liberation. Austen's work, in contrast, reinforces the gender and class conventions of her moment even as it satirizes them. Austen, White decides, is thus far less appealing than George Eliot, with her Shakespearean "richness and sweep and depth," her "rich maternal feeling" and her "tremendous staying power." Although she may lack Austen's "exquisite surface" (and the "fiery poetry of Emily Brontë"), Eliot remains titanic. In her attempts at sexual emancipation and freethinking, she is self-made, modern, a contemporary in a way that Austen is not. "I could have got on with her," White concludes, "as I probably could *not* have got on with the Brontes or Austen."[40] For West, Austen was an Enlightenment rationalist, working to emancipate herself intellectually in her novels, through a minute observation of contemporary social mores. For White, writing as a post-Freudian and an advocate of sexual emancipation, Austen seems a product as much as a chronicler of her age, and this is a major limitation.[41]

Sheila Kaye-Smith and G. B. Stern's contrapuntal Austen collection, *Talking of Jane Austen* (1944), argues a middle ground. Austen's novels powerfully evoke and carefully analyze their historical moment. Paradoxically, this historical fidelity allows modern readers to experience the novels as a singular world running parallel to theirs and thus to feel suspended, in reading, from their own time. As both writers acknowledge, this is potentially escapist—but it can also be therapeutic. Kaye-Smith, she tells us, discovered Austen when her own early fiction was not yet attracting critical attention; her time with Austen, and in Austen's time, helped her to suspend her anxieties about posterity. Stern's preoccupation with Austen began while she was trying to ward off a nervous breakdown during the bleakest days of World War I. Writing now during World War II, Stern praises Austen as a continuing haven of sanity in a world of darkness.[42]

As Virago reprints of their novels make clear, Kaye-Smith and Stern are ambitious, often fascinating writers in their own right. Stern's major work is a five-novel Galsworthian chronicle of a Jewish family in London, ruled by a matriarchal succession.[43] Kaye-Smith's best novels explore the rural settings and social issues associated with Eliot, Thomas Hardy, and Mary Webb. Set in mid-nineteenth-century Sussex, *The History of Susan Spray, the Female Preacher* (1931), for instance, chronicles an obscure millenarian sect based on the visions of a farm laborer, bolstered by the rural penury created by the Corn Laws, and eroded by an ambitious female preacher, who finds literary expression in (semifraudulent) biblical visions.[44]

If Stern and Kaye-Smith write novels strikingly unlike Austen's, their respective readings of her reflect their own strengths as writers. Stern is concerned primarily with characterization and kinship (minor characters, marriages in *Mansfield Park*), as with Austen as a chronicler of social forms: the education of women, the walk and the dance as courtship rituals, letter writing as a social practice. Kaye-Smith theorizes such concerns, intrigued by Austen's refusal to incorporate into her novels the world-historical events or even the routine social violence of her day. To Kaye-Smith she seems

> more reticent on "such odious subjects" than almost any other writer of her period—Lydia's news in *Pride and Prejudice* that "a private has been flogged"

> is almost the only reference . . . to the more brutal aspects of eighteenth-century life—which may be one reason why Jane Austen's novels appear so modern in comparison to those of Smollett, for instance, or Fielding, which are definitely dated by their violence. Who would guess while listening to the humane and enlightened talk of Captain Wentworth and Captain Harville . . . that the crews of their ships were sometimes partly, sometimes mainly, recruited by the cudgels of the Press Gang? Who would gather from the harmless sporting activities at Uppercross or Netherfield that poachers caught on those estates were probably transported for life?[45]

Her novels reflect a deeply ingrained sense of female proprieties. Yet Austen remains a painstaking social historian of her own moment, whose illumination of mores, class, and economic structure anticipate Victorian realists like Eliot. If Austen presents herself as a miniaturist, Kaye-Smith imagines her as an "etcher," with an acid that "bites sharply into its medium."[46] Even Austen's much-vaunted style is not, to Kaye-Smith's ear, a mannered one; emphatically post-Augustan and anti-Johnsonian, it works to capture the grammatical roughness and slanginess of colloquial speech.

In his *New Yorker* review essay "A Long Talk about Jane Austen" (1944), Edmund Wilson praises Kaye-Smith for her sensitivity to Austen's historicity. Yet he criticizes *Talking of Jane Austen* for its tendency to read the Austenian oeuvre out of time, by treating the novels as coexisting, interlocking fictions rather than as the traces of Austen's own developmental history. He also faults the book's lack of attention to aesthetic questions, its failure to consider Austen's achievement (virtually unique, he believes, among women authors) in shaping social observations *into* works of art.

Over the course of his essay, Wilson's initial acknowledgment of Stern and Kaye-Smith as "two of Jane Austen's sister novelists" gives way to cruder generalizations about women writers, including "the two ladies" under review. *Talking of Jane Austen* explores the authors' unease with the anomalous gender politics, Evangelical moralism, and prim tone of *Mansfield Park*, as with the problem of Fanny as a "creep-mouse." Wilson finds "this line of criticism in regard to *Mansfield Park*" so familiar as to be tedious; it "seems to represent a reaction which is invariable with feminine readers." He remembers his own initial reaction to the novel, in contrast, as "purely aesthetic" and completely positive, appreciative of the novel's formal perfection, "balance and harmony." Regarding Austen's heroines, he concludes, there may be a recurring difference in "the point of view of men readers" and that of "women ones." "The woman reader wants to identify herself with the heroine, and she rebels at the idea of being Fanny. The male reader neither puts himself in Fanny's place nor imagines himself marrying Fanny"; he remains free to concentrate instead on Austen's artistic technique. And Austen herself sides with the male reader.

> Whatever tone Jane Austen may sometimes take, what emerges and gives the book its value are characters objectively seen, form and movement conceived aesthetically. It is this that sets Jane Austen apart from so many other women novelists—whether, like the author of *Wuthering Heights* or the author of *Gone With the Wind*, of the kind that make their power felt by a projection of their feminine day-dreams, or of the kind, from *Evelina* to *Gentlemen Prefer Blondes*, that amuse us by mimicking people. Miss Austen is almost unique among the novelists of her sex in being deeply and steadily concerned, not with the vicarious satisfaction of emotion . . . nor with the skillful exploitation of gossip, but, as the great masculine novelists are, with the novel as a work of art.[47]

Women modernists remained preoccupied with the variety and discontinuity of a female tradition in literature, as with the question of how to build on the tradition of psychological analysis and formal innovation represented by female forerunners from Mme. de Lafayette to Emily Brontë. Wilson, in contrast, insistently conflates established "classic" novels by women with recent, popular, "trivial" fiction, while recycling characterizations of women's fiction in circulation already in the eighteenth century: that at bottom they are either escapist fantasies or gossip. Only Austen is able to transcend her gender, and nowhere more so than in the novel apparently most obedient to her period's codes of female subservience.

What interests Wilson not at all is why female readers are disturbed by *Mansfield Park*, as they are by Fanny's masochism, and why identification plays so central a role in their own reading experiences, to the exclusion of a "purely aesthetic" response. Women modernists, as we have seen, were interested both in female literary response and in their own identification with female characters and predecessors. White wonders whether her preoccupation with George Eliot as a writer would translate into the realm of social interaction. Were she somehow the contemporary of George Eliot, the Brontës, and Austen, which author would she have conversed with and befriended? In "Tradition and the Individual Talent" (1919), T. S. Eliot famously postulated the coexistence, across time and space, of literary geniuses in dialogue with one another. White reimagines this notion in terms closer to Kaye-Smith and Stern's reading of Austen's novels as all simultaneously present to their readers, *and* in terms of social interaction.[48]

Woolf wonders whether those contemporaries who insist on Austen's gentility are the same people who would disapprove of Woolf herself. At the same time, Woolf is critical of those who lump all women writers together. "Then there's the man," she writes in 1919, "who says I'm Jane Austen (but I'd much rather write about tea parties and snails than be Jane Austen)."[49] She herself is *not* Austen, indeed remains unsure—despite her admiration of Austen's "perfection"—whether she would want to be. Wilson will postulate apparently unbridgeable divides between the question of female identification with Austen and the problem of aesthetic form, as between the question of Austen's social historical acuteness and her status as an artist. Yet for women modernists, Woolf argues, these questions are intimately interrelated.

## Recasting the Roles: *The Optimist* and *The Rector's Daughter*

When E. M. Delafield and F. M. Mayor rewrite *Mansfield Park* and *Persuasion*, their fiction reflects simultaneously on Austen's historicity, her contemporaneity, and her transmutation of personal experience into art. Although now often reread as a novel engaged with the events of its day—the abolition of the slave trade, the French Revolution, political upheaval in the Caribbean—*Mansfield Park* used to be viewed as Austen's most quietist, ahistorical work. Delafield's updating reproduces both the novel's careful distance from and conscious echoes of world events. If Antigua and slavery lurk in the background of *Mansfield Park*, the memory of World War I lurks in the background of Delafield's *The Optimist* (along with a sense of India and Canada as colonial refuges). Here too, any foray from the household into the outside world leaves lingering traces in the characters, whether negative (shell shock) or positive (memories of the front's paradoxical freedom).

The focus of *The Optimist*, nonetheless, remains on an intimate, oppressive, familial microcosm, dominated by an overbearing patriarch. Like Sir Thomas Bertram, Delafield's Canon Morchard fails to understand his children—and the gap widens when Adrian, his spoiled, feckless favorite, insists on acting in amateur theatricals at a neighbor's house. The Canon finally agrees to attend the performance but judges it tasteless, another symptom of the cynical soullessness of the modern world. At the same time, Adrian's participation in the play (and an abortive love affair with a fellow thespian) represent a first break with the pious atmosphere in which he was raised, a break finalized by his callow plan to take orders so as to succeed to a local living, by his "fast," debt-ridden life in London, and by his journalistic work for an atheist newspaper.

As this summary suggests, Adrian is an amalgam of several *Mansfield Park* characters, in equal parts Tom Bertram, Edmund Bertram, and Henry Crawford. Delafield's recasting of Austen's female roles is more complex yet. *The Optimist* treats the three Morchard daughters with more sympathy than *Mansfield Park* does the Bertram sisters. Each of the Morchard women struggles to overcome her own passivity, to escape the suffocating embrace of father and family. Fortified by memories of her brief freedom working at a British Army canteen in France during the Great War, Valeria manages to marry and emigrate to Canada. Emphatically unemotional through most of the novel, Flora responds to mounting family pressures by becoming a religious fanatic, escaping into hysteria, then into a cloistered order. The oldest, Lucilla, has spent her childhood mothering her younger siblings. Under pressure from her father, she agreed to renounce a college education, to serve at home as his housekeeper and amanuensis for his theological magnum opus (doomed never to find a publisher). In early middle age, like Austen's Anne Elliot, Lucilla is full of regret for having allowed herself to be "persuaded" to this sacrifice. Yet she finds consolation in unsentimental realism about her situation, as in moments of principled opposition to her father's sentimental selfishness.

In their meekness and piety, the Canon's daughters refigure key aspects of Fanny Price. Delafield's novel suggests not only the survival but the proliferation of women in Fanny's dependent position: the St. Gwenllian of 1922 contains many more Fanny Prices than the Mansfield Park of 1814. Yet in the novel's most important change from Austen's prototype, Delafield also assigns part of Fanny Price's role to a male character, Owen Quentillian. In Woolf's historical fantasia *Orlando* (1928), the hero changes sex to mark the transition from one epoch and set of gender roles to another. Delafield's recasting of *Mansfield Park* is almost as dramatic in marking the difference between Austen's epoch and the early twentieth century.

An orphan raised with the Canon's children, Owen—like Fanny—functions as an insider-outsider observer of family dynamics and is shaped, into adult life, by his early interactions with the children and their father. He courts Valeria, counsels Flora, and, finally, on the novel's last pages, marries Lucilla, whose compassion has shielded him from his first days with the Morchards. Like his childhood companions, Owen struggles as an adult for a more egalitarian relationship to the Canon. His greatest act of rebellion is the publication of an essay on "The Sanctification of Domestic Tyranny," which extrapolates from his long-standing observations of life at St. Gwenllian to argue that "the parental instinct was only another name for the possessive instinct."[50] Yet as Owen and the Morchards realize when the Canon dies, this patriarch was more than a petty despot. In his limited, problematic way, the Canon was an idealist, determined to believe in a well-ordered world. He dies optimistic, ignoring the virtual collapse of his family, and ignorant of the damage he has done to his children. Unlike Sir Thomas, the Canon is *not* redeemed over the course of the novel, but those around him nonetheless develop a belated, surprised respect for his faith, despite its destructive effects.

In *Mansfield Park*, as feminist readers have long complained, Austen not only analyzes Fanny's meek passivity but presents her as the novel's primary figure of identification. Delafield circumvents this problem. By dividing Fanny's functions among several characters, and by using a male protagonist to articulate the novel's critical view of family life, she both evokes the plight of the downtrodden woman and disengages the reader from her masochism. Fanny is a redemptive figure, her character strengthened over the course of Austen's novel so that she can catalyze repentance in others. Owen is more aloof and analytic, a hardheaded, rationalist "prig." Powerless, even in adult life, to mount direct opposition to the Canon's controlling sentimentality, he nonetheless assists his fellow characters, one by one, to escape their father's grip. Unlike Fanny, then, he is a figure of agency and freedom in a family microcosm that traps the other characters. Because he is able to pass in and out of their world, he is able both to judge it and to help them reshape it. If Orlando had to become a woman in order to register the sensibilities of the modern era, Fanny Price had to become a man to gain full autonomy as a character, to liberate himself (and the women around him) from a suffocating domesticity, and to analyze, through writing, the familial structure of oppression. Although it is more overtly influenced by the feminism of *its* moment than *Mansfield Park* by late-eighteenth-century feminism, *The Optimist* is actually less sanguine about female self-liberation.

The astringent pessimism of *The Optimist* is both part of the novel's homage to Austen and characteristic of Delafield's work. Now remembered, if at all, for her humorous *Diary of a Provincial Lady* (1931), so popular that it spawned three sequels, Delafield is easily mistakenly characterized as a domestic chronicler in the line of Angela Thirkell and Jan Struthers or a comic complainer like Erma Bombeck and Peg Bracken. Yet her early novels are caustic. In *Consequences* (1919), a family's odd girl out is pushed into a convent and then into suicide. In *The Way Things Are* (1927), a woman trapped in the provinces with an absentminded, near-mute husband falls in love with a Londoner but is swept tragically back into domesticity. In *Thank Heavens Fasting* (1932) the debutante-system appears as a lifelong impediment to women's mental and emotional development. Even in *The Provincial Lady in Wartime* (1940), two women caught in the Blitz compare notes about their cripplingly sheltered childhoods, under the old system that forbade well-bred girls to travel alone or dress themselves, mend their own clothing or cook an egg. "We look at one another in the deepest dismay at these revelations of our past incompetences, and I say that it's no wonder the world is in the mess it's in today."[51]

Like other early-twentieth-century women writers, Delafield and Mayor drew at once on Austen and on feminist rhetoric to develop their own critique of female confinement. Some of these novelists return to the Gothic settings of convent and madhouse, or describe literal immurement: in her 1934 *Harriet* (based on a nineteenth-century criminal case), Austen biographer Elizabeth Jenkins describes how Harriet Woodhouse [!], an attractive, slightly retarded heiress, is lured into marriage by an unscrupulous fortune hunter, imprisoned in his house, and literally starved to death.[52] In the quietly devastating life stories chronicled in Mayor's *The Third Miss Symons* (1913), Elizabeth von Arnim's *The Pastor's Wife* (1914), May Sinclair's *Mary Olivier: A Life* (1919) and *The Life and Death of Harriet Frean* (1922), and Radclyffe Hall's *The Unlit Lamp* (1924), women are cowed into remaining at home, forced to tend elderly relatives or husbands, and deprived of an adult, autonomous life.[53] Such works identify the understated, unsentimental thread of tragedy in Austen's work: the fate of Charlotte Lucas, married to a fool to be married at all; the vision of Miss Bates left old, lonely, and impoverished; the frightened attempts of Fanny Price to please rich relatives; the efforts of Anne Elliot to serve her thankless family.

Much of F. M. Mayor's work centers on the spinster, as a figure tragically vulnerable to family pressures, yet capable of an autonomous mental life. Like Cassandra Austen, Mayor remained unmarried after her fiancé died of a sudden illness. And like Cassandra and Jane Austen, she took enormous pleasure in the companionship of her unmarried sister (in Mayor's case, her twin); their shared dissection of the staid social world around them became the basis of her fiction.[54]

Mayor's fiction is haunted by Austen. In "Miss De Mannering of Asham," modern characters are haunted by the ghost of the tragic title character, seduced and abandoned in 1805 by a rake who bears a strong resemblance to Willoughby and Wickham. In "Letters from Manningsfield," an unmarried vicar's daughter describes her life in a small, Highbury-like village. Partway through her correspondence, however, the wry Austenesque descriptions of local color begin to give way, as the letter-writer passes from reporting on the fairies spotted by her father's elderly parishioners to meeting a fairy herself, an encounter with the magical that leaves her deeply, uncharacteristically disenchanted with her lot in life, and with the prospect of eternal spinsterhood. By the final letters, however, she has recovered her usual equilibrium and found unexpected rewards in her acquiescence. Her parents show that they recognize her many sacrifices made for their sake, including an engagement, renounced long ago after her father fell ill. Now, in a macabre gesture, her mother gives her "a little ring as a symbol that I was happily married to her and Father and the village, for better for worse, in sickness and in health, till Death do us part."[55] And then, unexpectedly, as at the end of *Persuasion*, a prospect of ordinary marriage looms. After eighteen years, the heroine's old suitor renews his suit; she is not, after all, forgotten.

Mayor's *Rector's Daughter* is at once a more sustained attempt to update *Persuasion* and a close rewriting of *The Optimist*.[56] Mayor's novel places Austen and Delafield on an equal footing as templates. This represents a new approach to the question of a female literary tradition. The problem of how to absorb the example of one's forebears, without seeming anachronistic, is solved when one draws on contemporaries' reiteration of older prototypes. While taking over much of Delafield's setting, mood, and plot, Mayor also manages to fashion an homage to *Persuasion* out of Delafield's homage to *Mansfield Park*.[57] Mayor's rewriting thus recapitulates part of the developmental trajectory of Austen's own final years as a novelist.

Like Delafield, Mayor focuses her novel on a canon's daughter, who subordinates her own emotional needs to be a nurse to her retarded sister and a companion to her scholarly, self-absorbed, and apparently unappreciative father. "After dinner he brought forth his Cambridge University Calendar, which was to him as the peerage to Sir Walter Eliot": Canon Jocelyn is so preoccupied with academic pedigree that he distances himself from other clergy, even aspiring intellectuals. Mary Jocelyn takes a very different solace "in reading her favourite novels for an hour before dinner, finding in Trollope, Miss Yonge, Miss Austen, and Mrs. Gaskell friends so dear and familiar that they peopled her loneliness."[58] As in *Persuasion*, the selfless daughter devotes too much of her life to a selfish father, while the parent's attempt to regulate his children's lives almost ruins them. To break up his son's romance with Mary's best friend, Canon Jocelyn sends him to Canada, where he eventually marries. But Mary's friend stays true to his memory and grows old musing on her one brush with love.

Mary herself, it first appears, may be rewarded by the happy ending given Anne Elliot. In middle age, she falls in love with a neighboring curate. He realizes that he loves her, but then becomes infatuated with a beautiful, superficial younger woman and marries her instead. Soon disillusioned, the couple separate, and he comes to understand, as he confides to Mary, that he has missed lifelong happiness with her. Mary responds by avoiding him, recognizing the intensity of her own feelings, and forbidding herself a potentially adulterous entanglement, although her renunciation brings her close to madness. Then the curate's wife returns to him, disfigured and ill, and his renewed pity and passion once again eclipse his feelings for Mary.

In this modern-day *Persuasion*, Captain Wentworth marries Louisa Musgrove. It is he, therefore, who must regret his Anne Elliot, only to fall in love with Louisa all over again, after her accident.[59] In consequence, this Anne Elliot remains locked into her role of helpmate and silent sufferer: Mary not only faces the ultimate success of her lover's marriage but takes on the painful, soothing role of his wife's confidante. Eventually this intimacy too fades, and the death of Mary's father leaves her entirely alone. Yet the book does not end tragically. In dying, her father belatedly reveals his love for her; in death, he seems no longer a selfish tyrant but a figure fighting his own emotional isolation. Mary leaves Dedmayne Rectory and spends several happier years before dying herself. Her death, in turn, forces the curate and his wife to realize what they owe her. On the novel's last pages, the curate is overwhelmed by Mary's memory: the very rush of the wind brings back to him her quiet intensity and depth of character.

Even more than *The Optimist*, *The Rector's Daughter* adheres to its Austenian prototype, and nowhere more, paradoxically, than in its refusal of a conventional happy end. *Persuasion* gives "expression to our painful solitariness" but then gives hope that it may someday be assuaged. The Anne Elliots of the world, the reader hopes, will someday find consolation and due recognition; dying unmarried and unlauded, Jane Austen herself belatedly met the acclaim of posterity.[60] On the level of plot, Mayor refuses redemption. Yet her novel is almost hagiographic: Mary finds salvation in moral rectitude, and her memory lives on, ubiquitous as air.

Like *The Optimist*, *The Rector's Daughter* is more pessimistic than Austen about women's fates. Jilted before her lover actually proposed, Mary Jocelyn is denied even Anne Elliot's chance at self-determination. Yet her refusal to be persuaded into adultery represents (in and despite its conventionality) a firmness of moral choice that amounts to real agency. Her story ends not with romantic fulfillment but in a smaller, self-forged content: moral principles upheld, the respect of those she loves, the transformation of her deepest emotions into poetry.

In 1848 and 1850, Charlotte Brontë declared herself unable to see Austen's virtues as a novelist: lacking "sentiment," Austen was merely "shrewd and observant," her fiction "a carefully fenced, high cultivated garden."[61] Exploring the sensibilities raging beneath a repressed surface, Mayor's novel not only champions Austen's social vision but establishes the Brontës' indebtedness to her. Her novel moves from an initial, Austenian account of loneliness in family life to a final, Brontëan evocation of the soul transcending the body. *The Rector's Daughter* traces its lineage from *Persuasion*, via *Agnes Grey* and *Wuthering Heights*.[62] And like Delafield's Lucilla Morchard, Mary Jocelyn is a cleric's daughter in a long literary line that extends from Austen through the Brontës to Mayor herself, as well as a descendant of Anne Elliot and of *her* descendants, Jane Eyre and Lucy Snowe.

Even more than other Virago novels, *The Rector's Daughter* can be read as an homage to the Woolfian notion of a women's literary tradition, and to the particular Jane Austen of the early twentieth century: a spinster who found dignity and autonomy in celibacy yet continued to criticize the role of marriage in determining women's fates; an artist whose personal conventionality did not impede a compassionate moral vision. In forging art out of her own experience of isolation and suffocation, indeed, this Austen showed later women writers how to create transcendence from the quotidian, and how to create an aesthetic of their own.

## Notes

1. Sylvia Townsend Warner, *The Diaries of Sylvia Townsend Warner*, ed. Claire Harmon (London: Virago, 1994), 250; Warner was also the author of *Jane Austen 1775–1817* (London: Longmans, Green and Co., 1951).

2. Elizabeth Taylor, *A Game of Hide and Seek* (1951; reprint, London: Virago, 1986), 155–56; Elizabeth Jane Howard's introduction (v–xi) cites Elizabeth Bowen's sense of the novel as crossing *Persuasion* with *Wuthering Heights.*

3. "I have read Jane Austen so much and with so much enjoyment and admiration," writes Ivy Compton-Burnett, "that I may have absorbed things from her unconsciously." Compton-Burnett and M. Jourdain, "A Conversation," *Orion: A Miscellany* (London: Nicholson and Watson, 1945), 21.

4. Alone, confused, the pregnant heroine of Rosamond Lehmann's *The Weather in the Streets* (1936; reprint, London: Virago, 1981) reads *Mansfield Park* in bed, along with *Villette*, *Vanity Fair*, and *David Copperfield*: "[O]n, on . . . The characters so out of date, so vital, lived in her with a feverish, almost repellently heightened activity and importance, more real for their remoteness" (270). After an abortion, she reads *Pride and Prejudice* as she waits, still alone, to miscarry (293); in its social comedy and happy ending, Austen's early novel only underlines Olivia's isolation, uncertainty, and grief.

5. Southam 1987, 2:66.

6. George Saintsbury, preface to the 1894 Hugh Thomson illustrated edition of *Pride and Prejudice*, reprinted in Southam 1987, 2:218.

7. H. G. Wells, *Ann Veronica* (New York: Doni and Liveright, 1909), 221–22, 263, 267.

8. Southam 1987, 2:39.

9. Rebecca West, "Preface to *Northanger Abbey*" (1932), cited in Southam 1987, 2:297.

10. W. H. Auden, "Letter to Lord Byron" (1936), reprinted in *Collected Poems*, ed. Edward Mendelson (New York: Random House, 1976), 79, lines 105, 113–119. As Southam argues in his introduction to vol. 2 of Southam 1987, nineteenth-century women novelists like Julia Kavanagh, Margaret Oliphant, and Mrs. Humphry Ward also read Austen as an acerbic social critic; John Halperin's "Jane Austen's Nineteenth-Century Critics: Walter Scott to Henry James," in *Jane Austen: Bicentenary Essays*, ed. Halperin (Cambridge: Cambridge University Press, 1975), 3–42, juxtaposes the Austen family's portrayal of "their" Jane as "saintly, gentle . . . harmless" (27) with Kavanagh's remarks on her "cold views of life"

(23), and Oliphant's notes on Austen's "feminine cynicism" and "stinging yet soft-voiced contempt" (28).

11. Elizabeth Bowen, "Jane Austen," in *The English Novelists: A Survey of the Novel by Twenty Contemporary Novelists*, ed. Derek Verschoyle (London: Chatto and Windus, 1936), 100.

12. See, for instance, Anthony Trollope's *Chronicles of Barset* (1855–1867) and Oliphant's *Chronicles of Carlingford* (1863–1876); Oliphant's *Miss Marjoribanks* (1866; reprint, London: Virago, 1988) thus recapitulates the plot of *Emma* in the context of a multiwork series modeled on the Austenian oeuvre as a whole. In the twentieth century, see E. F. Benson's six-volume *Make Way for Lucia* (1920–39), and the chronicles of Angela Thirkell's Barsetshire (1936–59), as of Miss Read's Fairacre (1955– ).

13. See, for instance, Sara Jeanette Duncan's *The Imperialist* (1904; reprint, Toronto: McClelland and Stewart, 1990). Set in a Canadian Highbury, it places the Austenian town chronicle at the center of an economic world system.

14. Stella Gibbons, *Cold Comfort Farm* (1932; reprint, Harmondsworth: Penguin, 1977), 20. Gibbons's twenty-year-old heroine Flora plans to become a novelist in this Austenian vein, after a life of ladylike leisure: she will spend the next thirty years "collecting materials" and then write "a novel as good as *Persuasion*, but with a modern setting, of course."

15. Deidre Lynch, "At Home with Jane Austen," in *Cultural Institutions of the Novel*, ed. Lynch and William B. Warner (Durham, N.C.: Duke University Press, 1996), 159–92. Lynch points to detective novels set in the closed, semifeudal, pleasingly anachronistic world of the country estate or village. Yet such fiction can seem quasi-modernist in its epistemology, as it recasts Austen's interest in social semiotics: Agatha Christie's Miss Marple is a shrewder, faintly feminist descendant of Miss Bates.

The cult of Austen also leads to a revival of Regency romances and costume films, as to a lasting vogue for Regency decor. Characters in Ada Leverson's *Bird of Paradise* (1919; reprint, London: Chapman and Hall, 1951) thus inhabit a "little Chippendale flat, all inlaid mahogany and old-fashioned chintz, china in cabinets, and miniatures on crimson velvet," which "somehow suggested Hugh Thomson's illustrations to Jane Austen's books." While claiming that her characters are not "in the least degree like Miss Austen's heroines and their mothers," Leverson insists that one mother, obsessed like Mrs. Bennet with marrying off her daughter, "had much of the same querulousness" (227). Austen ostensibly creates an old-fashioned, decorous world, yet her genteel characters show a calculating asperity.

16. Virginia Woolf to R. W. Chapman, 20 November 1936, in *The Letters of Virginia Woolf*, ed. Nigel Nicolson and Joanne Trautmann (New York: Harcourt Brace Jovanovich, 1975–80), 6:87.

17. Virginia Woolf, "Jane Austen Practising," in *The Essays of Virginia Woolf*, vol. 3, *1919–1924*, ed. Andrew McNeillie (New York: Harcourt Brace Jovanovich, 1986), 334, 333.

18. Ibid., 331–32.

19. Rebecca West, "The Long Chain of Criticism," in *The Strange Necessity: Essays and Reviews* (1928; reprint, London: Virago, 1987), 264, 263–64.

20. Rebecca West, "The Strange Necessity," in *The Strange Necessity*, 13–198, esp. 78, 96–99. Like Auden, West compares Austen to Joyce, to find Joyce the more conventional and sentimental of the two.

21. A decade later, inspired by Virago's success and anchored by Dale Spender's *Mothers of the Novel: One Hundred Good Women Writers before Jane Austen* (London: Pandora, 1986), Pandora's (short-lived) Mothers of the Novel reprint series reconstructed the feminist novel writing (Mary Hays, Amelia Opie, Lady Morgan) of Austen's own era. Like the Virago series, Pandora's reprints featured newly commissioned introductions, written by contemporary women novelists, many of whom follow Spender in using Austen as a principle point of reference. Eva Figes's introductions to Maria Edgeworth's *Belinda* (1801; reprint, London: Pandora, 1986) and *Patronage* (1814; reprint, London: Pandora, 1986) discuss Austen's championship of Edgeworth and compare their handling of the courtship novel and of male characters.

22. See Brian Southam, "Criticism 1870–1940," in *The Jane Austen Handbook*, ed. J. David Grey (London: The Athlone Press, 1986), 102–9.

23. Angela Carter, *Several Perceptions* (1968; reprint, London: Virago, 1995), 4.

24. Virginia Woolf, *A Room of One's Own* (1928; reprint, Harmondsworth: Penguin, 1972), 5. Subsequent references will appear in the text.

25. Lettice Cooper's *The New House* (1936; reprint, London: Virago, 1987), argues Maureen Duffy in her introduction (vii–xv), is "in the Austen tradition rather than the more local Brontë" (ix). Virago reprints several Brontë-inspired novels, from Rachel Ferguson's revenant novel *The Brontës Went to Woolworths* (1932; reprint, London: Virago, 1988) and May Sinclair's biographically inspired *The Three Sisters* (1914; reprint, London: Virago, 1984) to novelistic redactions of *Wuthering Heights* like Beatrix Lehmann's *Rumor of Heaven* (1934; reprint, London: Virago, 1987) and Rosamond Lehmann's *The Ballad and the Source* (1944; reprint, London: Virago, 1982). Eliot is a more subdued presence in the series. Cooper's introduction to Winifred Holtby's *South Riding* (1936; reprint, London: Virago, 1988), v–ix, compares it to *Middlemarch*. (A biographer of Eliot, Cooper in her own 1938 *National Provincial* offers a full-scale recasting of Eliot's novel.)

26. In *Jane Austen* (New York: Farrar, Straus and Cudahy, 1949), Elizabeth Jenkins admonishes against the pervasive impulse to pit Austen against the Brontës or Eliot. "It is not that Jane Austen possessed a more interesting mind or a more varied imagination than her successors; it is a foolish method of appreciation that exalts *Persuasion* at the expense of *Middlemarch* or of *Jane Eyre*" (339). The Virago Modern Classics works rather to exalt later writers *along* with Austen. Yet they also use Austen's novels as a standard against which to describe or measure "secondary" works of fiction."

27. F. R. Leavis, *The Great Tradition: George Eliot. Henry James. Joseph Conrad* (New York: New York University Press, 1964), 5, 7.

28. Elizabeth Jane Howard, introduction to Elizabeth Taylor, *The Wedding Group* (1968; reprint, London: Virago, 1985), v. The first Virago Modern Classic, Antonia White's *Frost in May* (1933; reprint, London: Virago, 1978), reprints a

1948 essay by Elizabeth Bowen that praises White's style for being "precise, clear and unweighty as Jane Austen's" (9).

29. Sally Beauman, introduction to Ada Leverson, *The Little Ottleys* (New York: Dial Press [American reprint of Virago], 1982), vii–xvi: viii.

30. Beauman, introduction to E. H. Young, *Jenny Wren* (1932; reprint, London: Virago, 1985), v, xii. Beauman's introduction to Young's *The Misses Mallett (The Bridge Dividing)* (1922; reprint, New York: Dial Press, 1985), vii–xvi, argues that it is inspired by the author's youthful memories of Bristol much as Austen was inspired "by the spas of eighteenth-century England" (vii); Georgina Battiscombe's afterword to Yonge's *The Clever Woman of the Family* (1865; reprint, London: Virago, 1985), 368–72, compares her "limited" historical vision to Austen's proverbially narrow range and locale.

31. Tamie Watter, introduction to Mrs. Humphry Ward, *Marcella* (1894; reprint, London: Virago, 1984), vii–xvi; Paul Binding, introduction to Jane and Mary Findlater, *Crossriggs* (1908; reprint, London: Virago, 1986), vii–xiv. Helen McNeil's introduction to Jenkins's *The Tortoise and the Hare* (1954; reprint, New York: Dial Press, 1983), 1–6, applies Jenkins's observations about Austen's plots to Jenkins's own novel.

32. Emily Eden, *The Semi-Attached Couple and The Semi-Detached House* (London: Virago, 1979). The cover also cites Lord David Cecil's comparison of the two: "The kind of English lady whose most delightful representative is Jane Austen . . . clever, sensible, delightful . . . a zestful, worldly-wise interest in her fellows and a sparkling sense of humour."

33. Gaby Weiner, introduction to Harriet Martineau, *Deerbrook* (1839; reprint, New York: Dial, 1983), vii.

34. Bel Mooney, Afterword to E. H. Young, *Chatterton Square* (1947; reprint, London: Virago, 1987), 369.

35. Jane Marcus, introduction to Rebecca West, *The Judge* (1922; reprint, London: Virago, 1989), 4.

36. Margaret Kennedy, *Troy Chimneys* (1953; reprint, London: Virago, 1985), 200. Anita Brookner's introduction (vii–x) cites this passage (viii) as key to Kennedy's aesthetic.

37. Catherine Carswell, *The Camomile* (1922; reprint, London: Virago, 1987), 132.

38. Catherine Carswell, *Open the Door!* (1920; reprint, London: Virago, 1986). Lawrence excoriated "the mean Jane Austen" as an "old maid" who is "thoroughly unpleasant, English in the bad, mean, snobbish sense of the word." Austen's narrow view of social life is due not only to intensifying class struggle but to her own enforced chastity. D. H. Lawrence, "A Propos of Lady Chatterley's Lover" (1929), in Lawrence, *Sex, Literature and Censorship: Essays*, ed. Harry Moore (New York: Twayne, 1953), 119.

39. Antonia White, *Diaries 1926–1957*, ed. Susan Chitty (London: Virago, 1992), 30 November 1937, 115.

40. Ibid., 15 June 1938, 196–97. A sense of Austen's repression inspires similar ambivalence in Woolf. When Ethel Smyth announces a "mad Jane Austen mood" (126), she declares her own preference for the Brontës: "whatever 'Bloomsbury'

may think of JA., she is not by any means one of my favourites. I'd give all she ever wrote for half what the Brontes wrote—if my reason did not compel me to see that she is a magnificent artist. What I shall proceed to find out, from her letters, when I've time, is why she failed to be much better than she was. Something to do with sex, I expect; the letters are full of hints already that she suppressed half of her in her novels—Now why? (Virginia Woolf to Ethel Smyth, 20 November 1932, *Letters of Virginia Woolf,* 5:127).

41. See also White, *Diaries,* 196: "February 19, 1948. To me, Jane Austen's 'perfection' is highly suspect and though I *enjoy* her (who wouldn't) I don't really admire her. . . . I think she is the most bourgeois of all writers. She has certain ethical standards which are not always reducible to mere good breeding, but of all writers she must be one of the least 'spiritual.' Her whole mainspring is materialistic. She is really the last of the 18th century writers with their terror of 'enthusiasm.' "

42. In their 1945 interview, Compton-Burnett and Jourdain evoke Austen's putative escape from history to justify their own "fleeing the bombs" to take refuge from the war in Lyme Regis. Under such circumstances, Compton-Burnett argues, Austen and Mary Mitford "would both have fled, and felt it proper to do so"; she only wishes that she "could really feel it equally proper." Compton-Burnett and Jourdain, "A Conversation," 20.

43. See *The Matriarch* (1924; reprint, London: Virago, 1987) and *A Deputy Was King* (1926; reprint, London: Virago, 1988).

44. Sheila Kaye-Smith, *Susan Spray* (1931; reprint, London: Virago, 1983).

45. Sheila Kaye-Smith and G. B. Stern, *Speaking of Jane Austen* [American title for *Talking of Jane Austen*] (New York: Harper & Brothers Publishers, 1944), 29. In the sequel, *More Talk of Jane Austen* (London: Cassell and Co., 1950), Stern continues to read Austen anthropologically, while Kaye-Smith ruminates on sociological and historiographical questions.

46. Kaye-Smith and Stern, *Speaking of Jane Austen,* 31.

47. Edmund Wilson, "A Long Talk about Jane Austen" (1944), in Wilson, *Classics and Commercials: A Literary Chronicle of the Forties* (New York: Farrar, Straus and Giroux, 1950), 197, 199–200, 200, 200–201.

48. One thinks here of the imaginary dinner symposia staged in Hendrik Van Loon, *Van Loon's Lives* (New York: Simon and Schuster, 1942), in Judy Chicago's *Dinner Party* (1979), and in Caryl Churchill's play *Top Girls* (London: French, 1982). Characters in Elizabeth Taylor's *A Wreath of Roses* (1949; reprint, London: Virago, 1994) elaborate "tea-parties for English literary ladies": "Jane and Ivy" arrive "at the door together and wait there, looking at one another's shoes"; Virginia arrives late; "Elizabeth Barrett taking up all the room on the sofa." Most problematic are the Brontës: Emily "wouldn't come in at all . . . stood up the road and eyed the gate," Anne "looked into her lap" with trembling hands, while Charlotte "came too early" and then "wrecked" the party with her "inverted snobbery." Ancients and moderns meet as equals, yet the party disintegrates: "Everything went wrong" (36).

49. Virginia Woolf to Margaret Llewelyn Davies, 16 November 1919, *Letters of Virginia Woolf,* 2:400. In a diary entry of 28 November 1919, Woolf is "irri-

tated" at Katherine Mansfield's review of *Night and Day.* "I thought I saw spite in it. A decorous elderly dullard she describes me; Jane Austen up to date." "But I had rather," she adds on 5 December, "write in my own way of 'four Passionate Snails' than be, as K.M. maintains, Jane Austen over again." *The Diary of Virginia Woolf*, vol. 1, *1915–1919*, ed. Anne Olivier Bell (New York and London: Harcourt Brace Jovanovich, 1977), 314, 316.

50. E. M. Delafield, *The Optimist* (New York: MacMillan, 1922), 241.

51. E. M. Delafield, *The Provincial Lady in Wartime* (1940; reprint, Chicago: Academy Chicago Publishers, 1986), 315.

52. Elizabeth Jenkins, *Harriet* (1934; reprint, Harmondsworth: Penguin, 1980).

53. Mayor, *The Third Miss Symons* (1913; reprint, London: Virago, 1979); May Sinclair, *Mary Olivier: A Life* (1919; reprint, London: Virago, 1980); Sinclair, *The Life and Death of Harriet Frean* (1922; reprint, London: Virago, 1980).

54. Like "Jane Austen before her," Janet Morgan argues in her introduction to *The Rector's Daughter* (1924; reprint, London: Virago, 1987), v–xx, Mayor learned "that when there is little else," minor events and skirmishes "transform domestic life into a seething battlefield and, cleverly deployed, make what were Parish Notes into a Saga" (xiii).

55. F. M. Mayor, "Letters from Manningfield," in *The Room Opposite and Other Tales of Mystery and Imagination* (London: Longmans, Green and Co., 1935), 73.

56. For a nonfeminist rewriting of *The Optimist* and *The Rector's Daughter*, see Richard Aldington, *The Colonel's Daughter* (New York: Doubleday, Doran and Company, 1931). Here spinsterhood leads to hysteria.

57. *Persuasion*, Mayor claimed, was the greatest influence on her rendering of emotional life. Sybil Oldfield, *Spinsters of This Parish: The Life and Times of F. M. Mayor and Mary Sheepshanks* (London: Virago, 1984), 315 n. 7.

58. Mayor, *The Rector's Daughter*, 47, 24.

59. In *The Squire's Daughter* (1929; reprint, London: Virago, 1987), Mayor herself returns to describe the marriage between staid curate and "flighty" woman from the wife's standpoint. Similarly, Lehmann's *The Weather in the Streets* and *The Echoing Grove* (New York: Harcourt Brace Jovanovich, 1953) explore the consequences of an affair from the differing perspectives of wife and mistress. Such novels mirror the high modernist "perspectivalism" of Woolf's *The Waves* or Lawrence Durrell's *Alexandria Quartet.*

60. "That small, sly Jane," Elizabeth von Arnim notes in her diary in 1938, after rereading *Pride and Prejudice*: "scribbling away about entirely ordinary people, and behold immortality!" Leslie de Charms, *Elizabeth of the German Garden* (Garden City, N.Y.: Doubleday and Co., 1958), 375.

61. Southam 1987, 1:126–8.

62. The wish to synthesize Austen and the Brontës is recurrent, as is the fear that the mixture will be unpalatable. When Elizabeth von Arnim's *Vera* (1921; reprint, London: Virago, 1988) receives bad reviews, John Middleton Murray comforts the novelist that as "a *Wuthering Heights* written by Jane Austen," it is not immediately legible to critics: quoted in de Charms, *Elizabeth of the German Garden*, 224.

# 7

## Free and Happy: Jane Austen in America

MARY A. FAVRET

WRITING IN the *American Mercury* in 1924, Arthur Bingham Walkley, an Englishman, wonders whether Austenites exist in America. "I can no more conceive an American reader getting excited about Highbury and Box Hill . . . than I can myself about Appomattox or Old Point Comfort. Nor," he continues, "do I think that Miss Austen had any sympathy with the democratic ideal."[1] Putting aside for a moment Walkley's equation of the sites of British fiction with those of American history, we might take up his question of the appeal of Jane Austen for American readers who do hold some sympathy with the democratic ideal. In recent studies on the history of Austen's reading publics, we have learned how audiences in her homeland manufactured around Austen a complex but abiding English national identity. In the late Victorian period, admiration for Austen concentrated on a pious, domestic femininity, at ease in a sanitized preindustrial world. The turn of the century foregrounded instead a heritage of refinement and wealth, featuring high society, "stately homes, gardens and hand-crafted artefacts"; while in the years between the major twentieth-century wars, Austen's world was stripped down to represent simple values, the security of home, and the "smallness" of England's "Home Counties."[2] Even the more marginalized figure of "the Divine Miss Jane," promoted in the first decades of this century by a coterie of urbane, upper-class Englishmen, remains exclusively English in its affiliations.[3] As Roger Sales has reminded us, "[the] association between Austen and Englishness," which arose in the early years of this century, remains to this day "particularly powerful" among Austen compatriots.[4] Together with Shakespeare, Jane Austen has become for the English "the most English writer." So how can an American profess a love for Jane Austen without surrendering to Anglophilia?

Mixing Austen's history with that of the United States might seem to exacerbate the problem. From 1775 to 1817, the span of her life coincides almost exactly with the United States' divorce from England and its efforts to forge an independent national identity (the Monroe Doctrine, for instance, was announced in 1823). During Austen's lifetime, two wars were fought between the newly hostile nations, the latter of which could have involved one of her naval officer brothers. We might be tempted to say that her novels represent the values of a political system Americans had violently rejected. And yet it seems rather silly to judge our response to a writer according to such crude historical data. Even if we were to identify Austen with the most God-fearing, king-loving, snobbish sort of Englishness alive in the reign of George III and George IV, how quick should American readers be to read like ardent republicans and aggrieved colonists? This is not to deny the ineradicable ties between the United States and England, but rather to point the question of American responses to traces of colonialism, felt culturally, socially, and otherwise, and to consider Jane Austen's place in that response.[5] Other questions, equally difficult, follow from this one: where do we locate the limits of national identification, or dis-identification (in the case of some Americans and England)? At what moments and in what situations does the nationality of a reader or writer become pliable, or even eradicable? Within the complex of pleasures, projections, elisions, and consolations that feed readerly identification, we find that the defining contours of any icon—even the "most English" Jane Austen—can be set in motion.

The pages that follow offer a history of Jane Austen's reception in America, primarily in the last decades of the nineteenth century, when her reputation first became established among the literati and in the popular literary journals, then moving into the first decades of the twentieth century. It follows Gauri Viswanathan's suggestion that the teaching—and reading—of English literature in the postcolonial world "can no longer be studied with Britain as its only or primary focus." In her analysis of British literature and English rule in India, Viswanathan reminds us that it would be wrong to assume that the presence of a predominantly British literary curriculum in a former colony gives evidence of "an unmediated assertion of cultural power."[6] I want to extend her thoughts beyond school curricula to the literary culture more generally. Yet the story of Jane Austen in America is not necessarily representative of the fate of British literature in America; Austen does and does not become something altogether new when she hits these shores (fulfilling thereby a fundamental American, not English, myth). In other words, to some readers on this side of the Atlantic, she no longer looks English, nor are her novels naturally rooted in a Great Tradition of British Literature. Rather than simply adopting Austen as a means of acquiring cultural capital (though that surely happened), readers performed their American-ness by accepting Austen as one of their own. By making Austen into something they wanted to recognize as American, these readers became American themselves.

This essay documents what some of Austen's American fans enjoyed, admired, and promoted in her work. It generally steers clear, however, of one tradition among Austen's American readers which emerged at the beginning of this century and continues to this day: that is, the avowedly Anglophilic and primarily touristic strain.[7] This strain does at times overlap with others, but the patterns of reading that interest me here move in another direction. They tend to dissociate themselves from England and from the historical person, Jane Austen, who lived and died there. Indeed, a dominant pattern among these American admirers of Austen neglects Chawton Cottage, Steventon Parsonage, the Royal Navy, rooms at Bath, the Anglican Church, and the English countryside; Jane Austen, for these readers, is about something else. And that something else might be named, loosely, freedom and the pursuit of happiness.

Of course, Austen has had her American detractors. Ralph Waldo Emerson, the man who defined the American Scholar, if not American thought itself, found Austen's fiction revolting: "[It is] vulgar in style, sterile in invention, imprisoned in the wretched conventions of English society, without genius, wit, or knowledge of the world. Never was life so pinched and narrow. [Her main subject] is marriageableness. . . ." "Suicide," Emerson concludes, "is more respectable."[8] Mark Twain's distaste for Austen was even more elaborate than Emerson's. There were two writers whose prose Twain found unreadable: Edgar Allan Poe's and Jane Austen's (a strange pairing). Poe's work, Twain wrote, he might read if paid to, but never Austen's. Speaking about libraries aboard ships, Twain offered that "one omission alone [the works of Jane Austen] would make a fairly good library out of one that hadn't a book in it." His most telling comments about the novelist appeared in a manuscript fragment entitled "Jane Austen": "Whenever I take up 'Pride & Prejudice' or 'Sense & Sensibility,' " Twain begins, "I feel like a barkeeper entering the Kingdom of Heaven"; he had no idea what to do there, except "detest all her characters, without reserve."[9] The animosity in Twain's analogy looks more perplexing than funny, but the perplexity unravels a bit if we recall the obvious differences between Austen's gentry, in large part exempt from working for a living, and Twain's bartender, a member of the commercial class who measures his pleasure by the pint rather than by the acreage of his estates.

Here we have two representatives of American-ness repudiating Austen in no uncertain terms. Emerson's antipathy for the topic of marriageableness and Twain's rabid discomfort with Austen's paradise align them with a familiar story about the American literary tradition: its aversion to domesticity and social convention; its fascination with the individual, the loner; its yearning for open spaces, unclaimed vistas, Huck Finn lighting out for the territories.[10] This is a distinctly masculine tradition, uneasy about any contact with the feminine; its founding father reportedly James Fenimore Cooper, author of the Leatherstocking tales. Most accounts of this tradition, however, fail to mention that Cooper, challenged by his wife to write a "better novel" than the stuff they had been reading together, published his first work, *Precaution* (1820) in direct imitation of Jane Austen's *Persuasion* (1818). And though he would subsequently adopt, with greater success, the historical romances of Walter Scott, Cooper never abandoned an emphasis on "marriageableness," even as he turned it in a distinctly American—and racial—direction.[11]

Lurking in these snippets about Jane Austen's place among nineteenth-century avatars of American literary masculinity, we find the distinctive features of Austen's reception in America in the nineteenth and early twentieth centuries, when American literature was establishing its independence from England. In Cooper's case, we find the identification of Austen's fiction with something new and better, something Americans might adopt as their own.[12] In Emerson's diatribe against marriageableness, we find him distancing himself from the realm of social convention and prosaic feelings. Other American readers, however, would credit Austen herself with this same sort of distance, claiming her as an astute critic of the marriage market. Warren Burden Blake, writing in *Scribner's Magazine* in 1914, cites these lines about Charlotte Lucas from *Pride and Prejudice* in order to correct Emerson: "Without thinking highly of either men or matrimony, marriage had always been her object, it was the only honorable provision for well-educated young women of small fortune, and, however uncertain of giving happiness, must be their pleasantest preservative from want." If Jane Austen were living today, Blake reflects, she "would see through many of our modern make-believes . . . and would write another *Pride and Prejudice*."[13] If you twist the lens just a bit, as Blake does, Austen becomes the bachelor's ally, in her own way as free from matrimonial and sentimental prisons as Emerson could want. Finally, taking another look at Twain's image of Austen's paradise, we might discern the suggestion that Austen is capable of offering a different sort of world, free from some of the burdens of a laborer's daily life. These three notes—the possibility of a new, better something; the desire for distance from emotional or social demands; and the creation of another, more leisurely world—though muted in the foregoing examples, ring loudly and distinctly in the records of other American readers of Jane Austen, bestowing on her work a particularly American sound.

---

To find out just how American Jane Austen can be, we need only turn to her most influential U.S. advocate, William Dean Howells, one of the premier men of letters in late-nineteenth-century America, and certainly its leading proponent of literary realism. For Howells, Austen is to be admired for her "perfection of form," the "symmetrical lines" upon which her novels are built.[14] But alongside her technical refinement, and inextricable from it, are the novelist's "originality and independent spirit," miraculously freed from the conventions of the English novel and its moralism. For Howells, and he will be echoed by a host of other American readers, the technical perfection of Austen's realism offers a sort of aesthetic package that he makes geographically portable. In *Criticism and Fiction*, published in 1891, Howells wonders why English writers, given the radiant example of Austen's "refined perfection," failed to follow her lead. The answer turns out to be the "poor islanders' " bad taste. While "Continental Europe [and, obviously, this American critic] ha[ve] the light of aesthetic truth," England remains in provincial darkness, using a criticism based on "special and personal" interests, rather than on the scientific principles that would illuminate Austen's virtues.[15] Even as they appear Cosmopolitan rather than English, however, Austen's virtues are appropriated by Howells for America. He compares her simplicity and honesty to "Mr. Jefferson's," her artistry to Nathaniel Hawthorne's (*C&F*, 221; "JA," 315). He then invokes Emerson to differentiate the English from the American novel. " 'I ask not for the great, the remote, the romantic,' " he writes, borrowing from *The American Scholar*; " 'I embrace the common, I sit at the feet of the familiar and the low. . . . Man is surprised to find that things near are not less beautiful than things remote' "(*C&F*, 321–32).[16] English fiction, for Howells, is entrenched in concerns with "the great, the remote, the romantic," while American fiction seeks something "new": the common, near, and everyday. In this light, Austen's work looks, to Howells, amazingly Emersonian and American. (He conveniently forgets the glories of Pemberley or the attractions of Donwell Abbey.) "It takes rare virtue," Howells remarks, "to appreciate what is new, as well as to invent it"; yet newness and invention, he insists, are the terrain of the American novel, as they are Austen's terrain (231). Austen, says Howells, "was the first to write a thoroughly artistic novel in English" ("JA," 316); she seems to have handed that accomplishment on to American, not English, writers.[17]

To be an American artist, in Howells's terminology, is to be honest, simple, and unflinchingly devoted to the highest demands of art. In short, it is to be what he calls "modern." In another essay, Howells explains that Jane Austen "shows herself to be more modern than all her predecessors and contemporaries and most of her successors"; she is "distinctively modern." ("JA," 328, 329 and passim). This modernism, an American ideal, expands beyond the merely formal and aesthetic to be a matter of character and politics. Howells insists upon the "courage" and independence" of Austen's brand of realism ("JA," 315, 318, 328, 332), and that courage and independence soon "distinguish everything she did" until she becomes a sort of freedom fighter (329). Reading *Pride and Prejudice*, Howells dwells on the famous scene between Elizabeth Bennet and Lady Catherine De Bourgh, concluding that "it is impossible . . . not to feel that [Elizabeth's] triumph is something more than personal: it is a protest, it is an insurrection. . . . An indignant sense of the value of humanity as against the pretensions of rank, such as had not been felt in English fiction before, stirs throughout the story." "In *all* the novels of Jane Austen," Howells claims, we find "a revolt against the arrogance of rank" ("JA," 319; my emphasis). What could more endear her to American sensibilities? Even as he transplanted Austen, Howells used her (together with Emerson) to construct a definition of the American writer. Welcoming "simple, natural and honest" writing like Austen's, Howells suggests to his audience, allows modern Americans to gain "a firmer hold upon our place in the world" (*C&F*, 193).

Faced with Howells's use of Austen to mark the American writer with a particular brand of realism, we might consider that Howells's critics, engaged in the "romantic revival" at the end of the nineteenth century, also adopted Jane Austen as their darling. Contesting the stringency and implicit elitism of the realist camp, advocates of the romantic revival offered an alternative set of values for legitimating the nation's reading. As Nancy Glazener has recently written, "Whereas realism promoted good citizenship through self-discipline and self-denial,"—virtues found inherent in Austen's style—the romantic revival, deeply tied to notions of leisure and pleasure, "marked the legitimation of consumerist motives for reading."[18] Here too Austen's fiction becomes a standard. Agnes Repplier, one of the most accomplished publicists of the romantic revival, maintains that "there are such things as satisfaction and happiness," and they are found in books. Unlike other romance revivalists, Repplier does not write to promote the works of such contemporaries as Robert Louis Stevenson and Rudyard Kipling; instead she turns to the early nineteenth century: Scott, Byron, Charles Lamb, and Austen. But her consumerist logic, full of metaphors of eating and diet, choice and individuality, undergirds the larger movement. In linking literature with education and discipline, she worries, "we have abandoned the effort to be pleased." By depriving ourselves of choice, in reading materials as in diet, we are deprived of "that hourly happiness which should be ours in dining." Jane Austen helps makes the point for her: "Like Mr. Woodhouse," she writes, the "regulators of reading" (whom she allies with Howells) "are capable of having the sweetmeats and asparagus carried off before one's longing eyes and having baked apples provided as substitute." And against the tendency of contemporary novelists to moralize, Repplier recalls Lady Bertram's ineffectual strictures to her daughters not to "perform anything inappropriate."

As objects of choice and purveyors of pleasure, books (and here she means primarily novels) promote their own version of democracy. According to Repplier, books lack reserve and discretion toward "different classes of persons"; they speak differently to different individuals. At the same time "it is precisely because of the *independence* assumed by books that we have need to cherish our own *independence* in return"—an independence she habitually identifies with choice. "Not one of them would give itself freely to us at the dictation of a critic."[19] In another essay by Repplier, this mixture of self-possession and adaptability exactly identifies the writer Jane Austen.[20]

In contrast to Howells's insistence upon the new, advocates of romance emphasized the pleasures of the familiar and comfortable; thus Repplier titles her essay "Our Friends, the Books." And few books seem cozier than the six novels of Jane Austen. According to Donald G. Mitchell, writing in 1897, "She wrote many good old-fashioned novels which people read now for their light and delicate touches, their happy characterization, their charming play of humor, and their lack of exaggeration. She makes you slip into easy acquaintance with the people of her books as if they lived next door."[21] "In these dark days of ethical and unorthodox fiction," Repplier suggests, Austen provides "matchless tales which are our refuge and solace." Her mastery of conversation, "that sincere and pleasurable intercourse," becomes, in Repplier's reading, the perfect union of the pleasurable and the amicable, played out in leisurely fashion.[22] The desire for the comforts available in Austen's world could be accommodated within the late-century logic of consumerism without looking Anglophilic. As Thomas Wentworth Higginson points out, "[T]he American habit of mind is essentially cosmopolitan" and goes shopping to each country for "the best of its kind." From England, then, the American sees fit to import neither science nor politics nor sport, but rather "those accessories of high-bred life which promote daily comfort and convenience, the organization of a large household, the routine of social life."[23] In this view, Austen's novels provided a very satisfactory product for domestic consumption.

The legacy of this alternative reading of Austen will emerge again later in this essay, but for the time being it serves to register how Austen, perhaps uniquely, was able to appear on both sides of the late-century struggle to define the role of literature in America. Even the gendered logic through which much of this debate transpired—with the realists pegged as effete, shrill, didactic, and domestic and the romancers boasting their adventurousness, sense of history, and movement; or, conversely, the realists applauded for their virtuous self-discipline and the romancers faulted for escapist flights of fancy—such logic disappeared when the figure of Austen was raised. Higginson, the editor of Emily Dickinson and an astute cultural critic, charmingly makes this point in his 1888 collection *Women and Men*. "It certainly looked at one time as if Miss Austen had thoroughly established the claims of her sex to the minute delineation of character and manners, leaving to men the bolder school of narrative romance," he observes. However, "it is the men, not the women, who have taken up Miss Austen's work, while the women show more inclination . . . to the novel of plot and narrative." With Austen as his pivot point, then, Higginson concludes, "It is plain that women novelists, like men, incline sometimes to one branch of the art, sometimes to another," and that "personal preference" and "fashion," rather than "any tendency growing out of sex," determines the choice.[24]

Whereas realists would stress the work of art, and thus the professional expertise of the artist, their opponents would look to the practice—and pleasure—of the reader (for them, the ideal writer was, like Austen, "content to tell a story").[25] In these distinct emphases, both sought a definition of American independence, and, as we will see later, a means of venturing toward a new world. As Glazener points out, the struggle between realism and romance took place on two sides of the same coin. "One could view the distinction between [the two] as a version of th[e] symbolic separation between the ethics of production (culminating in the self-sustaining nation) and of consumption (culminating in the trade-dependent nation), which are systematically interdependent but have been acculturated in incompatible ways."[26] Jane Austen, offering a model of disciplined production *and* a world of leisured, domestic pleasures, helped American readers reconcile the irreconcilable.

---

Despite the significant impact of the romantic revival, most American men and women of letters at the turn of the century responded primarily to Howells in an effort to carve out their place in the world. They embraced Austen as one of their own, identifying her with what was "modern" and placing her ahead of her time. But the terms of Howells's praise could be inflected in a variety of ways. Deidre Lynch has recently suggested that Austen provides "a cultural site supportive of new inventions." American readers bear out this thought to an extreme, making Austen the source of an almost mechanical or technical novelty.[27] In the course of celebrating the novelist for the high resolution and fidelity of her art, readers turn her fiction into a sort of machine. Thus Henry Wadsworth Longfellow, as early as 1839, remarks that Austen's work offers "a capital picture of real life, with all the little wheels and machinery laid bare like a patent clock." In subsequent decades, the type of machine changes, but Austen's mastery of it remains constant. Putting down the patent clock, she takes up the camera: "Henry James and Howells . . . are the lineal successors of Miss Austen," Higginson writes, in a common assessment; "they all belong to the same photographic school." Readers will be "impressed and electrified by her marvelous photographic reproduction of social shades of conduct," proclaims another admirer in 1897. In their 1932 textbook, Robert Morss Lovett and Helen Sard Hughes follow Howells in distinguishing Austen from the two primary types of nineteenth-century fiction in England, what they call the propagandist and the romantic, both of which betray a certain lack of scientific objectivity. For them Austen is an innovator who "owes her later fame to the singleness of purpose and the technical success with which she cultivated" her work. The love of technique often collapses into the love of the technological per se. She was a "precisionist," according to a 1913 essay in the *Sewanee Review*, linking Austen with a contemporary school of American painters devoted not only to realistic technique but also to the celebration of American technology (ocean liners, factories, skyscrapers, etc.). She modeled a "silvery perfection," according to another admirer. Though these readers praised Austen for the "return to nature" she had given the novel, they nonetheless characterized the medium of that return in the language and values of an increasingly technological society. She became the idol of a culture of engineers. According to Princeton professor Gordon Hall Girould, in his 1942 textbook, Austen created a more efficient, streamlined product than her competitors. A sustained "continuity of movement," and a "closely linked series of events" characterize her innovations. "The incomparable smoothness of texture, the neatness of execution. . . . was [*sic*] not a mere trick of giving a polished surface, it was a matter of structural organization." In the midst of World War II, Girould could admire Austen for what looked like good old American technical and organizational know-how, refined by a modernist sensibility. But in 1969, watching the Vietnam War and the Apollo moon landing, two products of American technical ingenuity, the writer Eudora Welty would give a different cast to Austen's novel machinery. Explaining that Austen's appeal for late-twentieth-century readers lay in the "noise" and "velocity" of her fiction, Welty develops the image of Austen's writing as a sort of futuristic tank or guided missile:

> Each novel [she writes] is a formidable engine of strategy. It is made to be—a marvel of designing and workmanship, capable of spontaneous motion at the lightest touch and of travel at delicately controlled but rapid speed toward its precise destination. It could kill us all . . . ; it fires at us, all along the way, using understatement in good aim. Let us be thankful it is trained not on our hearts, but on our illusions and our vanities.

Turning around the critical commonplace that says Austen never attended to the warfare that marked her lifetime, Welty remarks, "She could be our Waterloo; she *is* our Waterloo." Welty's "our" is not marked as a national identification: her essay addresses present and future generations of readers. And yet the metaphors that explore her preoccupations allow Welty to give Austen agency within a specifically American destiny in 1969.[28]

All these appeals to Austen's technical prowess, as different as they are, help accommodate Austen to a culture that identifies itself with the cutting edge. Like Americans of the new century especially, Austen was always ahead of her time.[29]

In wedding Austen's stylistic advances to their own sense of technological sophistication, moreover, early-twentieth-century readers made her an icon of emotional and moral detachment, ahead of the curve but also above it all.[30] Austen's novelty could thereby be converted into a sort of liberating distance. English readers, such as Charlotte Brontë, had begun in the Victorian period to criticize Austen's emotional detachment, while George Henry Lewes and Margaret Oliphant worked to soften and forgive it. D. H. Lawrence had extended these concerns, remarking on Austen's "sharp knowing in apart-ness." Americans found this characteristic unapologetically attractive: considered one way, it positioned Austen with them, one step outside of British society yet fully authorized to have fun with it. Thus Austen's satire gained a special appeal for American readers, who enjoyed assigning to her this description of Elizabeth Bennet: "She dearly loved a laugh,"[31] particularly when the laugh was on the English. Part of the joke of the novels, accordingly, rested on the readers' recognition, with Austen, that English country life was confoundedly boring: "She paints a society which . . . presents the fewest salient points of interest and singularity to the novelist," writes J. B. Shaw in 1849 in his *Outlines of General Literature*, "—we mean the society of English country gentlemen."[32]

Considered another way, the characteristic detachment that American readers found in Austen's prose became for them the instrument of social freedom.[33] J. F. Kirk, writing in 1853, introduces this angle of interpretation. For him, Austen has perfected a new sort of impersonality in her novels: "[T]he authoress herself is never visible, never even peeps from behind the curtain." As a result, each novel suggests a sort of hands-off approach to its characters: "The characters are not described, they exhibit themselves in action and in speech; and there are no works of prose fiction in which the individuality of all the actors is so well maintained."[34] "Her novels are impersonal," agrees another reader, ten years later. "Miss Austen herself never appears." For that reason, it seems "her characters are living people, not masks behind which the author soliloquizes."[35] "Unlike many English novelists," write Lovett and Hughes in their 1932 textbook, "[Austen] does not surrender herself to her characters, but holds herself in a studied detachment from them."[36] A later textbook reiterates this point, combining it with appreciation for Austen's masterful technique: "[I]n all the novels the action develops essentially from the characters involved, and in all of them the design is so perfect as to be quite unobtrusive."[37]

According to these readings, Austen operates at an almost godlike distance from the world of her novels: "Her world," explains Eudora Welty, "may of course easily be regarded as a larger world seen at a judicious distance—it would be the exact distance at which all haze evaporates, full clarity prevails, and true perspective appears." At this distance, says Welty, the novelist perfects her comic gift, seeing her subject "indeed in the round."[38] As a result of this authorial distance and circumspection, Austen's characters operate freely, almost independently of their creator. The author's "miraculous" gift for writing conversation, Repplier claims, gives her characters "individuality" and independence.[39] "She bequeathed to posterity just people," writes Warwick James Price in 1913, "whom it is easier to understand than to describe, for they evolve themselves, and so tell their own stories."[40] As John Halperin has more recently put it, Austen's characters may eventually be educated into "a realization of the evils of excessive subjectivity," but that excessive subjectivity is nevertheless allowed to display itself fully.[41] Austen is seen as freeing her characters to "be themselves" as if they inhabited a noncoercive realm. As I mentioned earlier, recognition of this element in Austen's writing had not escaped British critics. Virginia Woolf joins Welty and others in imagining Austen at a supernatural distance from the world: "One of those fairies who perch upon cradles must have taken her a flight through the world directly she was born. When she was laid in the cradle again, she knew not only what the world looked like, but had already chosen her kingdom."[42] Woolf's fantasy, however, comes to rest with a kingdom and a monarch, something American readers avoid. For them Austen is a "pioneer," discovering a new world where individuals speak and act without moral and ideological constraint. Thus Welty implicitly links her image of Austen with American astronauts landing on the moon.[43]

There seems to be some oscillation here: Austen turns a dispassionate eye on the world of British society, with its conventions and idiosyncracies; at the same time, she creates in her novels a new world of free agents, a world that looks vaguely American. We can understand some of this oscillation by looking at Austen alternately through the lenses of the realist and the romantic. For the advocates of romance and readerly consumption, a new world is created through the act of reading that, even as it encourages readers to make friendly with the characters on the page, also insists upon an individual's right to make this world her own. Realists, on the other hand, rely less upon the creation of a new world than upon departure from an old one: the detachment of the author gives *her*, if not her reader, independence and room to maneuver. In either case, a utopian sort of "elsewhere" is produced. A later American critic, John Halperin, merges these two late-nineteenth-century responses to Austen's fiction, making it the instrument of the downfall of an old world and the discovery of a wholly new one. Austen writes the sort of novel that, according to Halperin,

> frees the reader from his [preexisting] world and allows him to transmigrate to the world of the novel itself—and then keeps him there, prohibiting him from returning to his own world. . . . [These novels] provide a world of [their] own, if it is to be purely autonomous, and thus it cannot propagate moral and philosophical systems. . . . [It] is a realistic genre, a genre of inner reality. In establishing that inner reality it must abolish the outer one.

For Halperin, of course, this new world is a thoroughly abstract one, a mental America that is nonetheless totally real.[44]

This promise of a world that offers us a new inner reality should be familiar to readers of American literature. Richard Poirier, another Ameri can scholar, wrote in 1966 a study of Hawthorne, Emerson, Thoreau, Twain, and James, titled *A World Elsewhere*, in which he argues that the idea of the New World has made American writers "addicted" to the possibility of building "new structures of the mind and . . . language," "a world elsewhere," or, in other words, the sort of "inner reality" Halperin finds in Austen. And, curiously enough, Austen is the only English writer to make an extended appearance in Poirier's study, alongside her great admirer Mark Twain. Through a long comparison of Austen's *Emma* with Twain's *Huckleberry Finn*, Poirier makes a compelling case for the similarity of the crucial scenes of each novel: Huck's recognition that he has hurt Jim's feelings and Emma's recognition that she has slighted Miss Bates. Despite their differences, Poirier argues, the two novelists share an emphasis on the importance of "acknowledging and sifting through differences" and developing "a delicacy towards the feelings of others." And although Poirier will maintain that Austen writes "in the true English style," "with the confidence that English society gives" her, he nevertheless sees a streak of American-ness in Emma, who like Huck is "susceptible to imaginative flight beyond the social group," and who, in making up stories about her acquaintances, is "trying . . . to reform society in her own imagination,—to create, like an American hero, a new environment for herself."[45] The urge to create a new world, which Poirier and others will say is characteristically American, carves out a space for itself in Jane Austen's fiction.

---

I want to linger for a moment on Poirier's reading of Austen, which has helped me understand another aspect of Austen's appeal for American readers. Up to this point, I have traced a tradition among American readers who sever Austen's ties with England and accommodate her to an

American perspective, a view that aligns itself with innovation, technical and technological mastery, and an almost scientific objectivity that operates at a distance from social convention and emotions; readers also incorporate Austen into the pursuit of pleasure, consumer choice, and the possibility of creating a new world. But Poirier's reading takes us back to that alternative nineteenth-century American masculine tradition (Cooper, Emerson, Twain, etc.) and seeks to explain its unease with the novels of Jane Austen. According to Poirier, Austen finds the solution to, say, Emma's embarrassment within the structure of society, and society can finally accommodate her heroine. Writers like Twain or Hawthorne or Cooper, by contrast, cannot imagine such a flexible social order. For Poirier, Austen does *not* write at the same distance as these others. "The difference," he says, "lies in the problem in nineteenth-century American fiction of imagining personal relationships within the context of existent social environments. . . . Twain cannot provide Huck with an alternative . . . that has any viability within the social organization which the novel provides." And so Huck can only "light out for the territories." Whereas Austen is able to delineate "the threat of conformity and artifice [in society] *as well as* the opportunity for self-discovery," American writers have had difficulty finding ways to integrate their heroes into society of any sort.[46] Austen's appeal, then, rests in her seeming ability to integrate where American writers cannot. What remains unexplained here is why American writers of the last century got stuck in what Poirier calls "a limited view of the inclusiveness of social environments" and why Austen escaped it.

The unspoken answer, all too obvious in the case of Huckleberry Finn, is the legacy of slavery in the United States. At the same time that Agnes Repplier could imagine a sort of Ellis Island for literature ("There are no aliens in the ranks of literature," she writes, "no national prejudice in an honest enjoyment of art"), the nation could not shake off the knowledge that theirs was not an inclusive society.[47] In racist best-sellers like Madison Grant's *The Passing of the Great Race* (1916) and *Alien in Our Midst* (1930), the presence of racial difference especially would be offered up as the reason for the failures of union in the new world. Integration via marriage—Austen's consistent solution to alienation—was extremely difficult to imagine, let alone achieve, in a racialized society. The disappointments of Reconstruction, together with the waves of new immigrants in the 1880s to 1930s, intensified the racial anxiety of white Americans, so that Anglo-Saxon nativism, a belief in the superior genetic endowment of the Anglo-Saxon "race" and in their capacity for self-government, coupled with a fear of racial mixing and Mendelian degeneration, found popular, scientific, and governmental support. Central to this rising, racialized understanding of American society was the question of marriage and breeding.[48] A 1939 report issued by the Special Commission on Immigration and Naturalization of the Chamber of Commerce of the State of New York could claim with confidence that "to guide the evolution or development of a nation or race, it is necessary to establish racial standards. To hold the country against all would-be alien invaders, whether they serve as enemies in battle or as friendly immigrants, and to set up standards for the admission of outside reproductive stocks into the mate-selection of the established race."[49] Scrupulous attention to marriage choices, of the kind Austen modeled, could thus be regarded as a means of maintaining distinctions between "aliens" and the "established," that is, Anglo-Saxon, race and thereby securing the future of the nation.

I want to suggest now that another of the reasons for Austen's rising appeal in the United States, especially in the decades around the turn of the century, was that her fiction allowed (white) Americans to construct a dream of themselves and their society—more advanced than England, technologically savvy, sophisticated, and independent—that secured racial homogeneity. This is not to say that English society in Austen's day was not aware of racial difference: indeed, the modern discourse of race, based on encounters between white colonizers and colonized people of color, had solidified by the early nineteenth century, when Austen lived. Yet, as the example of Sir Bertram's Antiguan plantations in *Mansfield Park* makes clear, slavery and the question of race could be kept at a distance; since the 1780s slavery had been outlawed in the British Isles.[50] When slavery does makes its appearance in one of Austen's novels, it has been bleached and sanitized: in *Emma*, Jane Fairfax complains of the white slave trade, referring to the market for governesses.[51] Of course it could be argued that any number of English novels would do the trick, if one were searching for the fantasy of a totally white, Anglo-Saxon society; but in fact the English novelists from whom Howells and others would dissociate Austen—Thackeray, Dickens, Brontë, Scott, Eliot—painted a society that wrestled with race in the form of Jews, Irish, and West Indian mulattos. In the later nineteenth and early twentieth centuries, Austen's homogeneous society emerged as especially (and problematically) suited to the needs of a nation struggling to renew itself in the aftermath of war. To the extent that white American readers identified with Austen and found consolation in her fiction, they also were willing to imagine themselves rid of the legacy of racial slavery, the trauma of Civil War, and the difficulties posed by mass immigration. Recalling Walkley's comment, which opened this essay, we begin to recognize the trade-off American fans might enact while reading Austen: "I can no more conceive of an American reader getting excited about Highbury and Box Hill . . . than I can myself about Appomattox," site of General Robert E. Lee's surrender to General Ulysses S. Grant.

I will offer just a few examples to support this thought, which grows out of Poirier's juxtaposition of *Emma* and *Huckleberry Finn*. Hints of the desire to escape race surface in the many celebrations of the "normal people," the "just people," "the people next door" who populate Austen's novels: because "there are so many more of us [ordinary people]," writes one fan, than of the less than ordinary people who seem to get all the attention.[52] Sometimes a preoccupation with race becomes more distinct: "She had never heard of . . . 'the survival of the fittest,' " explains a 1930s textbook in a final flourish, "yet [Austen's novels] are all consumed with a condition fundamental to the future of families and the race: viz., the right mating of individuals." Thus, it continues, "she reveals the enduring quality of English society, the strength of the fabric woven by the upper middle-class, the clergy and the country gentlemen." This is the same textbook which had earlier insisted that Austen "lacks many of the qualities and interests which characterize serious English fiction."[53] But when it gets down to the "quality," "strength" and "future of the race," the severely homogeneous nature of Austen's English "families and social groups" grows attractive. In the 1940s, the issue of race in Austen takes another form. Laura Hinkley, in 1946, makes this observation: "[Austen] could have demanded with Henry James, 'What is character but the determination of incident? What is incident but the illustration of character?' " If we insert "race" where Hinkley and James have "character," we have two very profound questions about American history and literature.[54] But Hinkley moves in another direction, though still raising the specter of race: "(But, as a matter of fact," she admits in an aside, "incident is so often the illustration of such extremely alien character, Hitler's for instance)." Austen eliminates the specter for her: "Jane shut out everything alien," Hinkley says, with a relief that looks chilling next to the mention of Hitler. "Most of all, she created a tranquil, delightful world."[55] Poirier himself, writing during the height of the Civil Rights movement, cannot bring himself to acknowledge the significance of racial difference for American literature, instead enlisting Austen to transcend slavery and its legacy: having read *Emma*, he sees in *Huckleberry Finn* that "Negro slavery [is] only one aspect of a general enslavement—of feeling and intelligence within inadequate and restrictively artificial modes of expression."[56] Creating a new world for free expression, the sort of world readers imagined Austen creating for her characters, would make slavery disappear.

A deep-seated but never fully articulated sense of Austen's relationship to race and the trauma of slavery combines with the ordeals of World War II in the 1940 film version of *Pride and Prejudice*, starring Greer Garson and Laurence Olivier. Though it featured English actors and was written in part by well-known English author Aldous Huxley, this *Pride and Prejudice* was an undeniably Hollywood affair. Though the film was praised for its "faithfulness" to the text of Austen's novels, there were a few odd

2. Greer Garson as Elizabeth Bennet and Laurence Olivier as Mr. Darcy. Publicity still from the 1940 Metro-Goldwyn-Mayer *Pride and Prejudice*. Courtesy of the Museum of Modern Art, Film Stills Archive, New York.

changes that contemporary critics failed to mention. Most remarkably, the studio had insisted on moving the historical setting forward forty years, so that the story presumably took place in the 1850s. This change allowed the actors and actresses to be dressed in obviously *Gone with the Wind* fashion. Thus *Pride and Prejudice* takes place in an antebellum world, where Elizabeth Bennet looks and sounds suspiciously like Scarlett O'Hara. But where are the slaves, the plantations? Where is the war?

Pemberley, the estate in the novel that might have triggered thoughts of Tara, is never shown. The war, however, is signaled obliquely. In one scene, Elizabeth and her sister Jane sit in a room that prominently features a globe. Jane worries that she has received no letters from Bingley, that perhaps something has happened to him; and Elizabeth consoles her, assuring her that he will write and he will return home. With the image of distant lands before our eyes, it is easy to read this scene as if Jane were waiting for her man to return from a foreign war. Later, in an astounding and seemingly superfluous move, the film assembles the Bennet family in this same room, now filled with boxes and baggage. They have been forced out of their community, refugees now without a home. There are muted echoes here again of *Gone with the Wind* and the displacement caused by the siege of Atlanta. But the more immediate context of World War II might make us wonder whom these refugees really represent. In a series of repressions and avowals, the film cannot help reading Austen's novel into America's own traumatic history and the current global tragedy.[57]

I may be testing credulity here, hunting for connections and meaning in hopes of explaining what may, in the end, merely be anomalies, "alien" moments in Jane Austen's American legacy. Nevertheless, I do want to propose this: that if Jane Austen has a place in U.S. literary history—and I hope this essay has made that point at least—then that place cannot be properly imagined without some consideration of race and its legacy in the United States. A simple silence about race, either in Austen's own work or in the responses of her American readers, is never simple; nor does it give us the warrant to ignore the impact of race on our reading. The appearance and disappearance of race in Americans' discussions of Jane Austen, or of other violence in U.S. history, also suggest that national enthusiasms can operate as powerfully through what they refuse as what they embrace. Making Austen free and happy in America helped establish emerging definitions of a democratic nation, but it also encouraged the nation to "forget" race, slavery, and unhappiness. Tracing this history teaches us that Americans have a long and rich tradition of appreciating Jane Austen, but perhaps one that cannot or should not always keep Box Hill at a remove from Appomattox.

## Notes

This essay owes a great debt to the helpful suggestions of my colleagues Andrew Miller, Janet Sorensen, and David Nordloh, and to the editor, Deidre Lynch.

1. Arthur Bingham Walkley, "Mansfield Park and America," *American Mercury* 1 (1924): 320–22.

2. See Roger Sales, *Jane Austen and Representations of Regency England* (London and New York: Routledge, 1994; rev. ed., 1996), chapter 1; and Deidre

Lynch, "At Home with Jane Austen," in *Cultural Institutions of the Novel*, ed. Deidre Lynch and William B. Warner (Durham, N.C.: Duke University Press, 1996).

3. See Claudia L. Johnson's essay in this volume.

4. Sales, *Jane Austen*, 11.

5. The only mention of America in Austen's novels arises facetiously. Tom Bertram, aiming to distract a torpid Dr. Grant, launches this assault: "A strange business, this in America, Dr. Grant! What is your opinion? I always come to you to know what I am to think of public matters." Jane Austen, *Mansfield Park*, 119. If any discussion follows, it is lost to us.

6. Gauri Viswanathan, *Masks of Conquest: Literary Study and British Rule in India* (New York: Columbia University Press, 1989), 109, 108.

7. Early examples of this sort of response can be seen in Anna Waterston, "Jane Austen," *Atlantic Monthly* 11 (1863): 235–40; Anon., "Jane Austen," *Harper's New Monthly Magazine* 41 (1870): 225–33; and Oscar Fay Adams, "In the Footsteps of Jane Austen," *New England Magazine*, n.s., 8 (1893): 594–608.

8. Ralph Waldo Emerson, journal entry from 5 August 1861; cited in Southam 1968, 28.

9. Mark Twain, *The Mark Twain–Howells Letters: The Correspondence of Samuel L. Clemens and William D. Howells, 1872–1910*, ed. Henry Nash Smith and William H. Gibson, vol. 2 (Cambridge: Harvard University Press, Belknap Press, 1960), 769–70, 841, 770n. Besides Austen and Poe, Twain professed great disgust for the writing of James Fenimore Cooper. See his "Fenimore Cooper's Literary Offenses," the best-known of his forays into literary criticism.

10. See Leslie Fiedler, *Love and Death in the American Novel* (New York: Criterion Books, 1960), as well as Richard Poirier, *A World Elsewhere: The Place of Style in American Literature* (New York: Oxford University Press, 1966).

11. See Philip Fisher's illuminating comments on Cooper's *The Deerslayer* (1840), in his *Hard Facts: Setting and Form in the American Novel* (New York: Oxford University Press, 1987): "Cooper is often faulted for not having freed himself, as a writer of adventure novels, from a core of marriage intrigues. However, in *The Deerslayer* the marriage questions restate in a unique and profound way the central matters of names, competing claims, and the right to extend claims through time" (51). Fisher points out that the plot of *The Deerslayer* structures itself around five possible marriages, and that those marriages reinforce the racial boundaries between white Euro- and Native American populations.

12. Despite his desire to write a new sort of novel, Cooper's effort with *Precaution* was severely compromised as an American production. Part of the novel's failure "resulted from his attempt to pass the work off as English . . . for fear that an American work would not be well-received." Donald Ringe, *James Fenimore Cooper*, updated edition (Boston: Twayne, 1988).

13. Warren Burden Blake, "The Business of Marriage," *Scribner's Magazine* 55 (1914): 531–31. See also Edmund Wilson, "A Long Talk about Jane Austen," *A Literary Chronicle, 1920–1950* (Garden City, N.Y.: Doubleday and Company, 1950), 302–9, where he insists upon Austen's "emotional detachment" from matters of marriage; and Laura L. Hinkley, *Ladies of Literature* (New York: Hastings House Publishers, 1946): "Jane . . . was so happy without being married, can we

believe that her delicious play of mind could ever have settled down in conjugal or maternal affections?" (85).

14. William Dean Howells, "Jane Austen," *W. D. Howells as Critic*, ed. Edwin H. Cady (London and Boston: Routledge and Kegan Paul, 1973), 315. The essay was first published in three parts in *Harper's Bazaar* in 1900, under the title "Jane Austen's Heroines." Cady follows the slightly revised text of Howells's *Heroines of Fiction* (New York and London: Harper's & Brothers Publishing, 1901). Hereafter cited as "JA."

15. William Dean Howells, *My Literary Passions and Criticism and Fiction* (New York and London: Harper's & Brothers Publishing, 1910), 221–33. Hereafter cited as *C&F.* The remarks on Austen first appeared in an "Editor's Study" column of *Harper's Monthly* in 1889 and later in *Criticism and Fiction*, which first appeared in 1891. Howells strategically ignores Austen's growing popularity in England, but he might, like Henry James, have attributed it to "provincial and special and personal" causes.

16. Howells quotes, with some mistakes, from *The American Scholar.* See Ralph Waldo Emerson, *Selections from Ralph Waldo Emerson*, ed. Stephen E. Whicher (Boston: Houghton Mifflin, 1959), 78.

17. Several readers of Austen follow Howells in detaching her from the English tradition: Edmund Wilson, in his "A Long Talk about Jane Austen," finds Austen's literary affiliations "freakish" and "queer," her comedy "natural to the latin [*sic*] people," rather than the Anglo-Saxon. He names Austen and Dickens as the only two English novelists "who belong in the very top rank" along with the great French and Russian writers (302–3). Thomas Wentworth Higginson worried that Austen had been made, by Howells and others, the origin of the school of French naturalists: "There is something extremely grotesque in this situation, and yet, there is much truth in this theory." "Men's Novels and Women's Novels," in his *Women and Men* (New York: Harper & Brothers, 1888), 156. See also Robert Morss Lovett and Helen Sard Hughes, *The History of the Novel in England* (Boston: Houghton Mifflin Company, 1932), 169. John Halperin continues this tradition: "In method and range of interests she is more like James [and Proust], it may be, than like . . . Eliot, Thackeray, Trollope, or Meredith": *The Language of Meditation* (Elms Court, Mass.: Arthur H. Stockard, 1973), 17.

18. These paragraphs owe a great debt to Nancy Glazener's masterful study *Reading for Realism: The History of a U.S. Institution, 1850–1910* (Durham, N.C.: Duke University Press, 1997), esp. chapter 5. Quotation from 148.

19. Agnes Repplier, *Essays in Miniature* (New York: Charles I. Webster, 1892), 12, 14, 69, 25–26 (my emphasis). In three essays—"Our Friends, the Books," "Old Maids," and "Conversation in Novels"—in this collection, which typifies Repplier's brand of criticism, Austen serves as a central figure. See Glazener's excellent discussion of Repplier's contributions, *Reading for Realism*, 149–58.

20. See Repplier's essay "Old Maids," esp. 157.

21. Donald G. Mitchell, "A Hampshire Novelist," in his *English Lands, Letters, and Kings*, vol. 3 (New York: Charles Scribner's Sons, 1897), 266.

22. Repplier, "Conversation in Novels," 66, 64.

23. Thomas Wentworth Higginson, "The Swing of the Pendulum," in *Women and Men*, 25.

24. Higginson, "Men's Novels and Women's Novels," in *Women and Men*, 156–60.

25. Repplier, "Conversation in Novels," 66. See also Glazener, *Reading for Realism*, 163–64 on the appeal of the storyteller.

26. Glazener, *Reading for Realism*, 162.

27. Deidre Lynch, "At Home with Jane Austen," 162.

28. Longfellow's journal entry is quoted in Southam 1968, 2:25. On Austen and photography see Higginson, "Men's Novels and Women's Novels," in *Women and Men*, 157; Mitchell, *English Lands, Letters, and Kings*, 3:171; and Charles Townsend Copeland, "Miss Austen and Miss Ferrier; Contrast and Comparison," *Atlantic Monthly* 71 (1893): 836–46. Lovett and Hughes write in *History of the Novel*, 165. Warwick James Price, in his essay "Grandmother's Favorite Novel," *Sewanee Review* 21 (1913): 480–89, refers to Austen as a "precisionist." Laura L. Hinkley refers to her "silvery perfection" in *Ladies of Literature*, 102. Girould writes in *The Patterns of English and American Novels: A History* (Boston: Little, Brown, and Company, 1942), 192. For Welty's essay, "The Radiance of Jane Austen," see *The Eye of the Story: Selected Essays and Reviews* (New York: Random House, 1978), 3–13. Another warlike version of Austen can be found in the anonymous 1911 poem "To Jane Austen," *Atlantic Monthly* 108 (1911): 572–73:

> Thou seekest truth, and when 'tis found
> Thou dost its sportive whims confound; . . .
> It dreads thy logic's bristling fence,
> Thy files of serried evidence,
> Thy panoplied, embattled sense,
> Irrefragable Jane!

29. The refrain is common: see Burden Blake, "Business of Marriage"; Hinkley, *Ladies of Literature*; and especially Howells, "The Immortality of Jane Austen," *Harper's Magazine* 127 (1916): 958–66. "Why was she so persistently, so increasingly . . . alive? . . . [B]ecause as the world civilized and enlightened to her level, so far above the average of her own time, the world must hold her in ever-widening appreciation and affection. With every succeeding generation she must be more read, and . . . more loved" (961).

30. As Edmund Wilson puts it, echoing her two great nineteenth century admirers, George Henry Lewes and William Dean Howells, Austen "was unique among novelists of her sex in being deeply and steadily concerned not with the vicarious satisfaction of emotion. . . . nor with the skillful exploitation of gossip, but with the novel as a work of art" ("A Long Talk about Jane Austen," 306).

31. Gamaliel Bradford, Jr., "Portrait of a Lady," *North American Review* 197 (1913): 819–31. See also Edmund Wilson, "A Long Talk about Jane Austen," on Austen's affinity with classical comedy; Q.K., "Jane Austen," *New Republic*, July 28, 1917), 356–67; Hinkley, *Ladies of Literature*; and Burden Blake, "Business of Marriage."

32. J. B. Shaw, *Outlines of General Literature* (Boston, 1849), 129.

33. One especially modernist version of this detachment will read it as a supreme manifestation of the artist, and a sign of Austen's distinction from the "rest

of her sex." See especially Wilson, "A Long Talk about Jane Austen," following along the lines of Lewes and Howells.

34. J. F. Kirk, "Thackeray as a Novelist," *North American Review* (July 1853), quoted in Southam 1968, 143.

35. Hinkley, *Ladies of Literature*, 102.

36. Lovett and Hughes, *History of the Novel*, 168.

37. Girould, *Patterns of English and American Novels*, 163.

38. Welty, "The Radiance of Jane Austen," 7. Yet, Welty maintains, Austen should not be read through the lens of alienation: "Jane Austen's frame was that of *belonging to her world*" (her italics, 10).

39. Repplier, "Conversation in Novels," 64.

40. Price, "Grandmother's Favorite Novel," 488.

41. Halperin, *Language of Meditation*, 148.

42. Virginia Woolf, *The Common Reader*, First Series, ed. Andrew McNeillie (1925; New York: Harcourt Brace Jovanovich, 1984), 136.

43. Price, "Grandmother's Favorite Novel," 483; and Welty, "The Radiance of Jane Austen," 13.

44. Halperin, *Language of Meditation*, 15. Halperin gets his ideas about the "autonomous novel" from Ortega Y Gasset's treatise *The Dehumanization of Art* (1925).

45. Poirier, *A World Elsewhere*, viii, 159, 160.

46. Ibid., 176, 153 (my italics).

47. It is worth quoting at length this remarkable passage from Repplier, for it gives a sense of how a writer like Austen could be "naturalized" by an American reader. "If they come from afar, or are compatriots of my own, they are equally well-beloved. There are no aliens in the ranks of literature, no national prejudice in an honest enjoyment of art. The book, after all, not the date or birthplace of its author, is of material importance. . . . [T]he volume that has crossed the seas, the volume that has survived its generation, stand side by side with their newborn American brother, and there is no lack of harmony in such close companionship" ("Our Friends, the Books," 16).

48. The classic study of the history of nativism in the United States is John Higham, *Strangers in the Land: Patterns of American Nativism, 1860–1925*, reprinted by arrangement with Rutgers University Press (New York: Atheneum, 1963). See esp. chapter 6.

49. Harry H. Laughlin, *Immigration and Conquest*, a report of the Special Commission on Immigration and Naturalization of the Chamber of Commerce of the State of New York (New York: Chamber of Commerce, 1939), 6.

50. See Edward Said, "Jane Austen and Empire," in *Contemporary Marxist Literary Criticism*, ed. Francis Mulhern (London: Longman's, 1992), 97–113. Originally published in 1989 in *Raymond Williams: Critical Perspectives*, ed. Terry Eagleton (Oxford: Polity Press, 1989), 150–64. For a rejoinder to Said, see Moira Ferguson, "*Mansfield Park*, Slavery, Colonialism, and Gender," *Oxford Literary Review* 13 (1991): 118–39.

51. A mulatto woman is rumored to arrive in *Sanditon*, Austen's last and uncompleted novel, but we never get a chance to see her. She is the only racially marked person referred to in all of Austen's writings.

52. Hinkley, *Ladies of Literature*, 85–86.

53. Lovett and Hughes, *History of the Novel*, 171, 166.

54. Hinkley, *Ladies of Literature*, 89. For a useful analysis of the function of race in the construction of American literary realism, especially in the work of Henry James, see Kenneth Warren, *Black and White Strangers* (Chicago: University of Chicago Press, 1993). Warren's reading of James's *The Portrait of a Lady*, given that novel's reliance on Austen's *Pride and Prejudice* and *Emma*, is especially suggestive in the context of this paper. See his chapter 1.

55. Hinkley, *Ladies of Literature*, 117.

56. Poirier, *A World Elsewhere*, 199.

57. Another departure from the novel occurs at the end of the movie, when Lady Catherine De Bourgh is revealed to have acted as cupid's emissary, her showdown with Elizabeth a mere ruse to determine the latter's true feelings for Darcy. Contemporary critics understood this move as an attempt to soften the issue of class division and to reinforce sympathy for the English—aristocrats or not—during wartime. See Robert Lowsa-Peebles, "European Conflict and Hollywood's Reconstruction of English Fiction," *Yearbook of English Studies* 36 (1996): 1–13.

# 8

## In Face of All the Servants: Spectators and Spies in Austen

*with special reference to the 1995 adaptation of* Persuasion

ROGER SALES

*Persuasion*, set in 1814, is a highly topical text that debates questions about who will, and who deserves to, win the peace at the apparent end of the Napoleonic Wars. The 1995 BBC TV adaptation, a self-contained film version screened in cinemas as well as on television, opens with Admiral Croft being rowed out to a ship of the line. He inspects the sailors on board and then, in the messroom, announces to the officers that the war is over, Napoleon is exiled in Elba, and so they can all go back to somewhere called home. The narrative has movement and pace. It starts being intercut almost immediately with another one that also has urgency. Sir Walter Elliot's extremely halfhearted battles on the home front to conquer his debts are very far from over. A council of war has been called at Kellynch to deal with this crisis. While the navy celebrates victory, Mr. Shepherd and Mrs. Clay, and then Lady Russell, hurry toward this home.

Mr. Shepherd, the family lawyer, is met by two grooms. He is greeted much more angrily by some of Sir Walter's creditors, who have to be restrained by the underbutler. Five servants in livery come out to meet Lady Russell, one of them carrying a stool so that she can dismount gracefully from her carriage. These two arrivals quickly convey the nature of the problem. Sir Walter has been squandering far too much money on maintaining an ostentatious lifestyle, of which this veritable army of servants is such a crucial part. In the kingdom of the vain, valets and valetism reign supreme.

*Persuasion* is not the only recent adaptation that opens with images of male comradeship before moving back to the more restricted domestic world of the heroine. The 1995 BBC TV serialization of *Pride and Prejudice* opens with two buddies, Darcy and Bingley, galloping furiously around the countryside in search of a house rather than a wife. The foregrounding of heroes is in danger of disrupting Austen's romance plots. Her heroines are usually placed in the uncomfortable position of having to solve the mysteries of masculine motivation and movement with only half-buried signs and muffled clues to help them. But in the TV serial we actually see Darcy attempting to come to terms with the hurt, and love, that he feels after Elizabeth's rejection of his proposal. We know where he is, what he is doing, what indeed he is wearing, as well as having clear indications about what he is thinking. This serialization led to a mock-hysterical period of Darcymania.[1] His emotional turmoil, smouldering looks, and damp white shirt were allowed to steal the show from the heroine.

The television version of *Persuasion* stays closer to the text's romance conventions. Captain Wentworth disappears completely from the action after the visit to Lyme until he arrives in Bath. Yet there is still a sense in which television makes heroes more knowable and understandable earlier on than they are in Austen's novels. It is also usually the case that the villains, through their transparent looks and mannerisms, can be instantly recognized as such. So the tension in the romance plot—for instance, over whether Anne Elliot will read the signs in time to see through William Walter Elliot, the heir presumptive—is all but lost. We may know, or hope, that she will, but there still needs to be just a little more suspense.

The representation of masculine identities will be explored further here, given that it is such a distinctive feature of the 1990s versions of Austen. The main theme, however, will be a consideration of the roles servants play in these costume dramas, as a way of also highlighting how Anne herself is cast by her family as being little better than a servant. It will be argued that this particular adaptation finds important ways of visualizing how the Regency upper classes had to act out their lives "in face of all the servants," as somebody put it in 1815 after a high society elopement that will be considered later on here. Discussion of the adaptation itself will be followed by a brief look at some of the anxieties surrounding servants in Regency England using texts by Austen and others.

Earlier adaptations in serial form often tried desperately hard, out of a sense of cultural deference, to emphasize their faithfulness to the author's original text, whatever that might be. The 1990s versions are not nearly so reverential and are happy enough to be seen as readings and interpretations, sometimes jokey, frivolous ones as in the case of *Pride and Prejudice*. Although they often obscure themes, they can also send readers back to Austen's texts with important questions in mind that, if not completely neglected in the literary criticism, may nevertheless not have been given the importance that they deserve.[2] Servants themselves may be marginalized figures and yet, given the way in which Anne is cast by her family, service and subservience can also be seen as central themes.

Adaptations promote heritage myths of Austen, and yet they also contain shots that unsettle such cosy images. I have argued elsewhere that such moments occur in the 1980 television version of *Pride and Prejudice*.

There is a recurring shot of one or more of the Bennet sisters looking out a window. They watch events from which they have been excluded, such as the calls that take place when Bingley arrives in the neighborhood. They wait for events to happen over which they have no control, such as the delivery of letters from men to explain what is happening. This shot has a visual and thematic density that works against the emphasis elsewhere on elegant surfaces. The inevitable heritage images of historic homes and gardens lose some of their more conservative meanings when also visualized as genteel prisons. An elegant sash-window can be looked at, and looked through, in very different ways.[3] Julianne Pidduck notes that this window shot, the frame within the frame, also recurs throughout most of the 1990s adaptations and suggests that there is more of an emphasis here on the way in which the female figure at the window yearns to, and often does, transcend the confinements of gendered space.[4] I will consider images of servants, and service, in *Persuasion* to see whether they too produce unsettling moments that can in turn produce meanings from the written text itself.

As noticed, viewers become conscious of the hovering presence of servants very early on. Even before the appearance of household servants meeting and greeting the arrivals at the big house, a gardener is seen raking the grass as the carriages pull into the drive. These servants are at one level merely stage decoration, in every sense of the word extras. They are just there to remind us, as is the almost obligatory crunch of posh carriage wheels on immaculate gravel drives, that we are being invited to make a pleasurable return to a more leisured world which has been lost.

Servants can, however, perform other functions that often contradict such safe, nostalgic images of English heritage. Austen adaptations in general, and this one in particular, provide important reminders, present in the novels themselves but not always so openly displayed, of the way in which gentry life was a drama that had to be acted out daily in front of an audience of servants without whom a leisured lifestyle would have been impossible. Private life was in fact extremely public, a series of events in the stage-play world of the country house. This, in turn, raises questions about where we as spectators might be positioned. We are often, too often, invited to eavesdrop on dinner-table conversations. This can be seen as providing us with a privileged and therefore pleasurable access to an exclusive world. Yet, as will become more apparent, the camera itself, and therefore the viewers, often wait at table in the sense that the recurrent circling, hovering shot of the gentry eating and drinking is from the point of view of a servant. We may become part of this other world, but there are also times when we are made conscious of our ever so humble place within it.

This uneasy sense of belonging and yet not quite belonging is also the position in which Anne finds herself. She is like Fanny Price in *Mansfield*

*Park* in being a part of the family and yet apart from them. Fanny is a "quiet auditor of the whole" (123), during the theatrical rehearsals but also more generally. Anne, like a servant, eavesdrops on conversations that are taking place in domestic interiors between those who consider themselves to be her betters. She hears some things but not others. She tends to listen, and think, rather than speak and is often talked about as if she were not there. When she does find her voice, it is sometimes rendered inaudible by competing ones. She is made painfully aware that she is a nobody who should not get in the way of her superiors. This, too, is the servant's position: to perform useful actions and yet still to remain a spectator rather than an actor.

The discussion of Sir Walter's financial problems begins in the drawing room. Anne is late for it and so takes up a position that is distanced from the family circle. She quietly listens to the dialogue and watches the actors. She enters carrying a bunch of keys, indicating that she is the housekeeper in all but name and is presumably late because she has been undertaking domestic tasks. Hand-props quickly establish her subservient status. Later on, she comes down the stairs holding lists, items once again associated with a housekeeper. She keeps discreetly out of the way while Admiral Croft is being shown around the house: not seen and not heard.

The drama about the debts continues over lunch. Two servants stand motionless behind Sir Walter, but the shots are not being taken from their point of view. They sometimes come, however, from the perspective of an unseen servant who is waiting at the other end of the table. An estate worker trudges slowly and wearily past the window while the family is eating, suggesting connections between the worlds of leisure and work. The impassive faces of the servants behind Sir Walter perhaps betray hints of dumb insolence, or possibly it is just sheer boredom. A job that involved listening to him pontificating about the arrangement of his hair and the perfection of his complexion is not one to be undertaken at all lightly. Anne, like the other servants, also has to endure his vain monologues in silence. Later on, after he has eventually been persuaded to let the house to Admiral Croft, he instructs Anne to see that the other servants are civil to their new master. It is far beneath his dignity to talk to them himself. Anne is being asked to carry on being a go-between, relaying a message from the upstairs world to the downstairs one.

Elizabeth Elliot, accompanied by Mrs. Clay, makes a self-consciously dramatic exit from the house to take a carriage to Bath. They sweep toward the main door. Viewers can clearly see sullen domestic servants lined up to the left of this door. If looks could kill, then Elizabeth and Sir Walter would be dead long before they ever reached the safety of the carriage. It is not immediately clear who is to the right of the door. Elizabeth, with no sense of irony, leaves the great house still overplaying the part of mistress of it. She barks out instructions to this unseen figure by the door: "I haven't had time to speak to the gardener so here is the list of plants for Lady Russell. This is the list of books and music that I must have sent to Bath. And you'd best catalogue all the pictures and clear your rubbish out of the storeroom."[5] Only as she is laying down the domestic law like this does it becomes apparent that she is delivering these orders to Anne. Sir Walter adds insult to this injury by lamenting the fact that he never had a son, when it is his turn to leave the house. Anne is being ritually humiliated because she is being publicly humiliated, in face of all the servants.

Sir Walter and Elizabeth cast themselves as paternalistic and philanthropic guardians of Kellynch, cruelly forced out by hard times, in a play that is a complete travesty of events. The stony-faced spectators lined up for their sentimental departure come from a different play. The estate workers have also gathered on the other side of the drive to form part of the audience. There is no sorrow written over these faces, just sullenness. It is suggested that the household servants would have had some opportunities to piece together information about the collapse of the family fortunes. News of Sir Walter's bankruptcy probably came as more of a shock to the estate workers, given that keeping up appearances was very much his style as well as his complete substance.

The adaptation, while conveying an important sense of the stage-play nature of gentry life, may still exaggerate (or modernize) the access that household servants did in fact have to the affairs of their employers. It is only souls of indiscretion such as Lydia Bennet who openly gossip about intimate family matters while the servants are still waiting at table. A waiter actually has to be sent away at the George Inn to prevent the embarrassment of her gossiping about Wickham and Mary King in front of him. The normal etiquette, whether at home or elsewhere, was for such intimate matters to be discussed, if at all, after the servants had withdrawn, indicating gentry anxieties about the presence of spies.[6] Elizabeth Bennet is worried that her mother's hysterical, and therefore unguarded, response to Lydia's brazen letter to Mrs. Forster will mean that all the servants at Longbourn will know of the family scandal that same day.

Adaptations are often caught in a double bind. Heritage concerns demand the presence of servants as decorative extras to provide a visual shorthand that announces quality of life. This in turn reinforces the quality of the various individual products, including Englishness, that are being displayed and showcased. Yet the narrative would grind to a complete halt if all that these servants, and in turn the viewers, heard was the smallest of small talk deemed appropriate for their ears.

Anne certainly needs no instructions from her arrogant sister in how to pack up the house. She does this quietly and methodically, supervising maids and other servants. Family portraits are removed from the walls.

Although Anne is in charge, there are still some shots in which her appearance among the dust sheets transforms her once again into the figure of a housekeeper. She then departs in a farm wagon, complete with a pig and some geese, rather than in a carriage. Viewers are given one last glimpse of the gardeners, burning dead leaves on the grounds. Is this the end of an era? *Persuasion* is still often seen as being an autumnal novel even though critics like Claudia L. Johnson have shown the false nature of some of the assumptions on which this claim is based.[7] It is also the case, again as argued by Johnson and others, that the worlds of the gentry and the navy are not as far apart as might have been suggested by the intercut narratives in the opening sequence. Wentworth, and indeed Mrs. Croft, are lesser gentry even though Sir Walter has great difficulty in coming to terms with this fact.

Anne merely exchanges one form of servitude for another. When she arrives at Mary Musgrove's house in Uppercross, she is shown in by a maid who then disappears. This means that almost immediately she has to start performing menial tasks, such as clearing up the toys that are strewn dangerously all over the floor. She becomes even more of a governess figure when young Charles Musgrove injures himself by falling out of a tree. Mary eventually swans off for a big dinner at the big house, leaving Anne to serve as the nurse, governess, and indeed mother. According to Mrs. Musgrove senior, Mary manages her servants just as badly as she manages her children. The nursery maid, Jemima, is reported as being extremely flighty. After young Charles's accident, Anne has to control the servants as well as the children.

It is shortly after this accident that Wentworth makes his entrance as far as Anne is concerned, he and his party being announced by the maid. He is shot with a slightly tilted camera to emphasize his physical stature and presence. This, and other visual tricks, leave no doubt that the hero of the romance has finally arrived. It is therefore difficult to take his flirtations with Henrietta and Louisa Musgrove as being particularly threatening, either to Anne or to the girls themselves. Both girls are instantly recognizable as being silly and shallow. Austen almost describes them as such, but the instant visual images lower the tension and suspense of the romance quite considerably. *Persuasion* may be an unconventional romance given that Anne, approaching a dangerous age, is older than other heroines and will be returning to rather than discovering her first love. There are still, however, more conventional uncertainties about the hero's intentions that in the adaptation tend to get lost.

Wentworth recounts some of his daring exploits at sea during a dinner-party scene. He boasts about prize money, although in the domestic sphere he himself and his wealth are the prize, and he knows it only too well. This scene goes on for four minutes of television time, even though there is in fact no clear indication in the novel that it actually takes place at dinner time. We are given something approaching Wentworth's point of view, with shots of these silly girls staring adoringly at the camera. But the standard shot is one that is from the point of view of an unseen servant waiting at table. The camera goes slowly round the table, hovering deferentially at the shoulder of almost all the guests. It is a scene that has a long history in British television with popular programs from the 1970s such as *Upstairs Downstairs* helping to establish its conventions.

Distinctions between British and American production values are sometimes very hard to make. The 1995 film version of *Sense and Sensibility*, scripted by Emma Thompson, starred other British character actors but was financed by Columbia Pictures. *Persuasion* itself was made in association with WGBH/Boston and a French coproducer. There is, however, still a case for saying that close associations with Hollywood tend to produce adaptations that are less interested in the spectacle, if this is what it is, of the gentry at table. *Emma* may contain many characters who are almost totally obsessed with food, and yet the 1996 Hollywood version of it offers only relatively short, sharp dinner-table scenes. In contrast, the 1996 ITV version, made by the *Pride and Prejudice* production team, gives more space to both servants and the food that they cultivate, prepare, and serve. They work hard to transform Box Hill into a dining space appropriate for the gentry, complete with long tables and chairs.[8] Hollywood adaptations of Austen, going back to the 1940 version of *Pride and Prejudice*, have always privileged romance and character (shading into caricature) over loving attempts to reproduce what passes for historical, heritage detail.

The way in which the dinner party may at times privilege Wentworth's point of view raises important questions about narration. A problem for Austen adaptations has always been what to do about the narrator's voice, which has sometimes been very clumsily and inappropriately translated into dialogue for the heroine and others. There are problems as well in rendering the thoughts of a heroine, which have also been put into dialogue that jars. As Ros Ballaster notes, this particular adaptation seems uncomfortable about narration.[9] The camera may have to fill the space created by the absent narrator, and yet it is unsure how to do this consistently and effectively. The servant's point of view is one of many adopted. This dinner party is the occasion on which Mrs. Musgrove indulges herself in "large fat sighings" (68) over the death of her completely worthless son. She is roundly and soundly criticized, indeed abused, for doing so in the novel. There are heritage concerns that may explain why the adaptation avoids this unsettling moment, which has always troubled those critics who prefer a safer, tamer, and gentler version of Austen. There may also have been more purely technical reasons for its omission, given that the sharp critique is delivered by the narrator.

The problem of instant recognition that has already been identified also takes its toll during the visit to Lyme. Benwick is a single and singularly unattractive man badly in want of a bath and a life. He is a very low-rent Lord Byron indeed. It is difficult to imagine for a moment the flicker of romance that Anne feels for him before her judgment thankfully gets the better of her. Her private thoughts on whether he will get over his bereavement are translated into dialogue that makes her voice more confident than it is in the novel at this stage.

Problems are also caused by the appearance of William Walter Elliot, the heir presumptive. He is not called upon to say anything much at Lyme, but he looks distinctly sly and shifty. It is his servant, gossiping with the waiter at the inn, who provides the clues to his identity. When Elliot starts opening his mouth more later on, he positively oozes insincerity and over-familiarity. His manner, when not shifty, is simpering and fawning. He flatters but is incapable of deceiving viewers, who must wonder why on earth somebody as sensible and capable as Anne is unable to see straight through him.

The romance text has all but broken down at this point. The rival suitor, or demon lover, in Austen's fiction is often characterized by the hypnotically seductive power of his voice. Even Fanny Price might not have been able to resist Henry Crawford had not her affections been engaged elsewhere. This is a voice that is unfortunately very rarely heard in adaptations, in which slow, mannered, allegedly period delivery takes precedence over a charm that is as destructive and dangerous as it is delicious and delightful. Ironically enough, the closest anybody has come to reproducing this truly charming voice is Alan Rickman when playing the part of stuffy, if considerate, Colonel Brandon in *Sense and Sensibility.* Marilyn Butler may be right to point out that in the novel itself William Walter Elliot is not nearly so much of a temptation as are characters such as George Wickham and Frank Churchill.[10] Perhaps the adaptation, through better casting, could and should have made him just a touch more tempting and tasty. The charm has to be there in the first place for it to be broken.

Despite problems caused by the bad casting of new male characters, the excursion to Lyme still captures important themes. Anne becomes quite radiant when she recognizes how Wentworth has noticed the way in which an apparently complete stranger gazes at her. The network of gazes is well done. The location filming and wide-angle shots, and more particularly the big, bright, and breezy seascapes, provide a real sense of release from the interiors at both Kellynch and Uppercross. Anne has passed through the window. Until Louisa's accident, smiles do not have to be reined in, and the background music is upbeat and uplifting.

This adaptation begins at sea, as indicated, with a sequence that establishes the world of male friendship and comradeship. This theme resurfaces at Lyme when Wentworth is reunited with Benwick and Harville. Yet variations on it have also been present before this. Charles Musgrove becomes a much more substantial and likeable character than he is in the novel. Like his sisters, he too falls very quickly under the spell of the gallant Captain. They enjoy their boys' own activities together, such as shooting, when, that is, Wentworth's adoring female fan club do not insist on being present as well. Wentworth's stories of high risks on the high seas enthrall Charles as much as the others. He casts his own admiring gazes and glances to Wentworth's end of the table. They call each other by their first names, even though they are very new acquaintances. They also engage in boyish, or laddish, banter that seals their intimacy. Charles asks Wentworth whether a letter, which we learn is from Harville proposing a visit to Lyme, is a love letter, as if the Captain does not have more than enough offers of love in his life. He is told that it is not, but that he too would love Harville once he had met him. Anne, who has arrived back before the rest of the walking party in Admiral Croft's gig, is passing around mugs of hot chocolate in this scene. She is waiting on, or serving, the others.

Charles gets great satisfaction from his association with the navy. His buddy Wentworth strides about Lyme in a swanky, smart uniform that reveals the contours of his body. The *Pride and Prejudice* adaptation displayed the male body in a more knowing, jokey way. Yet something broadly similar is also happening here, and the body beautiful in question is being shown off to men such as Charles as well as to women. Charles may admire Wentworth, but, back in Uppercross, Henrietta's loyal suitor was speechless with envy when he first met him. Wentworth was dancing a touch or two too intimately with Henrietta at the time. Either whichway, his body becomes a center of attention.

Charles's credentials as a likeable sidekick are enhanced by the way in which he is given a wife-from-hell. Austen is certainly caustic about Mary Musgrove, as she is about all imaginary invalids. Yet Charles's boorish neglect of her, together with the way in which society offers few other professions for women, are held to be at least partly responsible for her bad behavior. His fondness for hunting weasels and rats is not meant to endear him. He had proposed to Anne before marrying Mary. The adaptation, by transforming him into a jolly good chap (he gallantly proposes the trip to Lyme as a leaving present for Anne), casts more doubt than there should be over her powers of discrimination. Mary may behave badly, and yet, in the novel, it is her gossipy letter to her sister Anne which breaks the news that Benwick and Louisa have become an item. This unlikely event is introduced into the adaptation by Admiral Croft, which provides yet another example of the way in which male characters are allowed to become more central.

There may be a thespian in-joke about the way in which Charles's part is expanded into almost a leading role. The character is played by Simon Russell Beale, a classical actor specializing in black camp well known for, among other things, his portrayals of Marlowe's Edward II and Shakespeare's Richard III. He seems, initially at least, a surprising choice to play an oafish country sportsman like Charles in something as safe as an Austen adaptation. Being Russell Beale, however, he is always in danger of acting the others off the screen and beyond. Although Amanda Root and Ciaran Hinds both look right, and act well, as Anne and Wentworth, the presence of Royal Shakespeare Company heavyweights may be crowding their performances. Susan Fleetwood turns in a meticulously imperious performance as Lady Russell. Corin Redgrave minces about in coats of many colors that a Regency dandy like Sir Walter would not have been seen dead in, lisping as he goes. It is not just the hero and his new buddy who are in danger of encroaching upon the theatrical space of the actress who plays Anne.

One of Russell Beale's earlier performances for the Royal Shakespeare Company was in Nick Dear's *The Art of Success* in 1986. The choice of Dear to write the screenplay for *Persuasion* might also have been seen, initially, as an unlikely one. His work until then had been for theater and radio. *The Art of Success* brutally exposes the artistic, moral, and sexual corruption of William Hogarth's world. The underworld is populated by prostitutes and criminals. The overworld is equally corrupt and corrupting: rakes debauch themselves and anyone else on whom they can lay their trembling hands. The Prime Minister and the Queen indulge in highly sexualized power games. Another of Dear's history plays, *In the Ruins*, deals with King George III's madness (before Alan Bennett's popular play and screenplay on the same subject) and contains a story about how Admiral Lord Nelson, after his death at Trafalgar, was embalmed in a cask of brandy to prevent his body from decomposing when it was being brought back to England for burial.[11] Such grotesque stories do not appear in Austen's account of the navy at war. The combination of Dear and Austen is a self-consciously unusual one on the surface and as such is part of a pattern in 1990s adaptations. Andrew Davies's version of *Middlemarch* enjoyed success in 1993, and yet some of his other work on modern sexual comedies and political thrillers did not immediately suggest him for *Pride and Prejudice*.

Important concerns have been expressed by Ballaster and others about what happens when male writers, actors, and directors start colonizing spaces that have traditionally been female, and some of these have already been addressed here. Still, what Dear's stage background allows him to do is to bring out the theatricality of the novel's world. This is not to say that his screenplay is stagy in the sense of being slow, static, and old-fashioned. If anything, the reverse is true. It is rather to suggest that he is able to capture and examine the stage-play nature of a world in which parts, including that of the spectator, are performed very self-consciously. Roger Michell, the director who worked with this screenplay, was another deliberately unlikely choice given his dislike of period drama. He provocatively declared, sounding like a bad-boy rock star, that he had tried to "trash the hotel room of the BBC classic."[12] Pidduck argues that his highlighting of the servant's part, and thus economic power relations, can be seen as an attempt to introduce modern concerns into period drama.[13]

Lyme opens up possibilities for both romance and male friendship that are then apparently shattered when Louisa has her fall. Anne eventually finds herself in the much more claustrophobic world of Bath, looking out windows. Part of its claustrophobia comes from a return to a world with the constant, hovering presence of servants who spy on the various dramas as they unfold. Sir Walter has two liveried servants stationed at each end of his drawing room at Camden Place. They stand behind Sir Walter when dinner is served, for extra decoration rather than for functional purposes. The camera circles the table as a servant would, hovering deferentially by each character. All family business, including arguments, is acted out in front of, or in face of, the servants. First Mrs. Clay and then Elizabeth flounce off from breakfast when Anne declares her intention to keep her appointment with Mrs. Smith rather than go to visit Lady Dalyrymple. Once again, Anne's thoughts, this time about similarities between Mrs. Smith and Mrs. Clay, are translated awkwardly into dialogue. The whole of Bath is crawling with servants. Social status is announced by the style as well as the quantity of any retinue. Lady Dalrymple is flanked by two black page boys when the Elliots finally pluck up enough courage to call on her. The Marchioness de Thierry in the 1987 BBC TV version of *Northanger Abbey* has one black page boy who accompanies her to the ballrooms in Bath. As David Dabydeen has argued in relation to portrait painting in this period, such page boys functioned as exotic, expensive pets or trophies.[14]

When Anne visits Mrs. Smith, she meets Nurse Rooke and playfully accuses her of being a spy for using her position as a midwife to learn the secrets of the families that she visits. Nurse Rooke, who is given a voice in the adaptation but not in the novel, admits that she likes to keep her ears open.[15] Although not as clear in the adaptation as it is in the novel because of the problems surrounding narration, it is her eavesdropping and surveillance that help to uncover the plots being hatched by William Walter Elliot. The adaptation brings out Anne's affinity with servants, while at the same time probably overstating it. When, in the novel, she calls at Westgate

Buildings, she does not notice who opens the door for her. It might have been just a maid, she thinks, when questioned about it by Mrs. Smith, but it was in fact Nurse Rooke. Anne sees no one, or nobody. She is like the servants and yet also very unlike them.

Nurse Rooke is represented as being a benevolent spy, whereas there is something much more malevolent and menacing about the way in which Sir Walter's servants contemptuously watch him. This adaptation may be concerned to show off and display heritage products, but it also finds ways of visualizing a particular Regency set of anxieties about how servants might use family secrets, including sexual ones, to embarrass their employers. To take just one historical example, Lady Anne Abdy, the niece of the duke of Wellington and the wife of Sir William Abdy, eloped with Lord Charles Bentinck in 1815. They had planned this elopement when they met earlier at Worthing. Regency watering places were associated in fact as well as in the fictions of Austen and others with dangerous liaisons. The two lovers, displaying little originality, called themselves Captain and Mrs. Browne and set up a lovenest in Greenwich. The Abdy family were not very hopeful about being able to limit the damage to Sir William's reputation. As one of them wrote, Lady Anne "left Hill St in so public a manner with Lord Charles, in face of all the servants in the mews that I much doubt and fear the possibility of its being kept secret, added to which her servants and ours can not be kept silent."[16] These fears came home to roost. Somebody, quite possibly a servant, tipped off the *St James's Chronicle*, which produced a knowing, gossipy article, much like that read out aloud by Mr. Price about Maria Rushworth and Henry Crawford's elopement in *Mansfield Park*. Although the Abdy clan were worried about both sets of servants gossiping about family secrets, they were more than happy to recruit servants from the Greenwich establishment to reveal intimate details when Sir William petitioned for divorce in the House of Lords. Servants could facilitate, or service, an elopement, and yet this also gave them power to expose it.

It was, after the event, a very different kind of servant who probably did most damage to Sir William's reputation. He made the great mistake of calling in a tearful state on the courtesan Harriette Wilson for consolation, thus assuring himself of a place in her gossipy, scandalous, and highly popular *Memoirs* (1825). She can only just stop herself from laughing out loud at this sad figure who, in her worldly opinion, thoroughly deserved to be cuckolded several times over in the great game of hearts. A later attempt at a love letter from him addressed to "Dear, Pretty Miss Wilson" is treated with lofty disdain. She just quotes a fragment from the beginning and then majestically declares that the "rest of this eloquent epistle may be dispensed with."[17] She published and he was damned.

Wilson's *Memoirs* is not as far away from the world of Austen's novels as may be supposed, for she is an overstated version of Lydia Bennet. They are both party animals who are out for a good time. All the rest is merely propaganda from Mr. Collins's conduct books. They both laugh a lot, chatter incessantly, eat heartily, play naughty practical jokes, get easily bored when not the center of attention, and have a passion for men in uniforms. Harriette, like Lydia, follows the army to Brighton, although under the protection of her current aristocratic lover rather than that of a colonel's wife. She parades around in a form of military uniform, becoming the toast of the officers' mess and, more generally, the life and soul of any party.

In *Sense and Sensibility*, Colonel Brandon's plans to elope to Scotland with his cousin Eliza are foiled by a servant, although it is not clear whether this is by accident or by treacherous design. The Bertrams in *Mansfield Park* are unable to hush up Maria and Henry's elopement because it is impossible to silence the servant who has been involved it: "[T]he servant of Mrs Rushworth, the mother, had exposure in her power, and supported by her mistress, was not to be silenced" (411). This servant is still serving her mistress, of course, while at the same time shifting the balance of power between them. Wickham, himself the son of a senior member of the household staff at Pemberley, recruits another servant there, Mrs. Yonge, the governess or companion, to help him when he attempts to elope with Georgiana Darcy. He believes that he can trust her again when he elopes with Lydia. She, no longer in service at Pemberley for obvious reasons, finds them lodgings in London and probably reveals where they are to Darcy only when he pays her enough money. She is a mercenary figure, who comes close to ruining the reputations of both Georgiana and Lydia. She makes a living by renting out rooms and would have been only too happy to let Wickham and Lydia stay with her if any space had been available. The world of organized prostitution is not very far away.

These events are reported in the novels in question rather than shown directly and explicitly. Similarly, the five underservants who become discontented and potentially disobedient during the theatrical rehearsals at Mansfield Park remain in the very margins of the text. Yet, in the case of elopements, it is possible to see the figure of the potentially powerful servant (or former servant) as being both marginal and central. It could indeed be argued that these texts banish to their margins deep anxieties that would otherwise prove to be too destructive. Austen's novels are, in more general terms, places where deferential servants are usually talked about but not heard.[18] Elopements and other scandals nevertheless convey almost unthinkable ideas about how very precarious this deference might be. Other novelists from this period certainly offer much more explicit representations of servants who had exposure in their power. William Godwin's *Caleb Williams* (1794) deals with the consequences for an upper servant of his compulsion to discover his master's darkest secrets. A dead servant's papers in Charlotte Smith's *Celestina* (1791) hold the key to Celestina de Mornay's true origins, which her enemies try to obscure by getting a decoy, or false, servant to spread rumors. Jemima in Mary Wollstonecraft's *Maria, or the Wrongs of Woman* (1798) is the daughter of servants who then becomes one herself. Through her own experiences, which include rape by her master, she is able to expose, if not right, the sexual double standards that lie at the very foundations of allegedly respectable households. Austen's novels are markedly different in emphasis and agenda when dealing with servants. Yet these differences should not be pushed to the point where they obscure the fact that questions about power and exposure are indeed being raised in relation to servants.

Because servants, often aided and abetted by interested parties, had exposure in their power, concerted efforts were made to check their credentials before they were employed. The Servants' Character Act, which was passed in 1792, was aimed at preventing servants from either tampering with, or else fabricating altogether, their own references. Those found guilty were fined twenty pounds, a sum that was meant to be out of the reach of most offenders. If they could not pay this fine, the magistrates were empowered to send them to a house of correction for a period of hard labor. Part of the money raised by the fines that were paid went to those who informed against a servant using a false, or forged, character. Although potential employers may sometimes have pocketed this money, the intention of the act was to encourage other servants to become spies and informers. It attempted to recruit them to maintain surveillance of the downstairs world and thus to safeguard the household from shady characters who could turn downstairs into a sinister, threatening underworld.

The appointment of servants, particularly senior ones such as butlers and housekeepers, was often preceded by a careful vetting process that was carried out by a number of women pooling their knowledge. Mrs. Bland was enlisted to help Mary Heber and her family find a new butler toward the end of 1792. Mrs. Bland contacted several of her friends for names and was eventually in a position to interview candidates. Only one of these appeared suitable. He could be given a "character" by his former employers. Mary Heber nevertheless picked up a rumor from elsewhere, perhaps from other servants, that this butler allegedly had a habit of actually helping himself much too freely to the contents of the wine cellar. Mrs. Bland investigated again: "Of being discharged when in Liquor the time you named, he did not deny—nor was he turned away for it; 'twas he Left his place as he Preferred a steady good family to that of being in the Hurry of a Lord's."[19] This vetting process was designed to make sure that employers avoided sleeping, or perhaps not sleeping, in the same house as the enemy.

Returning to *Persuasion*, it is clear that Sir Walter makes yet another spectacular error of judgment when he encourages Mrs. Clay to take up residence in Camden Place in Bath as a companion for Elizabeth without the thorough investigation of her "character" that both Anne and Lady Russell sensibly conduct. He does not inquire about her failed marriage and is utterly uninterested in the welfare of her two children. Anne is humiliated not just by being treated as a servant but also by having her place usurped by one. Mrs. Clay, the enemy and spy within, humors the humorless Elizabeth and sets about using her considerable sexual charms to ensnare the vain Sir Walter into marriage. This is a part of the plot that is uncovered through the benevolent espionage of Nurse Rooke and Mrs. Smith. They can explain why William Walter Elliot is so keen to marry Anne as quickly as possible in order to prevent his inheritance from being taken away from him. Mrs. Clay, an upper servant certainly, is still yet another Regency servant who eventually acquires associations with sex and scandal. There is an elopement. Both she and the heir presumptive abandon their opportunistic schemes to marry into the Elliot family, and they set up an establishment together in London. Reports about Mrs. Yonge in *Pride and Prejudice* get close to the world of organized prostitution, closer than some still imagine is remotely possible in an Austen novel even though Eliza's story in *Sense and Sensibility* is also concerned with the sexual underworld. The ending of *Persuasion* likewise offers a very brief glimpse of the world of Harriette Wilson, the kept mistress, which was inhabited for a time by Wollstonecraft's Jemima before she became a common prostitute.

Mrs. Clay's price may turn out to be marriage to the heir and thus eventually the role of mistress of Kellynch. Austen comments that in her inability to wait any longer for Sir Walter, her "affections had overpowered her interest" (236). Affections in this context suggests sexual desire. Tony Tanner and others have wondered how much significance to attach to the fact that, at Sir Walter's suggestion, Mrs. Clay has been slapping on Gowland's lotion to try to keep her freckles at bay. This product contained mercury, which had been used extensively in the treatment of syphilis.[20] The representation of Mrs. Clay as a sexually predatory and mercenary character is not, however, at all dependent on this single interesting but inconclusive reference. Anne, Lady Russell, and, according to Mrs. Smith, the whole of Bath society know only too well what sexual game she is playing.

The figure of the servant can be a piece of period decoration, an extra reinforcing safe heritage messages about the quality of gentry life and thus also the quality of the production in which they are appearing. But their presence can also be much more menacing and threatening, as it is when Sir Walter and Elizabeth leave Kellynch. This scene in particular, but also other ones set in Bath, show the gentry world to be one that did not offer many opportunities for a retreat into the private. Performers were almost always on display. Despite their protagonists' taking the precaution of waiting until servants had gone, romances, arguments, and sexual encounters still often had to be acted out in front of, or in face of, an audience of real and potential spies. The Austen texts draw attention to this aspect of gentry life—for instance, the anxieties that all the servants will be gossiping away about Lydia's indiscretions—yet adaptations, through camera angles, stage positionings, action-props, and visualization more generally can highlight the nature of this surveillance and the pressures that it caused. Servants may not always be seen, or recognized, by their employers, but this does not prevent them from seeing. The same filmic techniques can also underline the uncomfortableness of Anne's position, caught somewhere between the upstairs and the downstairs world. This position is one that we as viewers come to share with Anne. We are invited to big houses and allowed to watch their inhabitants eating, drinking, and holding conversations. But we often do so from the position of a servant, made aware of the distance between us and those around the dinner table. The diners hold the power because they hold the stage. Yet we learn some of their secrets and so perhaps have our own form of power over them.

## Notes

1. I deal with the reception of this serial in an afterword to *Jane Austen and Representations of Regency England* (London: Routledge, 1996), "Austenmania," 227–39. I expand and develop this argument in "It's That Man in Tight Trousers Again: Dishy Mr Darcy Carries on Camping in a Raunchy Regency Romp also Called *Pride and Prejudice*," in *Jane Austen and Cinema*, ed. Judy Simons (London: Athlone Press, forthcoming).

2. Studies of servants in Austen's work include Judith Terry, "Seen but Not Heard: Servants in Jane Austen's England," *Persuasions* 10 (1988): 104–16, and Janet Todd, "Servants" in *The Jane Austen Handbook*, ed. J. David Grey (London: Athlone Press, 1986), 377–79. Todd does not deal with *Persuasion*. For representations of servants in fiction more generally, see Bruce Robbins, *The Servant's Hand: English Fiction from Below* (Durham, N.C.: Duke University Press, 1993), a very wide-ranging study that illustrates the strengths and weaknesses of a particular form of New Historicism. I deal with aspects of the "servant problem" in Regency England in "The Maid and the Minister's Wife: Literary Philanthropy in Regency York," in *Women's Poetry in the Enlightenment: The Making of a Canon 1730–1820*, ed. Isobel Armstrong and Virginia Blain (Basingstoke: Macmillan,

1999), 127–41. The servant as spy is discussed in Anthea Trodd, "Household Spies: The Servant and the Plot in Victorian Fiction," *Literature and History* 13 (1987): 175–87.

3. *Jane Austen and Representations of Regency England*, 25. For a discussion of access to knowledge in *Pride and Prejudice*, see Judith Lowder Newton, *Women, Power and Subversion: Strategies in British Fiction 1778–1860* (Athens: University of Georgia Press, 1981), chapter 2. This is anthologized in *New Casebooks: Sense and Sensibility and Pride and Prejudice*, ed. Robert Clark (Basingstoke: Macmillan, 1994), 119–44.

4. Julianne Pidduck, "Of Windows and Country Walks: Frames of Space and Movement in 1990s Austen Adaptations," *Screen* 39 (1998): 381–400.

5. This is my transcription of the dialogue from the 1995 BBC Worldwide Ltd Video. The speech is shorter, sharper, and therefore ruder in performance than it is in the published version of the screenplay. See *Persuasion by Jane Austen: A Screenplay by Nick Dear* (London: Methuen, 1996), 10. The title suggests what has become a familiar form of double authorship. Rebecca Dickson argues that the adaptation makes Elizabeth more obnoxious than she is in the novel: "Misrepresenting Jane Austen's Ladies," in *Jane Austen in Hollywood*, ed. Linda Troost and Sayre Greenfield (Lexington: University Press of Kentucky, 1998), 44–57. A number of other essays in this collection notice that this adaptation is more realistic in its representations of class and gender, without always recognizing that it also offers some heritage pleasures.

6. For more details, see Robbins, *The Servant's Hand*, 126–28.

7. Claudia L. Johnson, *Jane Austen: Women, Politics, and the Novel* (Chicago: University of Chicago Press, 1988), 144–45.

8. For a discussion of other scenes involving servants, such as strawberry picking at Donwell and the harvest supper at the end, see Edward Neill, *The Politics of Jane Austen* (Basingstoke: Macmillan, 1999), 143. The adaptation is wrongly attributed to the BBC.

9. Ros Ballaster, "Adapting Jane Austen," *English Review*, September 1996, 10–13. In addition to questions about narration, Ballaster suggests ways in which the traditional female spaces of the romance are in danger of being colonized by men. For another good account of 1990s adaptations, see Judy Simons, "Classics and Trash: Reading Austen in the 1990s," *Women's Writing* 5 (1998): 27–39. This is a special issue devoted to Austen that contains important studies. Both Ballaster and I have been influenced in our views on heritage cinema/television by Andrew Higson, *Waving the Flag: Constructing a National Cinema in Britain* (Oxford: Clarendon Press, 1995), and also by his subsequent publications. *Persuasions* 18 (1996) includes valuable commentary by Patrice Hannon and Deborah Kaplan on recent adaptations.

10. Marilyn Butler, *Jane Austen and the War of Ideas*, rev. ed. (Oxford: Clarendon Press, 1987), 280.

11. For more details, see Nick Dear, *The Art of Success and In the Ruins* (London: Methuen Drama, 1989).

12. As quoted in Catherine Bennett, "Hype and Heritage," *Guardian*, 22 September 1995.

13. Pidduck, "Of Windows and Country Walks," 398. As will be clear, I still see such potentially radical maneuvers as being compromised by more traditional heritage concerns. Pidduck's argument is on safer ground when it draws attention, albeit speculatively, to Margaret's expanded role in *Sense and Sensibility* as offering a "more dynamic feminist future," 391. A broadly similar claim is made about the final shot of *Persuasion* showing both Anne and Wentworth on board a frigate.

14. David Dabydeen, *Hogarth's Blacks: Images of Blacks in Eighteenth Century English Art* (London: Dangaroo Press, 1985), 23.

15. This section of the novel, in the wider context of nursing, is dealt with in some detail in John Wiltshire, *Jane Austen and the Body* (Cambridge: Cambridge University Press, 1992), 165–96. See also *Jane Austen and Representations of Regency England*, 192–99.

16. As quoted in Hugh Farmar, *A Regency Elopement* (London: Michael Joseph, 1969), 30. The evidence of servants, which was often discredited, figured prominently in this period in many other "crim. con," or adultery, cases involving members of the upper classes. It was also a key feature in the trial of Queen Caroline in 1820.

17. *Harriette Wilson's Memoirs of Herself and Others*, ed. James Laver (London: Peter Davies, 1929), 126. For a brief description of her career, see Jane Aiken Hodge, *Passion and Principle: The Loves and Lives of Regency Women* (John Murray: London, 1996), 112–16. For more details, see Angela Thirkell, *The Fortunes of Harriette: The Surprising Career of Harriette Wilson* (London: Hamish Hamilton, 1936). The comparison with Lydia Bennet, although not made explicitly, is nevertheless at times implied.

18. Exceptions include Thomas's reasonably long account of how he had sighted Lucy Steele, now Mrs. Ferrars, in Exeter in *Sense and Sensibility.* As soon, however, as he has performed this particular function, he is perfunctorily dismissed along with the tablecloth.

19. As quoted in Francis Bamford, *Dear Miss Heber: An Eighteenth Century Correspondence* (London: Constable, 1936), 137.

20. See Tony Tanner, *Jane Austen* (Basingstoke: Macmillan, 1986), 237.

# 9

## Jane Austen and Edward Said: Gender, Culture, and Imperialism

SUSAN FRAIMAN

### See Jane Sit

What is it about Jane Austen that makes headlines? *Mansfield Park* (1815) takes up relatively little space in the vastness of Edward Said's *Culture and Imperialism* (1993), yet one reviewer after another has seized on Austen's novel as emblematic of the cultural tradition Said shows to be inextricable from European colonialism.[1] Topping Michael Gorra's full-page review for the *New York Times Book Review*, for example, is the eye-catching question, "Who Paid the Bills at Mansfield Park?" Gorra goes on to highlight the discussion of Austen as "one of the best chapters" in Said's book. Irving Howe, in the pages of *Dissent*, though denying the relevance of colonial Australia to *Great Expectations*, lingers approvingly over Said's suggestion that slavery in Antigua is the dark underbelly of *Mansfield Park*. Likewise John Leonard, reviewing *Culture and Imperialism* for the *Nation*, begins his analysis of Said's sequel to *Orientalism* with a striking image of Austen: "See Jane sit, in the poise and order of *Mansfield Park*, not much bothering her pretty head about the fact that this harmonious 'social space,' Sir Thomas Bertram's country estate, is sustained by slave labor on his plantations in Antigua." His next paragraph renders Said on Albert Camus in similar terms, as a character in his own imperialist primer ("Watch Al run away"), but by then the device has lost its sting. And while reviewers friendly to Said repeatedly cite Austen as definitive proof of his claims, hostile reviewers invoke her with even greater vehemence as *Culture and Imperialism*'s most incredible example.[2]

If, as Leonard implies by omission, Jane Austen is not only "pretty" but "little," why the apparently big role in Said's exposé of the canon's partnership with imperialism? For one thing, as W.J.T. Mitchell notes in his piece for the *London Review of Books*, Said himself places Austen first in his lineup of cultural suspects.[3] He does this, I think, partly for chronological reasons, arguing that not only the venturesome *Robinson Crusoe* but also the stay-at-home novels beginning with Austen prepared the way for Kipling's and Conrad's more overt colonial thematics later in the century (*CI*, 75). But Mitchell suggests another explanation for the foregrounding of Austen that Gorra, Howe, and Leonard unself-consciously reproduce: "The choice of *Mansfield Park* (and of Jane Austen) as Said's opening literary example is a way of forcing this issue [of the novel's complicity with colonialism] into the open." For it is, as Mitchell observes, because of the tacit sense precisely of Austen's "littleness," the genteel narrowness of her concerns, that word of her hand in the plundering of Antigua gets our attention. A similar logic is at work in Eve Sedgwick's notorious linking of "Jane Austen and the Masturbating Girl" (1991).[4] Juxtaposing *Sense and Sensibility*'s screening of sex with nineteenth-century antionanist writings, Sedgwick herself, no less than the journalists who wagged their heads at it, plays upon the oxymoronic scandal of such a pairing. In spite of much revisionary work on this author, the yoking of gentle Jane to sex, subversion, or slavery still has the power to shock, registering thus the persistence of Austen's reputation for piety as well as the ongoing nature of debates between proponents of various new Austens and defenders of the old. The context for these remarks about Austen's place in Edward Said's influential book is my own investment in the woman writer that feminist critics have variously and laboriously wrested from the fray—a contradictory figure neither pretty nor little, with widely engaged interests and independent views, more self-conscious and profane than the flatly conservative figure of *Culture and Imperialism*. Said's typing of Austen leads me, finally, to consider the larger gender logic underlying his postcolonial project. For those of us who would mobilize Austen for a critical analysis of male and female roles, Said's otherwise radical work shows how tempting it remains to read her in keeping with traditional views.

## The Fully Acculturated Englishman

The cherished axiom of Austen's unworldliness is closely tied to a sense of her polite remove from the contingencies of history. It was Q. D. Leavis (1942) who first pointed out the tendency of scholars to lift Austen out of her social milieu, gallantly allowing her gorgeous sentences to float free, untainted by the routines of labor that produced them and deaf to the tumult of current events.[5] Since Leavis, numerous efforts have been made to counter the patronizing view that Austen, in her fidelity to the local, the surface, the detail, was oblivious to large-scale struggles, to wars and mass movements of all kinds. Claudia L. Johnson (1988), for example, has challenged R. W. Chapman's long-standing edition of Austen for its readiness to illustrate her ballrooms and refusal to gloss her allusions to riots or slaves—and has linked this writer to a tradition of frankly political novels by women.[6] It is in keeping with such historicizing gestures that Said's *Culture and Imperialism* insists on *Mansfield Park*'s participation in its moment, pursuing the references to Caribbean slavery that Chapman pointedly ignored. Yet while arguing vigorously for the novel's active role in producing imperialist plots, Said also, in effect, replays the story of its author's passivity regarding issues in the public sphere. Unconcerned about Sir Thomas Bertram's colonial holdings in slaves as well as land, and taking for granted their necessity to the good life at home, Said's Austen is a veritable Aunt Jane—naive, complacent, and demurely without overt political opinion.

I will grant that Said's depiction of Austen as unthinking in her references to Antigua fits with his overall contention that nineteenth-century European culture, and especially the English novel, unwittingly but systematically helped to gain consent for imperialist policies (see *CI*, 75). While defending the pleasures of many a specific text, Said agrees with critics such as D. A. Miller and Franco Moretti that the novel as a genre served conservative ends. It was, Said asserts, one of the primary discourses contributing to a "consolidated vision," virtually uncontested, of England's righteous imperial prerogative. Austen is no different from Thackeray or Dickens, then, in her implicit loyalty to official Eurocentrism (*CI*, 75). At the same time, Said's version of Austen in particular is given a boost by the readily available myth of her "feminine" nearsightedness. The advantage of beginning with Austen is, I have said, to grab us by the collar; but I think its effect is also to ease us in with a female novelist framed in reassuringly familiar ways. Sanctioned in large part by traditional scholarship, this rendering of Austen is further enabled, I would argue, by Said's highly selective materialization of her. I mean this in two senses. First, whereas in subsequent sections *Aida* is lovingly embedded within Verdi's corpus and *Kim* within Kipling's, and notwithstanding Said's claim that *Mansfield Park* "carefully defines the moral and social values informing her other novels" (*CI*, 62), this single text is, in fact, almost completely isolated from the rest of Austen's work. Yet had Said placed Sir Thomas Bertram, for example, in line with the deficient fathers who run unrelentingly from *Northanger Abbey* through *Persuasion*, he might perhaps have paused before assuming that Austen legitimates the master of Mansfield Park. If truth be told, Said's attention even to his chosen text is cursory: Austen's references to Antigua (and India) are mentioned without actually being read, though Said stresses elsewhere the importance of close, specific analysis. Maria Bertram is mistakenly referred to as "Lydia" (*CI*, 87)—confused, presumably, with Lydia Bennet of *Pride and Prejudice*. And these are just a few of the signs that *Mansfield Park*'s particular complexity—including what I see as its moral complexity—has been sacrificed here, so ready is Said to offer Austen as "Exhibit A" in the case for culture's endorsement of empire.

But the picture of Austen is disembodied in not only a textual but also a larger social sense. Though recontextualized as an English national in the period preceding colonial expansion, Austen's more precise status, further, as an unmarried, middle-class, scribbling woman, remains wholly unspecified. The failure to consider Austen's gender, along with the significance of this omission, is pointed up by Said's more nuanced treatment of Conrad. According to Said, Conrad stands out from other colonial writers because, as a Polish expatriate, he possessed "an extraordinarily persistent residual sense of his own exilic marginality" (*CI*, 24). The result is a double view of imperialism, at once refuting and reinforcing the West's right to dominate the globe. As Said explains, "Never the wholly incorporated and fully acculturated Englishman, Conrad therefore preserved an ironic distance [from imperial conquest] in each of his works" (*CI*, 25). Of course Austen was not, any more than Conrad, "the wholly incorporated and fully acculturated Englishman." Lacking the franchise, enjoying few property rights (and these because she was single), living as a dependent at the edge of her brother's estate, and publishing her work anonymously, Austen was arguably a kind of exile in her own country. If we follow out the logic of Said's own identity politics, Austen, too, might therefore be suspected of irony toward reigning constructions of citizenship, however much, like Conrad, she may also in many respects have upheld them. The goal of this essay is to indicate where and, finally, to suggest why Said so entirely misses this irony. My point, I should stress, is not to exonerate Austen of imperialist crimes. Surely Said is right to include her among those who made colonialism thinkable by constructing the West as center, home, and norm, while pushing everything else to the margins. The question I would raise is not whether Austen contributed to English domination abroad, but how her doing so was necessarily inflected and partly disrupted by her position as a bourgeois woman.

## The Beauties of Mansfield

Said's opinion that Austen is culpably indifferent to slavery in Antigua depends on a repeated but questionable assertion: that Mansfield Park epitomizes moral order and right human relations; thus Sir Thomas's colonial endeavors, underwriting all this happiness, must be condoned if not actually applauded. Said is not alone in seeing *Mansfield Park* as a celebration of the real estate named in its title, with all its resonance of tradition, wealth locked up in land, property passed from father to eldest son. Tony Tanner's 1966 introduction to the Penguin edition is an elegant example of this opinion; Ruth Bernard Yeazell's attractive 1984 essay borrows from anthropology to reach a similar conclusion about the book's investment in reinforcing the boundaries of the Bertram property.[7] Such "conservative" readings inevitably cite the Portsmouth chapters toward the end of the novel, in which Fanny Price disowns her native city and petit-bourgeois family in favor of Mansfield and its harmonious ways—and Said's is no exception. What all of these overlook, however, is the extreme irony of Fanny's idealizing retrospection:

> At Mansfield [as opposed to Portsmouth], no sounds of contention, no raised voice, no abrupt bursts, no tread of violence was ever heard; every body had their due importance; every body's feelings were consulted. If tenderness could be ever supposed wanting, good sense and good breeding supplied its place; and as to the little irritations, sometimes introduced by aunt Norris, they were short, they were trifling, they were as a drop of water to the ocean, compared with the ceaseless tumult of her present abode. (391–92)

The confident sequence of negatives breaks down here with the concessionary "if" that allows the occasional absence of tenderness at Mansfield. This is followed by Fanny's unsure approach to an unoriginal metaphor—"as a drop of water to the ocean"—that attempts to discount the quantity of aunt Norris's cruelty. The conspicuous banality of Fanny's idiom sets it off, however, from that of Austen's narrator and indicates the degree of ironic distance from Fanny at this point.

But even had this description not unraveled on its own, we need only contrast it with the preceding three hundred pages to grasp its utter implausibility. The Mansfield we have seen has been nothing but contention, jealousy, and insensitivity to others. Fanny herself has been its most frequent victim, though one of Austen's themes is this heroine's inability to speak her hurt. Fanny, like the many critics who stress her passivity, is even less able to acknowledge her own pivotal role in Mansfield's bitter generational conflicts and consuming sexual jealousies. After all, Fanny has been exiled for flatly disobeying Mansfield's patriarch, and she has done so out of passionate illicit love for her cousin Edmund. Portsmouth, I agree with Yeazell, is crowded, chaotic, greasy, and alcoholic—awash with stereotypes of the urban poor. But for all this, it only literalizes what at Mansfield is disorder of a more profound and hypocritical kind. At Portsmouth, two sisters tussle over a silver knife. At Mansfield they wage an unspoken battle over Henry Crawford, as Mary and Fanny do over Edmund. Portsmouth is dirty. Mansfield is adulterous. Portsmouth's patriarch drinks, curses, and ignores his daughters. The father at Mansfield intimidates, exploits, and also ignores his daughters. Portsmouth is noisy. Mansfield's greatest evil is its dishonest silence.

Said's premise, therefore—that "Jane Austen sees the legitimacy of Sir Thomas Bertram's overseas properties as a natural extension of the calm, the order, the beauties of Mansfield, one central estate validating the economically supportive role of the peripheral other" (*CI*, 79)—is undercut by Austen's own critique of the moral blight underlying Mansfield's beauty, which she achieves not least by blurring the normative class opposition between Mansfield and Portsmouth. What Said calls a validation of the English estate as "home," justifying its subjugation of "abroad," I see as an inquiry into Mansfield's corruption that challenges the ethical basis for its authority both at home and, by implication, overseas. Austen does, it is true, ultimately allow Mansfield and some of its sinning inmates to be redeemed, and to this extent she reaffirms the governance of British landowners. As a crucial qualification, however, she declines to make her heroine the next mistress of Mansfield, though Tom Bertram's illness specifically raises the possibility that Edmund will inherit. Tom's survival, placing Edmund and Fanny temporarily at Thornton Lacey and finally not in Mansfield itself but its adjacent parsonage, suggests Austen's wish to register, even at the end, some disdain for what Mansfield represents. (There is, from the outset, a slap at primogeniture in the younger son's role as hero and the older's marked delinquency.) Said's designation of Fanny as Mansfield's heir (see *CI*, 84, 89) is therefore inaccurate. In fact, Austen pointedly counters the centrality of Mansfield in Fanny's heart by settling her firmly on its perimeter.

## Patriarchal Values

The character most closely identified with Mansfield Park and its colonial subsidiaries is, of course, Sir Thomas Bertram. Said thus argues not merely that Austen celebrates Mansfield but, more specifically, that she backs Sir Thomas in his domestic and colonial ventures. Austen is implicated through a series of equations aligning Fanny with her wealthy uncle, conflating Austen with her diffident heroine, and thereby tying the author herself to slavery, in spite of an ethical outlook that might seem to preclude this. Said remarks, for instance, that Sir Thomas's overseas possessions "give him his wealth, occasion his absences, fix his social status at home and abroad, and make possible his values, to which Fanny Price (and Austen herself) finally subscribes" (*CI*, 62). Said describes Sir Thomas as Fanny's "mentor" (*CI*, 89), and he is not the first critic to link uncle and niece, especially in their view of the young people's rage for home theatricals. I would point out, however, that when Sir Thomas sets sail, Fanny grieves not (as her cousins think) for him but, on the contrary, "because she could not grieve" (33). Likewise on his return, she feels only a resurgence of "all her former habitual dread" (176). And though Sir Thomas and Fanny are finally reconciled, the key moral and political confrontation of the book remains, in my opinion, that played out between this nobleman and the timid young woman who, astonishingly, stands up to him by refusing to marry Henry Crawford.

The significance of this confrontation is condensed for me by Fanny's response when asked point-blank whether her affections are engaged by another: "[Sir Thomas] saw her lips formed into a *no*, though the sound was inarticulate, but her face was like scarlet" (316). Here Fanny does and does not confess her terrible desire for Edmund. She mouths a denial but cannot quite speak it; moreover, the word of disavowal she attempts is countered by the somatic affirmation of her blush. Finally, while her "no" in this immediate context would suppress her longing, Fanny's "no" to Sir Thomas (and Henry) in the scene as a whole tacitly asserts her right to reject and also to love where she will. Turning down Henry, Fanny declares her passion for Edmund against all norms of female modesty. In addition, she condemns Henry's history of carelessness with women and questions the double standard that dooms the fallen woman while promising to reform the rake. Crossing Sir Thomas, she declines to enrich her family by sacrificing herself and so dishonors the ideals of female and filial obedience. Regarding the sexual politics of marriage, therefore, far from sharing Sir Thomas's values, Fanny stages a significant rebellion against them. Threatened by the givens of gender relations in her day, she murmurs a negative that is only partly muted by her uncle's dread presence.

If Fanny's values, in light of the gender struggle central to *Mansfield Park*, cannot without violence be assimilated to those of Sir Thomas, neither can Austen be simply identified with her characters. The collapsing of author into character would be questionable in any case, but especially so given what I have already suggested is Austen's ironic rendering of Sir Thomas and, at times, of Fanny herself. This brings me to Sir Thomas's Antiguan connection and why his West Indian plantation makes the brief appearance that it does. Said quotes the line revealing that Fanny's inquiry into the slave trade is met with a "dead silence," and seems to suggest that Austen's novel, like the Bertram household, has nothing to say about slavery, when in fact the organization of both is premised upon unfree people (quoted in *CI*, 96). My view, by contrast, is that Austen deliberately invokes the dumbness of Mansfield Park concerning its own barbarity precisely because she means to rebuke it. The barbarity she has in mind is not literal slavery in the West Indies but a paternal practice she depicts as possibly analogous to it: Sir Thomas's bid (successful in Maria's case if not in Fanny's) to put female flesh on the auction block in exchange for male status.[8]

For this and other domestic tyrannies, including the casual import and export of Fanny Price, the slave trade offers a convenient metaphor.[9] It is a figure made possible by the confluence of abolitionist and feminist discourses emergent in Austen's day, and it takes for granted—as several scholars have argued Austen did—that slavery is a moral offense. Later writers, notably Charlotte Brontë, would make more conspicuous use of slavery as a metaphor for class and gender wrongs among the gentry, but a rather explicit instance occurs in Austen's own next novel, *Emma* (1816).[10] In a well-known passage (surprisingly unremarked upon by *Culture and Imperialism*), Jane Fairfax likens the commodification of British women by the "governess-trade" to that of Africans by the "slave-trade," hinting that the sale of "human intellect" is no more tolerable than the sale of "human flesh."[11] From a feminist perspective, it seems all too obvious that in *Mansfield Park* slavery functions similarly: not as a subtext wherein Austen and Sir Thomas converge but, on the contrary, as a trope Austen introduces to argue the essential depravity of Sir Thomas's relations to other people. This is not to say that *Mansfield Park* takes much real interest in Antigua and its laborers per se; I agree with Said that they are largely elided and always subordinated to the English material. The imperialist gesture is to exploit the symbolic value of slavery, while ignoring slaves as suffering and resistant historical subjects. As such a symbol, however, slavery in *Mansfield Park* is far less incidental and inadvertent than Said suggests. Ideologically, moreover, the implications of its use are mixed: though evacuating the specific content of slavery in the New World, placing its greatest emphasis elsewhere, this figure also turns on a moment of imagined commonality between English women and African slaves, a potentially radical overlap of outrage.

## The Isle of Wight

Said makes clear that the defining affect of colonialism is arrogance. I have said that Austen's relation to colonialism may be complicated, though not entirely mitigated, by her protest on behalf of women like herself. As a footnote to this comment, I would like to look briefly at what she says about arrogance as a worldview. I think, for example, of *Persuasion*'s meditation on the arrogant occupation of space. Sir Walter Elliot and his daughter Elizabeth are unable to see beyond the bit of land they happen to inhabit, as if its contours and horizons, its interests and intrigues, were the only thing in the world. Emotionally, a reader of Said would recognize, the stage is set for imperial conquest, for such people go abroad only to discount the significance of other populations and outlooks. Anne Elliot, by contrast, is described as "nobody with either father or sister: her word had no weight; her convenience was always to give way;—she was only Anne."[12] With little sense of her significance at home, Anne need not travel very far to have her relative nobodyness confirmed and to wince at the solipsism of other Elliots.

> Anne had not wanted this visit to Uppercross, to learn that a removal from one set of people to another, though at a distance of only three miles, will often include a total change of conversation, opinion, and idea. She had never been staying there before, without being struck by it, or without wishing that other Elliots could have her advantage in seeing how unknown, or unconsidered there, were the affairs which at Kellynch-hall were treated as of such general publicity and pervading interest; yet, with all this experience, she believed she must now submit to feel that another lesson, in the art of knowing our own nothingness beyond our own circle, was become necessary for her.[13]

Austen's target here is the dying but still haughty aristocracy. Far from questioning colonialism, *Persuasion* celebrates (as a meritocratic alternative) the British navy that made it possible. Yet I cannot help thinking that her text here bears somewhat on Said's project of exposing the provincialism underlying colonialism. There is such sensitivity to the way self-importance manifests itself in space, and such severity about mistaking local agendas for "general" and "pervading" ones. Surely Anne's lesson in her "nothingness beyond [her] own circle" is an implicitly anti-imperialist one. Moreover, it suggests once again the crucial operation of gender in Austen, for Anne is able to learn this lesson—and Austen to teach it—because, as an apparently unmarriageable woman, she is exiled from power.

*Mansfield Park*, too, castigates people who, while pretending to worldliness, see nothing beyond their own noses, and even its upstanding heroine is occasionally blinkered by personal interest. Like *Persuasion*, this novel criticizes solipsism primarily as a constituent of personality, not of foreign policy, but there is one conversation in which the limitations of its characters are phrased in explicitly geographical terms. Complaining of their uncouth cousin, Maria and Julia Bertram mock Fanny's inability to "put the map of Europe together" or name the "principal rivers in Russia." They marvel especially at her bad sense of direction: "Do you know, we asked her last night, which way she would go to get to Ireland; and she said, she should cross to the Isle of Wight. She thinks of nothing but the Isle of Wight, and she calls it *the Island*, as if there were no other island in the world" (18).[14] Compared to the wealthy Bertrams, and even to her seafaring brother William, poor Fanny is, to be sure, less adept at manipulating nations, less masterful in her relation to the globe. The Bertram sisters are also right to boast of their superior fluency in chronologies of English kings and Roman emperors, for their schooling in hegemonic traditions has been more thorough than Fanny's. On the other hand, Fanny's navigational mode as described in this passage is itself a rather imperialist one, for it begins and ends by fetishizing a single island. This island not only happens to resemble Britain in its ability to eclipse others such as Ireland and Antigua, leaving it the exclusive point of reference, but bears a name suggesting the pseudoracial basis for its domination. Austen's major point here is clearly to satirize Maria and Julia's class condescension to their simple cousin, but I believe she also likens all three girls to one another and ridicules them for their lordly outlook upon the world. I offer this passage as additional evidence that Austen is both more aware and more critical of the imperial mind-set than Said appreciates; it catches her, indeed, in an attitude of irony toward "*the Island*" and its loyal subjects that inclines, gently, in the direction of his own.[15]

## Sensitive but Not Maudlin

*Mansfield Park* as I read it, then, has little patience with high-handed patriarchs, their eldest sons, Regency sexual mores, or traditional marital practices, and even England itself is not above criticism. Its irreverence—bearing out Austen's earliest juvenile sketches, resonating with the other mature novels, and anticipating the final, unfinished *Sanditon*—suggests to me a less complacent view of power relations, especially gender relations, than Said is prepared to acknowledge. His inattention to Austen's feminist critique of authority is both the logical result and an ideological cognate of his failing, similarly, to remark the last two decades of intensive feminist commentary on this writer. Asserting that "the best account" of *Mansfield Park* is Tony Tanner's (*CI*, 342 n. 36)—admirable when first published in 1966 certainly, but hardly definitive in 1993—Said appears curiously unaware of the revolution in Austen scholarship instigated by such figures as Nina Auerbach, Patricia Spacks, Lillian Robinson, Sandra Gilbert, Susan Gubar, and Rachel Brownstein, among others. He therefore feels free to list Austen among those evincing the conservatism of the novel form, arguing that "the consolidation of authority [in Austen, Balzac, Eliot, and Flaubert] includes, indeed is built into the very fabric of, both private property and marriage, institutions that are only rarely challenged" (*CI*, 77). Feminist accounts, by contrast, have brought out precisely Austen's tactful challenge to the gender injustices of both these institutions. Tying the novel's authorization of empire to the "authority of the author" (*CI*, 77), Said further overlooks what feminist critics since Virginia Woolf have seen as the anxious and impaired authority of the female writer. More disconcerting still than his neglect of revisionary axioms concerning nineteenth-century women writers is that Said makes no mention of Margaret Kirkham (1983) or Moira Ferguson (1991), previous scholars specifically addressing the slavery theme in *Mansfield Park* from a feminist perspective. And though he makes positive passing reference to innovative studies of imperialist discourses by Lisa Lowe (1991) and Sara Suleri (1992), he does not specify their chapters mobilizing ideas about gender. Nor is there any dialogue with his student, Suvendrini Perera (1991), whose book on empire and the English novel identifies the feminist Orientalism of texts such as *Persuasion* and *Jane Eyre*, while arguing that "home" was a construct policing British women as well as colonial "others." Even Gayatri Spivak, the most celebrated feminist postcolonialist, is altogether absent from *Culture and Imperialism*.[16] The pertinence of these names to Said's project is not, I hasten to say, their simple political correctness as females or feminists, but the way their analyses intersect with and would serve to complicate one that proceeds for the most part along a single axis.

While I am not the first to note the paucity of women and feminist criticism in Said's work, it remains a question how these exclusions can coexist with Said's oft-stated appreciation for feminism's political uses.[17] In a 1989 interview, for example, he described his excitement at feminist works by Joan Scott, Helen Callaway, and Jean Franco,[18] and in *Culture and Imperialism* he stresses the significance of women's movements in Egypt, Turkey, Indonesia, China, and Ceylon, whose participation in nationalist struggles, by voicing internal opposition, helped to make these less monolithic (see *CI*, 218, 266). Said's reading of *Kim* as "an overwhelmingly male novel" (*CI*, 136) is itself, at times, incipiently feminist, and he points out more than once the masculinism of much nationalist discourse. Of Aimé Césaire's use of "man" in *Cahier d'un retour au pays natal*, he observes parenthetically, "[T]he exclusively masculine emphasis is quite striking" (*CI*, 280), and another parenthesis conscientiously admits that Ali Shariati's alternative to orthodoxy "speaks only of 'man' and not of 'woman' " (*CI*, 334). The relegation of such glosses to parentheses is telling, however—they are safely contained, in no way reorienting Said's line of argument—as is the far more frequent tendency to quote sexist language without any comment. But the most obvious testimony to both interest and uncertainty regarding feminist agendas is offered by a passage from the book's introduction. Highlighting feminism's contributions to Middle Eastern and postcolonial studies, Said cites Lila Abu-Lughod, Leila Ahmed, and Fedwa Malti-Douglas, whose recent books on women have begun to redress what was once "an aggressively masculine and condescending ethos" (*CI*, xxiv). Following this, however, his terms of praise take an ambiguous turn; these works are, he declares, "both intellectually and politically sophisticated, attuned to the best theoretical and historical scholarship, engaged but not demagogic, sensitive to but not maudlin about women's experience" (xxiv). Why the sudden urge to reassure and qualify here? Why the worry lest scholarship by and about women turn out to be, as a function of the more lachrymose sex, embarrassingly soft and weepy? And why, finally, the seeming insecurity about "engaged" scholarship, the need to disparage the waved fist and tearful face as if they were, or so he implies, inconsistent with carefully reasoned criticism? Keeping these questions in mind, my next section speculates that the troubling sexual politics of *Culture and Imperialism* may be bound up with a largely subliminal strategy of opposition to imperialism, a gender allegory employing the "feminine" in unreconstructed ways—that is, as an essentially devalued category.

## Lady Bertram's Shawl

Poststructuralism would seem to have discredited for good any notion of absolute, impartial truth, and feminists have long since dismantled the old, hierarchized dichotomy between male/objective and female/subjective. Nevertheless, the quotation above speaks to how critics continue to stigmatize scholarship perceived to be heartfelt and also gender it as feminine. On the one hand, Said's defense of politically invested work by female scholars from implied charges of emotional excess justifies his own style of impassioned scholarship; on the other hand, by raising these charges specifically in relation to women, it also effectively distances the male author from a denigrated mode. The gender logic of this defense is reiterated later in the book, in a section devoted to the oppositional writings of four, male, Third World intellectuals: C.L.R. James, George Antonius, Ranajit Guha, and S. H. Alatas. Celebrating the political content of their work, Said insists he does not mean that "oppositional scholarship must be shrill and unpleasantly insistent" (*CI*, 258). Given the strong coding of "shrill" as feminine, this protest seems once again calculated to secure the gender status of work whose "masculinity" is endangered by the depth of its feeling. And it doesn't hurt, of course, that the exemplary four are male to begin with.

But the "masculinity" of anti-imperialist projects such as Said's is rendered insecure in another way as well. As many have observed, the tropes Said mapped so unforgettably in *Orientalism* veil the East in a cluster of "feminine" attributes. It is mysterious, sensual, beckoning, undisciplined, and naturally subordinate to a West imagined in correspondingly "male" terms—and Said notes in his new book that Europe makes use of a similar vocabulary to depict Africa, Australia, and other "distant lands" (*CI*, xi). As Suleri has remarked, this gendering of the colonial encounter persists in counternarratives protesting the "rape" of colonial peoples and places.

She argues further that the "colonial gaze" may actually regard the colonized less as female than effeminate, producing feelings of sexual panic in the male colonizer.[19] From the perspective of the Third World male, however, to the extent that his resistance is mediated by imperialist frameworks, it hardly matters whether he is constructed as "woman" or "effeminate" man, for in either case his normative masculinity is called into question. One function, then, of Austen's primacy in Said's account of European culture, along with the marked masculinity of the resistance cultures put forth in counterpoint, may be to invert the received gendering of the colonial couple: to "remasculinize" the colonized male (and emotional male critic). This is accomplished most obviously by the predominance of men and male quest plots in Said's discussion of anti- and postcolonial texts—James Ngugi's and Tayeb Salih's rewritings of Conrad's *Heart of Darkness*, for example (see *CI*, 210–11). But the gesture is completed by Said's more subtle characterization of early imperial culture as "feminine," which helps to explain the paradigmatic status accorded to Austen. For though his book takes on European culture generally and does in fact range widely among genres, nations, and eras, its argument nevertheless implies a kind of synecdoche in which this culture is best represented by the novel, the novel by the English novel, and the English novel by Austen. Said opens his reading of *Mansfield Park* by quoting Raymond Williams on Austen's limited perspective "from inside the houses" as contrasted with William Cobbett "riding past on the road" (quoted in *CI*, 84). While Said wants to go beyond Williams's class analysis, his Austen, too, is tied to and constrained by a domestic purview in a specifically gendered way. Defined thus, her work is offered as "the perfect example" (*CI*, 59) of the hegemonic geography emergent in the preimperialist period, centered on a Eurocentric formulation of the category "home." Positioned at the beginning of his genealogy and at the heart of his argument, Austen's fiction works, at least in part, to characterize as domestic and to sex as feminine the larger body of European culture.

In addition to its science of interiors, *Mansfield Park* as representative text has something else to offer the project of feminizing Europe. Demonstrating the careless, everyday use of colonial materials by Austen and her characters, Said cites Lady Bertram's request that Fanny's brother William sail to India, "that I may have a shawl. I think I will have two shawls" (quoted in *CI*, 93). Given that Lady Bertram dozes through *Mansfield Park*, a figure of indolence without a shred of moral credibility, it is risky to assume that her appetite for imported goods is approved by the management. What this passage does reinforce, however, is an image of Europe as the leisured consumer of more than one shawl, kept in luxury by the backbreaking labor of colonial workers. It offers, in other words, an inverted sexual metaphor in which the recumbent, feminized East rises to its

3. Henri Rousseau, *The Representatives of the Foreign Powers Coming to Hail the Republic as a Token of Peace*, 1907. Courtesy Giraudon/Art Resource, NY.

feet, and the veil that once symbolized its mysterious allure reappears as a shawl, a figure for the consumerism of a pampered and feminized West.

## A Token of Peace

The cover of *Culture and Imperialism* features a 1907 painting, *The Representatives of the Foreign Powers Coming to Hail the Republic as a Token of Peace*, which I look to for a final illustration of the gender politics underlying Said's anti-imperialism. The painting shows a phalanx of dignitaries in official dress, gathered ceremonially on some outdoor steps. Buildings just visible in the background, a tricolor in each window, suggest Paris. The diplomats face forward, clutching olive branches in gloved hands. Front and center are pink-cheeked men almost uniform in height and dressed in Western garb. Peeking from the back row are two ruddier faces and one brown. To the far right are half a dozen miscellaneous figures with complexions, clothing, and headgear vaguely suggesting Eastern and African origins. All of these are shorter than the Westerners and, to judge by their irregular positions and unmatched stances, have little sense of military discipline. The uneven outline of their heads makes a jagged falling off from the block of massed Westerners. Overhead is an awning topped with flags, but the non-Western representatives, exceeding this frame, are exposed to the elements. The most prominent flags, with one exception, are easily recognizable as those of Britain (the naval red ensign), France, and the United States. Those farther back include Italy and imperial Germany but seem mostly to have been improvised by the artist. Finally, there are three explicitly symbolic elements. First, receptacles of olive branches bear the labels "Paix," "Travail," "Liberté," and "Fraternité." Second, a small lion sits frowning in the foreground—persuaded, it seems, to lie down at last with the lambs. And third, standing to the left in profile, a larger-than-life woman wearing a flowing red gown, extends an olive branch over the heads of the company. She supports a shield that, though partly obscured, appears to read: "Union des Peuples."

It does not take long to realize that Said means this painting ironically. In this "union" under French auspices, as in the European novel, Enlightenment rhetoric and good intentions cannot disguise the fact that non-Westerners get left out in the cold. Western flags still get top billing, and if all men are equal, Western men are clearly more equal than others—more central, more imposing, and more knowable. This is a crucial political judgment to make, and Said has done so for many years with exceptional brilliance and conviction. Yet I turn, in closing, to the cover of *Culture and Imperialism* because its ironized female icon also begins to suggest the problematic status of women and the feminine in Said's text. In the painting I describe, the lone female figure is largely an abstraction, no less than the lion at her feet, the branch in her hand, and the shield at her side. Towering over the heads of European men, she stands for their blond, benevolent patronage—and, from Said's point of view, their hypocritical peace. The effect of the cover, therefore, like the argument inside, is to leave out actual women while feminizing the wiles of imperialist culture, scorning them in a language indebted to sexist gender norms. Women did, of course, help to rationalize imperialism, and Austen is guilty along with the rest. But Said's balance sheet still has her paying more than her share of the bills. This occurs in part because, like the angel of false peace, she, more than any other single figure, is made to bear the symbolic burden of empire. No wonder that, in Suleri's review of Said for the *Village Voice*, she uses Austen as a shorthand for those texts whose interest in imperialism is hidden from view: "For every Salman Rushdie, there is a

Jane Austen."[20] Moreover, because Austen is abstracted from her specific historical context, her Eurocentrism is uncoupled from what was for her as a woman her incompletely realized citizenship. Off-center in relation to the dominant culture, Austen was no more fully embraced by official fantasies of democracy than were the darker "foreign powers"—a fact her novels suggest she pondered. In reading Austen thus, it is not my intention to pick up the pieces of a shattered idol; like Said, I am more interested in secularity and imperfection. I offer this complicating view, rather, as a token of the hope I share with him for a more genuine and just union of peoples.

## Notes

This essay originally appeared in *Critical Inquiry* 21 (summer 1995). © 1995 by The University of Chicago Press.

For their advice and support, many heartfelt thanks to Chris Reppucci, Debra Nystrom, Rita Felski, and Eric Lott.

1. Edward W. Said, *Culture and Imperialism* (New York: Knopf, 1993); hereafter abbreviated *CI*.

2. Michael Gorra, "Who Paid the Bills at Mansfield Park?" review of *CI* in *New York Times Book Review*, 28 February 1993, 11; see Irving Howe, "History and Literature: Edward Said's *Culture and Imperialism*," review of *CI* in *Dissent* 40 (fall 1993): 557–59; John Leonard, "Novel Colonies," review of *CI* in *Nation*, 22 March 1993, 383. For negative reviews featuring Austen, see, for example, Rhoda Koenig, "Limp Lit," review of *CI* in *New York*, 1 March 1993, 119–20; review of *CI*, *Wilson Quarterly* 17 (spring 1993): 86–87; "Guilt and Misery," review of *CI* in *Economist*, 27 February 1993, 95. For an exception, see Michael Wood's "Lost Paradises," review of *CI*, *New York Review of Books*, 3 March 1994, 44–47, which endorses Said's thesis while taking issue, as I do, with his reading of *Mansfield Park*.

3. W.J.T. Mitchell, "In the Wilderness," review of *CI*, *London Review of Books*, 8 April 1993, 11.

4. See Eve Kosofsky Sedgwick, "Jane Austen and the Masturbating Girl," *Critical Inquiry* 17 (summer 1991): 818–37.

5. See Q. D. Leavis, "A Critical Theory of Jane Austen's Writings" (1941–42), reprinted in *The Englishness of the English Novel*, vol. 1 of *Collected Essays*, ed. G. Singh, 3 vols. (Cambridge: Cambridge University Press, 1983), 61–146.

6. See Claudia L. Johnson, *Jane Austen: Women, Politics, and the Novel* (Chicago: University of Chicago Press, 1988), xvi–xvii.

7. See Tanner, introduction to Jane Austen, *Mansfield Park*, ed. Tony Tanner (Harmondsworth: Penguin, 1966), 7–36. See also Ruth Bernard Yeazell, "The Boundaries of *Mansfield Park*," *Representations* 7 (summer 1984): 133–52.

8. Michael Wood points out that the "dead silence" passage follows directly on Edmund's remark to Fanny that she has recently become " 'worth looking at.' "

His sense of the connection thus made between the objectification of women and slaves agrees with my own (Wood, "Lost Paradises," 46).

9. Said himself refers to Fanny at one point as "a kind of transported commodity." But he goes on to stress her "future wealth," likening her expansion into Mansfield to Sir Thomas's into Antigua, so that Fanny-as-commodity becomes Fanny-as-colonialist (*CI*, 88, 89). I have already noted that Fanny does not, in fact, inherit Mansfield, but should add that, in any case, even the "best" marriage did not increase but actually contracted the personal wealth and rights of women in Austen's day. See Lee Holcombe, *Wives and Property: Reform of the Married Women's Property Law in Nineteenth-Century England* (Toronto: University of Toronto Press, 1983), and Susan Staves, *Married Women's Separate Property in England, 1660–1833* (Cambridge: Harvard University Press, 1990).

10. See Karen Sánchez-Eppler, "Bodily Bonds: The Intersecting Rhetorics of Feminism and Abolition," *Representations* 24 (fall 1988): 28–59, which discusses white feminist uses of the slavery metaphor in an American context. On Austen's opposition to slavery and on its role as a metaphor in *Mansfield Park*, see Margaret Kirkham, *Jane Austen, Feminism and Fiction* (Totowa, N.J.: Barnes and Noble Books, 1983), 116–19; Johnson, *Jane Austen: Women, Politics, and the Novel*, 106–8; and Moira Ferguson, "*Mansfield Park*: Slavery, Colonialism, and Gender," *Oxford Literary Review* 13, nos. 1–2 (1991): 118–39. On Brontë's ambiguous use of this metaphor, see Susan L. Meyer, "Colonialism and the Figurative Strategy of *Jane Eyre*," *Victorian Studies* 33 (winter 1990): 247–68.

11. Austen, *Emma*, 300.

12. Austen, *Persuasion*, 5.

13. Ibid., 42.

14. Said quotes the "map of Europe" line to illustrate Austen's preoccupation with spatial issues. Thanks to Scott Fennessey, whose unpublished paper "Conjunctions of Geography and Society in Austen's *Mansfield Park*" first got me thinking about the Isle of Wight.

15. For another instance of Austen's skeptical patriotism, see *Northanger Abbey*, in which the hero begins by chiding the heroine, "Remember we are English, that we are Christians . . . ," only to end with the ominous picture of England as a place "where every man is surrounded by a neighborhood of voluntary spies" (197–98).

16. See Lisa Lowe, *Critical Terrains: French and British Orientalisms* (Ithaca, N.Y.: Cornell University Press, 1991); Sara Suleri, *The Rhetoric of English India* (Chicago: University of Chicago Press, 1992); Suvendrini Perera, *Reaches of Empire: The English Novel from Edgeworth to Dickens* (New York: Columbia University Press, 1991); Gayatri Chakravorty Spivak, *In Other Worlds: Essays in Cultural Politics* (New York: Routledge, 1987) and *The Post-Colonial Critic: Interviews, Strategies, Dialogues: Gayatri Chakravorty Spivak*, ed. Sarah Harasym (New York: Routledge, 1990). Other more recent books on the nexus of gender and colonialism include Jenny Sharpe, *Allegories of Empire: The Figure of Woman in the Colonial Text* (Minneapolis: University of Minnesota Press, 1993), and Anne McClintock, *Imperial Leather: Race, Gender, and Sexuality in the Colonial Conquest* (New York: Routledge, 1994).

17. Aijaz Ahmad singles out Said's essay on *Mansfield Park* (first published in 1989), noting its failure to recognize upper-class women as "differentially located in mobilities and pedagogies of the class structure" (Aijaz Ahmad, *In Theory: Classes, Nations, Literatures* [London: Verso, 1992], 186). See also Fawzia Afzal-Khan, review of *CI* in *World Literature Today* 68 (winter 1994): 229–30. Afzal-Kahn laments Said's neglect of work by postcolonial feminist critics.

18. See Jennifer Wicke and Michael Sprinker, "Interview with Edward Said," in *Edward Said: A Critical Reader*, ed. Sprinker (Oxford and Cambridge, Mass.: Blackwell, 1992), 248–49.

19. Suleri, *The Rhetoric of English India*, 16. Joseph A. Boone elaborates on the West's coding of Arab males as homosexual. Noting that "Said's failure to account for homoerotic elements in orientalist pursuits is a telling omission," Boone reinforces my sense of Said's stake in realigning Eastern men with dominant conceptions of manhood (Joseph A. Boone, "Vacation Cruises; or, The Homoerotics of Orientalism," *PMLA* 110 [January 1995]: 92).

20. Suleri, "The Secret Sharers: Edward Said's Imperial Margins," review of *CI* in *Voice Literary Supplement*, 8 June 1993, 31.

## *Notes on Contributors*

BARBARA M. BENEDICT, Chair of English at Trinity College, Connecticut, has published *Framing Feeling: Sentiment and Style in English Prose Fiction, 1745–1800* (1994) and *Making the Modern Reader: Cultural Mediation in Early Modern Literary Anthologies* (1996), as well as articles on Jane Austen, book history, and eighteenth-century popular culture. She is currently completing a book entitled *Curiosity/Curiosities: Objects and Subjects of Literary Inquiry* and another book on female self-representation in Austen's work, entitled *Jane Austen and Material Culture.*

MARY A. FAVRET teaches English at Indiana University. She is the author of *Romantic Correspondence: Women, Politics, and the Fiction of Letters* (1993) and the coeditor, with Nicola Watson, of *At the Limits of Romanticism* (1994). She is currently working on two projects: a collection of essays on reading Austen and a book entitled *Invisible Violence: Romantic Thought.*

SUSAN FRAIMAN teaches English at the University of Virginia and is the author of *Unbecoming Women: British Women Writers and the Novel of Development* (1993). Her essay in this volume is part of her forthcoming book, *Cool Men and the Second Sex.*

WILLIAM GALPERIN is Professor of English at Rutgers University, New Brunswick, and the author of *Revision and Authority in Wordsworth: The Interpretation of a Career* (1989) and *The Return of the Visible in British Romanticism* (1993). He is currently completing another book, *The Historical Austen*, of which his chapter here is a part.

CLAUDIA L. JOHNSON is Professor of English at Princeton University. She is the author of *Jane Austen: Women, Politics, and the Novel* (1988) and of *Equivocal Beings: Politics, Gender, and Sentimentality in the 1790s: Wollstonecraft, Radcliffe, Burney, Austen* (1995), which was a finalist for the MLA's James Russell Lowell Prize. She is also the editor of the new Norton Critical Editions of *Mansfield Park* (1998) and *Sense and Sensibility* (forthcoming) and is currently at work on a book entitled *Jane Austen: Cults and Cultures.*

DEIDRE LYNCH teaches in the English Department of the State University of New York at Buffalo. She is the author of *The Economy of Character: Novels, Market Culture, and the Business of Inner Meaning* (1998), which was awarded the MLA Prize for a First Book, and the coeditor, with William B. Warner, of *Cultural Institutions of the Novel* (1996).

MARY ANN O' FARRELL is Associate Professor of English at Texas A & M University. She is the author of *Telling Complexions: The Nineteenth-Century English Novel and the Blush* (1997) and the coeditor, with Lynne Vallone, of *Virtual Gender: Fantasies of Subjectivity and Embodiment* (1999). She is currently at work on a project on representations of blindness in literature and film.

ROGER SALES is Professor of English Literature at the University of East Anglia in England. His most recent major publication is *Jane Austen and Representations of Regency England* (1994; revised edition, 1996). In addition to another book, *English Literature in History, 1780–1830: Pastoral and Politics* (1983), and many essays on the Regency period, he has also published books on Renaissance and contemporary drama (Shakespeare, Marlowe, Stoppard). He is currently working on three projects: *Servants and Society in Regency England*; *A Literary Life of John Clare*; and an anthology of women dramatists of the Regency period.

KATIE TRUMPENER teaches English, comparative literature, German, and film studies at the University of Chicago. Her book *Bardic Nationalism: The Romantic Novel and the British Empire* (1997) was awarded the British Academy's Rose Mary Crawshay Prize and the MLA Prize for a First Book. Her book *The Divided Screen: The Postwar German Cinemas* is forthcoming; she is now working on a book about modernists and their memories of the nursery.

CLARA TUITE lectures in English at the University of Melbourne, Australia. She has published articles on Matthew Lewis and on Malthus and Mary Shelley, and she is an associate editor of the *Oxford Companion to the Romantic Age* (1999) and coeditor, with Gillian Russell, of the forthcoming *Romantic Sociability: Social Networks and Literary Culture in Britain, 1770–1840.* She is currently completing a manuscript on Austen and cultures of Romanticism and post-Romanticism.

# *Index*


abolitionism: *Mansfield Park* and, 19, 154, 213
adaptations (of Austen novels for film and television), 4, 19, 83n. 2, 120, 180–82, 187n. 57, 188–203, 204n. 5; compared to the novels, 193–96, 198; representation of servants in, 19, 189–95, 198–203. *See also under individual titles*
America: Austen's reception in, 166–82
Anglophilia, 13; American antipathy to, 166, 168, 172
Armstrong, Nancy, 91
Auden, W. H., 143, 162n. 20
Austen, Cassandra, 59n. 3, 157
Austen, Frank, 94, 102
Austen, Henry, 83n. 2, 102
Austen, Jane: and Americanness, 18–19, 166–77, 186n. 47; canonization of, 23n. 14, 105–6, 117–19, 129; as conservative, 5, 63, 90–91, 107, 143, 145, 150–51, 207, 210; contemporary reviews of, 89, 91–92, 96, 98, 102–3, 106–10 (*see also individual reviewers*); and detachment, 18, 175–76, 183n. 13, 185–86n. 33; and Englishness, 13, 166–67, 177; and feminism, 19, 142–45, 207, 213, 215 (*see also* female literary tradition; Virago Modern Classics; women novelists); and gay men, 25–26; and the genealogy of English literature, 9–10, 20, 39, 147–48, 184n. 17; as literary foremother, 17–18, 39, 116–18, 121–25, 128–36 (*see also* influence: of Austen; women novelists: Austen's relation to); as popular writer, 8–10, 12–15, 63–65, 73–82, 184n. 15; on provincialism, 213–15; and race, 178–82, 186n. 51; and religious sentiment, 102; sexuality of, 25–27, 29, 36, 38, 133; as teacher, 10–11, 133, 138–39n. 41; and technology, 173–75. *See also specific works by title*
Austeniana, 46, 59nn. 3 and 4, 60n. 6; and gender, 12
Austen-Leigh, J. E. (James Edward), 115; *A Memoir of Jane Austen*, 11, 12, 18, 83n. 2, 118–19, 122, 146
Austen societies, 3, 16, 37–38, 58
authorship: Romantic redefinition of, 16, 63, 64, 68, 70, 74

back-crossing, 117, 131–36; defined, 131
Ballaster, Ros, 194, 197
Barron, Stephanie, 4
Barthes, Roland, 88
Beauman, Sally, 163n. 30
Bell, John, 68, 69
Benedict, Barbara M., 8, 16, 17, 83n. 3, 84n. 17, 85n. 25, 86nn. 35 and 42
Bentley, Richard. *See* Standard Novels series: Austen's novels in
Bersani, Leo, 25–27
Bessborough, Lady, 91–92
Blake, Richard A., 22n. 11
Blake, Warren Burden, 169
Bloom, Allan, 29, 40n. 10
Bloom, Harold, 121. *See also* influence: anxiety of
Blyton, W. J., 34, 42n. 23
Boone, Joseph A., 223n. 19
Booth, Wayne, 36–37, 39, 43n. 34, 56, 61n. 21
Bowen, Elizabeth, 143, 163n. 28
Bradley, A. C., 30, 32
Bristol, Michael D., 7, 22n. 6
Brodie, Laura Fairchild, 23n. 18, 112n. 18
Brontë, Charlotte, 41n. 12, 61n. 17, 164n. 48, 179, 213; her critique of Austen, 10, 29, 40, 49–51, 63, 110, 159, 175, *Jane Eyre*, 216; Woolf on, 148–49. *See also* Brontës
Brontë, Emily, 150, 153, 164n. 48. *See also* Brontës
Brontës, 146, 149–50, 153, 162n. 25, 164n. 48; pitted against Austen, 159, 162n. 26, 163–64n. 40, 165n. 62
Brophy, Brigid, 132
Burney, Frances, 87–90, 94, 146
Butler, Judith, 28
Butler, Marilyn, 195
Byron, Lady, 92–93, 101

canonicity, 24n. 23, 145; and popularity, 8–10
canonization: of Austen, 23n. 14, 105–6, 117–19, 129, 136–37n. 14; of the novel, 121–22, 129
Carswell, Catherine: *The Camomile*, 149–50
Carter, Angela: *Several Perceptions*, 145
Castle, Terry, 27–28, 39, 120, 133, 139n. 44
Cecil, Lord David, 30, 35, 38, 42n. 27, 163n. 32
Chapman, R. W., 9, 30, 34, 119, 207–8
circulating libraries: catalogs of, 69–72; fees charged by, 67, 85n. 24; and formula fiction, 71–78; and literacy, 68; packaging of novels in, 71; titles and subtitles of novels in, 71–74; and the violation of cultural hierarchies, 16, 65–74, 82
closet, the, 11, 127, 128, 136
Colley, Linda, 120
colonialism. *See* Empire, British
Compton-Burnett, Ivy, 116, 160n. 3, 164n. 42
Connolly, Cyril, 123, 130
Conrad, Joseph, 207, 209, 218
conservatism: of Austen, 5, 15, 63, 90–91, 107, 143, 145, 150–51, 207, 210; of Austen's critics, 7; of the novel form, 87–98, 103–11, 208, 215
*Constantia; or, the Distressed Friend* (Anonymous), 74, 85n. 32
consumerism: and Austen's novels, 171–72, 218–19; and empire, 218–19
Cooper, James Fenimore, 168–69, 178, 183n. 9; *The Deerslayer*, 183n. 11; *Precaution*, 169, 183n. 12
country house novel, 17, 115–36; canonization of, 117–23; cultural functions of, 123–25; heterosexual imperatives of, 128–30; as literary inheritance, 115–17
cult audience: 8–9; and the Internet, 3–4; of Shakespeare, 10. *See also* Janeites; reading
cultural capital, 12, 18, 167
cultural hierarchies. *See* high and low culture
culture, popular. *See* high and low culture
curriculum: British literary, 13, 167

Dabydeen, David, 198
Davies, Andrew, 4, 197
Davy, Jane, 93–95
Dear, Nick, 197–98
decadence, 116–17, 126–27, 134
Decadence, 18, 117–19, 126–27, 131–36
de Certeau, Michel, 41n. 18, 90, 95. *See also* everyday, the
Delafield, E. M., 18; *The Optimist*, 144, 154–59
democracy, 18, 166, 171, 182, 221
details: in Austen's novels, 17, 97, 98, 101–2. *See also* everyday, the
Dickson, Rebecca, 204n. 5
didacticism, 10–11; of the novel, 17, 73, 89, 92–95, 107. *See also* regulation
domestic fiction, 96, 99–100, 109
Duncan, Sara Jeanette, 161n. 13

Edgeworth, Maria, 90, 93, 94, 105, 112n. 18; on *Emma*, 101
Edwards, Thomas R., 54–56
Eliot, George, 35, 61n. 17, 146, 148–50, 151, 152, 153, 162n. 26, 179, 215
Eliot, T. S., 153
elitism. *See* high and low culture
Ellman, Richard, 127
embarrassment, 8, 11, 58; Austen as an, 54–56; in *Persuasion*, 55–56; in *Pride and Prejudice*, 53
Emerson, Ralph Waldo, 171, 177, 178; on the familiar, 170; on "marriageableness" in Austen, 168–69
*Emma* (Austen), 36–37, 43n. 34, 47–49, 56, 61n. 21, 63, 79, 80, 95, 177–78, 179, 180, 213; contemporary response to, 96–102, 106, 112n. 18, 113nn. 23 and 31; film adaptation of (1996), 194; ITV/A&E adaptation of, 194; and Virago Modern Classics, 148, 149, 161n. 12
Empire, British, 132–33, 154; and English literature, 13, 167; and Said's reading of *Mansfield Park*, 19–20, 206–21
entails. *See* Austen, Jane: as literary foremother; influence: of Austen; inheritance
escapism, 34, 151, 153
everyday, the, 89–90, 93–95, 103–4, 106, 110–11, 170; as oppositional, 95–101. *See also* details

Favret, Mary A., 18–19
Fawcett, Millicent, 142
*Female Friendship: or the Innocent Sufferer* (Anonymous), 75–76
female literary tradition: 140–60; Austen's relation to, 141, 144–49; and the subordination of women, 150–51; Woolf on, 146–47
*Female Sensibility; or, the History of Emma Pomfret* (Anonymous), 75
feminism: 18, 107–8, 156–57, 215–16; and Austen, 19, 142–45, 207, 213, 215; and the suffragette movement, 140–42. *See also* female literary tradition; Virago Modern Classics; women novelists
Ferguson, Moira, 216, 186n. 47
Ferrier, Susan, 101, 105
Fielding, Helen: *Diary of Bridget Jones*, 4, 12
Fielding, Henry, 87, 152
Figes, Eva, 162n. 21
Findlater, Jane and Mary, 148
Firbank, Ronald, 7, 115, 116, 117, 130; *Valmouth: A Romantic Novel*, 117, 130–35
Fisher, Philip, 183n. 11
formula fiction, 71–78
Forster, E. M., 9, 17, 18, 26, 30, 39, 134, 138n. 30; *Abinger Harvest*, 123, 124, 125, 130; *Aspects of the Novel*, 37, 43n. 37; *Howards End*, 17, 116, 124–25; as inheritor of Austenian novel, 121, 122–30, 133, 138n. 32; *Marianne Thornton*, 124–25; *Maurice*, 116, 120, 124, 129, 130; on *Sanditon*, 115, 116–17, 123, 125, 126–29, 131, 134
Foucault, Michel, 90
Fraiman, Susan, 19–20
Freedman, Jonathan, 41n. 16
Freud, Sigmund, 126
friendship: with Austen, 14, 15, 16, 45–47, 56, 58–59; with books, 112n. 18, 172; in *Emma*, 47–49; as opposition and rivalry, 47–51, 61n. 17; in *Pride and Prejudice*, 51–54

Galperin, William, 11, 17
Garrod, H. W., 29–30, 35, 39, 43n. 41
Gaskell, Elizabeth, 143, 146
georgic poetry. *See* poetry, georgic
Gibbons, Stella, 161n. 14
Gilbert, Sandra M., and Susan Gubar, 97, 215
Gillaspie, Jon, 60
Gilson, David, 112n. 11
Girould, Gordon Hall, 174
Glazener, Nancy, 171, 173
*Gone with the Wind*, 19, 181–82
Gorra, Michael, 206–7
gossip, 11, 33, 37, 48, 106, 153, 185n. 30, 192, 199. *See also* details; everyday, the
Grant, Madison, 178
Graves, Richard Percival, 44n. 42

Hall, Radclyffe, 157
Halperin, David, 26
Halperin, John, 22n. 11, 160n. 10, 176–77, 184n. 17
Hamlyn, Hilda M., 85n. 29
Harding, D. W., 8, 34–36, 42nn. 24, 25, 26, and 28
Harrison, Frederic, 33
Hawthorne, Nathaniel, 170, 177, 178
heritage cinema, 22n. 8, 189, 190, 192, 194, 199, 202–3, 205n. 13
heritage industry, 6, 19, 119–20
heteronormativity, 25–27, 109; and novel studies, 32–33, 35–39, 43n. 34. *See also* Austen, Jane: sexuality of
heterosexuality: 25–30, 124, 130, 133, 134; compulsory, 120–21, 129, 131. *See also* heteronormativity; marriage; marriage plot; spinsterhood
Higginson, Thomas Wentworth, 172–73, 184n. 17
high and low culture, 5–6, 8–13, 22n. 12, 41n. 18; and circulating libraries, 65–82; the literary and the popular, 9–10, 16–17, 23n. 13, 63–82. *See also* readers: contention between
Hinkley, Laura L., 180, 183n. 13
Hogan, Charles Beecher, 112n. 11
homosexuality, 25–29, 32, 34–36, 138n. 28, 223n. 19; and literary inheritance (Austen's "queer nephews"), 17–18, 116–22, 128–36; and readings of *Emma*, 36. *See also* queerness
Housman, A. E., 39, 44n. 42
Howe, Irving, 206–7
Howells, William Dean, 18, 22n. 11, 185n. 30; on Austen, 169–74, 184nn. 15 and 17, 185n. 29
Hughes, Helen Sard, 174, 175

imperialism. *See* Empire, British
influence, 120–21; anxiety of, 121, 128–30; of Austen, 17–18, 117, 121–25, 128–36, 141, 147–49, 154–60
inheritance: literary, 17–18, 117, 121, 124, 125 (*see also* Austen, Jane: as literary foremother); of property, 115–16, 118, 124, 125, 134–35

*Jack & Alice: A Novel* (Austen), 76
James, Henry, 116, 177, 180, 184n. 15; and aestheticism, 41n. 16, 115, 126, 127; and Austen's legacy, 9, 177, 121–22, 136–37n. 14; *The Bostonians*, 134, 136, 139n. 46; and the closet, 127, 128, 180; *The Portrait of a Lady*, 17, 116
Janeite: history of the term, 12–15; in the *OED*, 42n. 23. *See also* Janeites; Janeitism
Janeiteism: in the early twentieth century, 31–33; masculinity and, 25–26, 30–31, 34–35; queerness and, 25–26, 32, 35, 38–39; as Victorian family enterprise, 118
Janeites: and film critics, 8; and professional literary critics, 3–4, 30–40. *See also* high and low culture; reading: nonnormative practices of
Jarman, Derek, 120
Jenkins, Elizabeth, 157, 162n. 26
Jenkins, Henry, 30, 41n. 16
Johnson, Claudia L., 15–16, 23n. 14, 108–9, 193, 207–8
Johnson, Samuel, 9, 39, 87, 113n. 31

Kaye-Smith, Sheila, 11, 164n. 45; as novelist, 151; *Speaking of Jane Austen* (*Talking of Jane Austen*) (with G. B. Stern), 36, 37, 144, 151–53
Kelly, Gary, 91
Kennedy, Margaret, 149
Kent, Christopher, 33, 42n. 21
Kimball, Roger, 25–29, 38, 39
Kipling, Rudyard, 171, 207; "The Janeites," 14, 15, 31–35, 37, 39, 41n. 19, 90, 108–9, 111; *Kim*, 208, 216
Kirk, J. F., 175
Knight, Fanny, 133
Knight, Marianne, 45–46
Knight, Richard Payne, 89–91, 104, 105

Lacoue-Labarthe, Philippe, and Jean-Luc Nancy, 114n. 36
Lascelles, Mary, 42n. 28
Lawrence, D. H., 29, 150, 163n. 38, 175
Leavis, F. R., 20, 38, 42n. 28, 129; *The Great Tradition*, 35–36, 42n. 27, 121–22, 146, 147–48
Leavis, Q. D. (Queenie), 42n. 27, 207
Lehmann, Rosamond, 160, 162, 165n. 59
Leonard, John, 206–7
Leverson, Ada, 148, 161n. 15
Lewes, George Henry, 10, 11, 17, 50, 60n. 16, 61n. 17, 83n. 2, 90, 109, 110–11, 175, 185n. 30
Lewis, C. S., 39
Liddell, Robert, 122
Linklater, Eric, 42n. 26
Longfellow, Henry Wadsworth, 173
Lovejoy, George, 74
Lovell, Terry, 83n. 4
Lovett, Robert Morss, 174, 175
Lucas, E. V., 23n. 14
Lynch, Deidre, 143, 161n. 15, 173

Macaulay, Thomas Babington, 10, 50, 109
Mangin, Edward, 68, 69, 79
manners: as gay, 38–39. *See also* novels: of manners
*Mansfield Park* (Austen): 17, 18, 28, 57–58, 62n. 22, 63, 75, 76, 78, 79, 102, 124, 135, 145, 148, 149, 151, 160n. 4, 183n. 5, 190–91, 199, 200; and abolitionism, 19, 154, 213; contemporary response to, 94–95, 112n. 18; and Delafield's *The Optimist*, 141, 144, 154–56; Edmund Wilson on, 152–53; and empire, 19–20, 179, 206–21, 222n. 9; feminist perspectives on, 207, 215–17; gender struggle in, 212–13; Said on, 19–20, 206–21, 223n. 17, 222n. 9
Marcus, Jane, 148–49
marriage, 33, 150, 160, 168–69, 196, 222n. 9; Austen's relation to, 9, 22n. 11, 183–84n. 13; and race, 178–79, 183n. 11. *See also* marriage plot; spinsterhood
marriage plot, 4, 15, 28–29, 35–38, 61n. 21, 101, 188–89, 195; Forster on, 129; readers' indifference to, 31–32; readers' interest in, 92–93; *Sanditon*'s departure from, 118–19, 133–35. *See also* reading: nonnormative practices of
masculinity, 188–89, 217–18; and Janeiteism, 25–26, 30–31, 34–35

Mayor, F. M., 18, 157–60, 165nn. 57 and 59; *The Rector's Daughter*, 144, 154, 158–60, 165n. 54
Menand, Louis, 8
Merchant-Ivory, 120
Merck, Mandy, 120
Michell, Roger, 4, 198
Michon, Cathryn, and Pamela Norris, 46, 59n. 5
Milbanke, Annabella. *See* Byron, Lady
Miller, D. A., 29, 34, 135, 208
Mitchell, W.J.T., 206–7
Mitford, Mary Russell, 113n. 31, 143, 146
modernism, 9, 17, 116, 144–46, 170, 174. *See also individual authors*
Mooney, Bel, 148–49
Moore, Thomas, 101
More, Paul Elmer, 7, 21n. 5
Morgan, Janet, 165n. 54
Morrison, Paul, 43
Mothers of the Novel series, 162n. 21
Mudrick, Marvin, 22n. 10, 36, 38, 42n. 28, 43n. 35
Murray, John Middleton, 165

Nafisi, Azar, 22n. 24
Nairn, Tom, 124
national identity, 33, 166–69. *See also* America: Austen's reception in; Anglophilia; Austen, Jane: and Americanness; Austen, Jane: and Englishness
National Trust, 12, 119
naturalization, 88, 98, 103–5, 107, 113n. 25, 118. *See also* conservatism: of the novel form; didacticism; probabilistic fiction; regulation
New Criticism, 43n. 34, 122
*Northanger Abbey* (Austen), 31, 63, 72, 74, 75, 76, 102–3, 198, 208, 222n. 15
nostalgia, 111, 119, 190. *See also* heritage cinema
novels: circulating, 63–82; and the everyday, 89–90, 93–101, 103–4, 106, 110–11; of manners, 122, 149; and regulation, 11, 17, 40n. 7, 87–89, 107–8, 110; three-deckers, 77–78. *See also* circulating libraries; domestic fiction; probabilistic fiction
novel studies, 5–8, 27–28; and heteronormativity, 35–39; professionalization of, 15–16, 41n. 16
novelty: circulating libraries and, 69, 78

O'Brian, Patrick, 4, 14
O'Farrell, Mary Ann, 10, 15
Oliphant, Margaret, 21n. 4, 160–61n. 10, 161n. 12, 175
originality. *See* authorship; formula fiction

Page, Norman, 138
Paglia, Camille, 139n. 46
*Past Times* catalog, 46, 59nn. 3 and 4, 60n. 6
Paulson, Ronald, 133
Pavlov, Ivan, 144
Perera, Suvendrini, 216
*Persuasion* (Austen), 18, 55–56, 63, 74, 76, 102, 133, 135, 161, 187–203, 205n. 13, 208, 213–14, 216; BBC/WGBH adaptation of (1995), 4, 19, 188–99, 202–3; and Mayor's *The Rector's Daughter*, 141, 144, 154, 158–60, 165n. 57
Pidduck, Julianne, 190, 198, 205n. 13
Platt, Arthur, 44n. 42
plot, 91–92, 101, 103; readers' indifference to, 32, 91, 109; Sir Walter Scott on, 97–98. *See also* marriage plot; details
Poe, Edgar Allan, 168
poetry, georgic, 120, 123, 130
Poirier, Richard, 177, 180
popular culture. *See* high and low culture
postcolonial theory: and gender politics, 19–20, 207–9, 215–21
Preston, Harriet Waters, 122
Price, Warwick James, 176
*Pride and Prejudice* (Austen), 17, 51–54, 63, 76, 85n. 25, 115–16, 151–52, 160n. 4, 165n. 60, 202, 208; MGM adaptation of (1940), 19, 180–82, 187n. 57, 194; BBC adaptation of (1980), 189–90; A&E/BBC adaptation of (1995), 4, 188–89, 194, 196; contemporary critical response to, 91–95, 97, 104–5; Howells on, 170; Saintsbury on, 141; Twain on, 168; Warren Burden Blake on, 169
probabilistic fiction, 87–91, 96, 103–4, 110. *See also* didacticism; everyday, the; naturalization; regulation
property. *See* inheritance: of property

queerness: of Austen, 27–29, 36, 38; and the country house novel, 116–17, 128–36; of the Janeites, 25–26, 32, 35, 39.

queerness *(cont.)*
*See also* heteronormativity; homosexuality; Janeiteism; spinsterhood

race, 19, 178–82, 183n. 11; in Austen's novels, 179–80, 186n. 51. *See also* Empire, British; slavery
Radcliffe, Ann, 76–77
Ransome, Arthur, 15
Raven, James, 83n. 7
readers: American, 166–82; contention between, 3, 7–8, 11–12, 25–40; female, 152–53; professional vs. popular, 3–8; in the Regency period, 63–82. *See also* circulating libraries; Janeites; novel studies; reading
reading: nonnormative practices of, 15–16, 30–31, 35–39, 91, 98–99, 101, 108–11, 112n. 18 (*see also* everyday, the: as oppositional); the politics of, 14–15. *See also* readers
realism, 39; versus romance, 9, 170–73, 176–77. *See also* didacticism; everyday, the; probabilistic fiction; regulation
Reeve, Clara, 87–91
regulation: the novel as form of, 11, 17, 40n. 7, 87–89, 107–8, 110. *See also* conservatism: of the novel form; didacticism; naturalization; probabilistic fiction
Repplier, Agnes, 3, 11, 171–72, 176, 178, 186n. 47
Richardson, Samuel, 87; *Pamela*, 77; *Sir Charles Grandison*, 64
Ritchie, Anne Thackeray, 11–12, 23n. 18
romance: American revival of, 171–73, 176; and novels, 9, 73, 81, 87–88, 99; *Sanditon* as, 131–35
romance plot. *See* marriage plot
Romilly, Anne, 94–95, 101, 104
Rosenblatt, Roger, 25–29

Said, Edward: *Culture and Imperialism*, 19–20, 206–21, 222n. 9; on *Mansfield Park*, 19–20, 206–21, 222n. 9; *Orientalism*, 206, 217
Saintsbury, George, 13–14, 24n. 24, 141, 142
Sales, Roger, 19, 21n. 3, 166
Sampson, George, 29
Samuel, Raphael, 24n. 21
*Sanditon* (Austen), 17–18, 67, 138n. 34, 139n. 46, 186n. 51, 215; as Decadent text, 130–36; and Firbank's *Valmouth*, 130–36; Forster's review of, 116–17, 123, 125, 126–29, 131, 134; publication history of, 118–19
Scott, Sir Walter, 17, 63, 64, 77, 89, 94, 104–5, 169, 171, 179; on *Emma*, 96–98, 103, 113n. 23
Sedgwick, Eve Kosofsky, 26, 28, 37, 39, 128, 136, 138n. 28, 138–39n. 41, 207
*Sense and Sensibility* (Austen), 26, 43n. 31, 63, 76, 77, 78, 148, 200, 202, 205nn. 13 and 18, 207; film adaptation of (1995), 4, 194, 195; contemporary critical response to, 91–92, 97; Rebecca West on, 144; Twain on, 168
servants, 83n. 10; in the 1995 BBC adaptation of *Persuasion*, 19, 189–95, 198–203; Servants' Character Act, 201; as spies, 192, 198–203, 205n. 16
Seymour, Beatrice Kean, 42n. 26
Shakespeare, William, 113n. 31, 122; Austen compared to 10, 13; cultural studies of, 21n. 3; fans of, 10
Shaw, J. B., 175
Silver, Brenda R., 22n. 12
Simon, John, 9, 22n. 10
Simons, Judy, 22n. 9, 23n. 13, 204n. 9
Sinclair, May, 157, 162n. 25
Siskin, Clifford, 24n. 23, 83n. 5
slavery, 19–20, 133, 145, 154, 178–82, 206–9, 211–13, 216, 222n. 10
Smith, Charlotte, 89, 201
Smith, H. F. Brett, 42n. 21
Southam, B. C., 11–13, 27, 39, 43n. 41, 83n. 2, 109, 133, 160n. 10
spectatorship, 190, 191, 192
spinsterhood, 9, 22n. 11, 36, 115, 126, 130, 131, 138n. 32, 143, 149–50, 157, 159–60. *See also* queerness: of Austen
Spivak, Gayatri, 216
Spurgeon, Caroline, 30, 32
Standard Novels series: Austen's novels in, 105–8
Stern, G. B.: 164n. 45; as novelist, 151; *Speaking of Jane Austen* (*Talking of Jane Austen*) (with Sheila Kaye-Smith), 36, 37, 144, 151–53
suffragette movement, 140–42
Suleri, Sara, 216, 217–18, 220–21

Summers, Montague, 26, 30
Swinburne, Algernon Charles, 39, 44n. 42

Tanner, Tony, 37, 202, 209–10, 215
Taylor, Elizabeth, 148; *A Game of Hide and Seek*, 140–41; *A Wreath of Roses*, 164n. 48
technology: *See* Austen, Jane: and technology
Thoreau, Henry David, 177
Todd, Janet, 62n. 22
Tonkin, Boyd, 8
Trilling, Lionel, 3, 4, 5, 8, 20, 29, 39, 43n. 39
Trumpener, Katie, 10–11
Tuite, Clara, 17–18
Twain, Mark, 168; *Huckleberry Finn*, 177–78, 180, 183n. 9

Uunila, Edith, 58

Vanita, Ruth, 24n. 21
Vernon, Lady, 94
Virago Modern Classics, 144, 154–160, 162n. 26; and modernism, 144–46; uses of Austen in, 147–49
Viswanathan, Gauri, 167
von Arnim, Elizabeth, 157, 165nn. 60 and 62

Walkley, Arthur Bingham, 166
war: Civil War, 181–82; Napoleonic Wars, 188; World War I, 31–33, 42n. 21, 151, 154–55; World War II, 174, 180, 187n. 57
Ward, Mrs. Humphry, 148, 160n. 10
Ward, John William, 93
Warner, Michael, 125
Warner, Sylvia Townsend, 140, 149
Watkins, Susan, 21n. 4, 46
Wells, H. G.: *Ann Veronica*, 141–42
Welty, Eudora, 174, 176, 186n. 38
West, Rebecca: on Austen, 142–44, 151, 162n. 20; *The Judge*, 148–49
Whately, Archbishop Richard, 10, 28, 89, 103–4
White, Antonia, 150–51, 163n. 28, 164n. 41
Wilde, Oscar, 39, 43n. 42, 119, 148
Williams, Raymond, 91, 218
Wilson, Edmund, 11, 36, 43n. 31, 183n. 13, 185n. 30; on *Mansfield Park*, 152–53
Winnett, Susan, 39, 43n. 39
Wollstonecraft, Mary: *Maria, or the Wrongs of Woman*, 201–2
women novelists: Austen's relation to, 141, 144–49, 154–60, 163n. 30; and the suffragette movement, 140–41. *See also specific authors*; female literary tradition
women's literary tradition. *See* female literary tradition
Wood, Michael, 221–22n. 8
Woolf, Virginia, 9, 22n. 12, 42n. 25, 123, 215; on Austen, 18, 46–47, 143, 153–54, 163n. 40, 164–65n. 49, 176; *Between the Acts*, 116; "Jane Austen Practising," 143; *Orlando*, 116, 155, 156; *A Room of One's Own*, 23n. 14, 146–47, 148
Wordsworth, William, 64

Yeazell, Ruth Bernard, 210
Yonge, Charlotte, 141, 142, 163n. 30
Young, E. H., 148–49, 163n. 30